INSIDE AMERICA'S CONCENTRATION CAMPS

Two Centuries of Internment and Torture

JAMES L. DICKERSON

Lawrence Hill Books

Library of Congress Cataloging-in-Publication Data
Dickerson, James.
Inside America's concentration camps : two centuries of internment and torture
/ James L. Dickerson.
    p. cm.
Includes bibliographical references and index.
ISBN 978-1-55652-806-4
1. Concentration camps—United States—History. 2. Imprisonment—United
States—History. 3. Torture—United States—History. I. Title.
HV8964.U5D53 2011
365'.450973—dc22

                                      2010017570

Interior design: Jonathan Hahn

Published by Lawrence Hill Books
An imprint of Chicago Review Press, Incorporated
814 North Franklin Street
Chicago, Illinois 60610
ISBN 978-1-55652-806-4
Printed in the United States of America
5 4 3 2 1

IN MEMORY OF HODDING CARTER—
more than a Pulitzer Prize–winning journalist,
he was a beacon that made a difference
in the lives of many who lived in a world without light

CONTENTS

Author's Note   vii

Introduction   ix

Prologue: From Sea to Shining Sea   1

PART I: NUNNA DUAL TSUNY (THE TRAIL WHERE THEY CRIED)

1   The Origins of Internment in Colonial America   13
2   Walking the Trail of Tears   27

PART II: CAMPS THAT WILL LIVE IN INFAMY

3   Pearl Harbor Under Attack   39
4   Executive Order 9066   61
5   Manzanar's Gateway to Hell   87
6   Life in an Arkansas Swamp   103
7   Eastward Ho to the Wild, Wild West   121
8   The Konzentrationslager Blues   145
9   Italian Americans Dodge a Bullet   161
10 Jews Turned Away from a New Promised Land   173
11 Finding Redemption in a Troubled Land   187

12 Prisoner, Go Home!   203

13 Righting the Wrongs   221

PART III: ASK NOT FOR WHOM THE BELL TOLLS

14 Modern-Day Internment   237

15 "Why Is This Thing Happening in This Country?"   245

16 Which Camp Will You Someday Call Home?   255

Acknowledgments   265

Notes   267

Bibliography   287

Index   297

AUTHOR'S NOTE

Unlike the concentration camps built in Nazi Germany during World War II, American concentration camps did not contain death chambers, and while there were instances in which prisoners were shot and killed by guards in the U.S. camps, there was no officially sanctioned systematic effort to exterminate prisoners.

Because of the emotional association of "concentration camps" with the Nazi Holocaust, one is hesitant to use that phrase in describing the American camps. However, President Roosevelt twice described the camps as concentration camps when publicly discussing the issue, and the joint Chiefs of Staff used the term early in 1942 when describing plans to house Japanese Americans targeted for removal from the Hawaiian Islands. Other government entities used politically correct words such as "internment camps" and "relocation centers" when describing their operations. One is reluctant to use either of those terms, since both seem callous and dismissive of the trauma experienced by innocent prisoners held behind barbed wire under armed guard.

Accordingly, "concentrations camps" will be used in this book, since the author feels that it is the most accurate description of the camps built by the United States over a span of nearly two hundred years.

The author also accepts the widely accepted definition of "Japanese American," "Italian American," "Native American," and "German American" as ethnic, racial, and cultural identities that are unrelated to citizenship.

INTRODUCTION

Concentration camps are not indigenous to America.

Neither is government-sanctioned torture.

Both were imported by white immigrants who either had a predisposition to torture and detention, based on cultural experiences in their homelands where torture and detention were an accepted means for governments to control those of different races and religions, or who, in a darker psychological twist, had been tortured and detained in their homelands and then exiled to America, only to succumb, during times of crisis, to their baser instincts to do unto others as others have done unto them. When you look at U.S. history, it is difficult to avoid the conclusion that for Americans whose families were desensitized by generations of abuse, government advocacy of torture and detention was a culturally acceptable means of imposing their will on people of different races, religions, and political beliefs.

Of course, the opposite reaction—revulsion to torture, religious and racial persecution, and political imprisonment—was a strong motivator for many immigrants who fled to America to escape those inhumane shackles of the human spirit that bound them in their homelands. Over the years these three unlikely groups—abusers, abuse victims, and crusaders against abuse—forged a complex witch's brew of cultural significance, one that ultimately came to define the American experience. Clashes based on those opposing views of life were inevitable.

Almost from the founding of the Republic, Americans have waged an uncivil war with one another over those defining issues. The War Between the States was fought over slavery, the ultimate poster child for torture and detention. Today the conflict continues, only this time the conflict is over Red State–Blue State differences about the role of government-sanctioned torture of individuals of different races and religions, imprisonment without trial, and the imposition of the death penalty.

At its core, government-sanctioned torture and detention are based on racism and religious persecution, with politics usually playing a secondary role. America was never the melting pot it was made out to be by myopic historians who have been slow to dig beneath the surface to identify the deep cultural divisions that have fractured Americans from one century to the next. Those who came to America to pursue economic gain tended to view torture as a legitimate tool with which to protect their wealth (favored were the rack, waterboarding, and the *garrucha*, which required the victim to be suspended from the ceiling with weights and pulleys attached to various appendages). By contrast, those who came to America to escape religious and personal persecution understandably viewed government-sanctioned torture and detention as unspeakable crimes that violated all concepts of human decency, although some eventually succumbed to their addictive lure as a means of protecting accumulated wealth. Those two opposing concepts of government morality have formed the dividing line for the cultural wars that have obsessed Americans for the past three centuries.

Concentration camps do not spring up in a vacuum. Almost always the seed is planted by armed conflicts in which the enemy is of a different race or religion. It is a small step for a state to depict all those of that race or religion as enemies of the state who must be removed from their homes and confined in concentration camps for the safety of the majority. Once confinement is achieved, the next step is for the state to subject those in the camps to torture under the rationale that it is necessary to protect the state. The question of innocence or guilt never arises because the victims are assumed to be guilty by virtue of their race or religion.

The story of America's concentration camps thus begins in the experiences of the earliest European societies, before white settlers came to the New World. Torture and detention predate Jesus Christ, but certainly his abuse and crucifixion establish him as the first high-profile torture and detention victim. It is not without incredible irony that when some white Christians first came to America they established torture and detention for anyone who violated the social norms of the era. In colonial America, women who talked too much, professed different religious beliefs (they were branded witches), or committed adultery were routinely tortured in public. They were detained in stocks, their heads and wrists locked painfully into place, they were subjected to the dunking stool, or they were whipped to a bloody pulp.

The process through which the abused become the abuser is a phenomenon that can be explained by contemporary psychology, which recognizes that few victims escape a traumatic past without residual damage and a deep-seated need to be accepted by the abuser. Psychologists and social workers are well aware of the frequency with which sexually abused children long for acceptance by their abuser and grow up to become abusive adults.[1] The same psychological principle applies to the cruelty that inhabits the dark corners of the political process: abuser and abused sometimes find common ground in their need to perpetuate dominance over others. It is a dysfunctional relationship that has defined our national character as much as anything else in our history.

My own ancestor, John Turner, whose kinsman Sir James Turner played an important role in Scotland's Killing Time, which resulted in the torture and detention of thousands of Scots, was himself subjected to the cruelties of the era before being banished to America. His experiences, offered in the following pages, are a good example of the complexities of this subject. Of course, Scotland was not the only country where torture and detention were a way of life. Similar horror stories surrounded immigrants from France, Germany, Italy, Spain, England, Ireland, and China, practically every nation that outsourced its dispossessed citizens to the United States.

As a democracy, America has evolved over the years in many respects, but one thing that has not changed significantly is the nation's continuing public debate over torture and detention.

PROLOGUE

FROM SEA TO SHINING SEA

Scotland's infamous Killing Time of the 1600s created waves that rolled across the Atlantic to the shores of America, carrying war-weary refugees in search of freedom. Those waves buffet American shores to this day.

The Killing Time was so named because of the bloody fighting that took place among Scottish Covenanters, Presbyterians who opposed English dominance over their religious lives; the armies of King Charles II and then later his brother, King James II, who attempted to subdue the Lowland Scots by placing the Scottish Presbyterian Church under the control of the Church of England; and Scottish Highlanders, most of whom were Roman Catholics, who frequently fought alongside the royal army against their Scottish countrymen in the South.

Throughout the 1600s, Scotland was a seething cauldron of passions, both political and religious. Much of the dissatisfaction had to do with Germany's Martin Luther, a district vicar who had challenged, during the previous century, the authority of the Catholic Church. His message sparked armed rebellion throughout Europe, leading to the Protestant Reformation. The Reformation was especially welcomed in Scotland, where for centuries battles had raged over whether the Scots would be governed by self-rule or by English kings. The Protestant approach to Christianity appealed to all classes of Scots, from noblemen to peasants, so much so that the Scottish parliament established a national Protestant religion named Presbyterianism. Scots were asked to sign a pledge of support called the Covenant. That prompted a confrontation with England, where control of the church was deemed the sole responsibility of the king.

It was into that world that James Turner was born in 1615. His parents lived in Dalkeith, about eight miles southeast of the Lowland city of Edinburgh, where his father, a portly man of jovial disposition, was the minister. By the time he was sixteen, James's parents and grandparents were convinced that his future was in the Presbyterian Church. He was educated at Glasgow College, and they wanted nothing so much as for him to enter the ministry and save souls to fight in the continuing struggle for Scottish freedom. James was eager to fight for such a righteous cause, but he was a reluctant student and saw himself more of a soldier than a minister. After receiving a master of arts degree, which he later belittled as being worthless, he traveled abroad to join the Swedish army, at that time the most revered in the world.[1]

After seeing a great deal of service in the Thirty Years' War, he returned to Scotland and was commissioned a major in the Scottish army, which at that time was led by Presbyterian Covenanters. After serving with the Covenanters for a time, he inexplicably changed sides and offered his services as a soldier to the Royal Army. Almost overnight he went from being the recipient of abuse at the hands of the Royal Army to a position in which he was commissioned to order abuse on behalf of the Royal Army.

In the beginning, the Covenanters were overjoyed by Turner's appointment, for they assumed that it meant that Charles II soon would grant their demands for a free Scotland, but they quickly learned that was not the case. The king was determined to impose his will on the Scots. Not only did Charles II not recognize Presbyterianism as Scotland's official religion, which is what the Covenanters had hoped for, but he made it a crime for any person not licensed by the Church of England to preach or pray, except in his own home with his family. Those who dared to pray outside their own homes were subject to fines, imprisonment, or banishment. Anyone who conducted an unauthorized religious service in an open field was guilty of a capital offense and subject to the death penalty. Those caught giving aid to Presbyterians were subject to the same harsh penalties. Despite those measures, Turner stood by his king, a decision that cost him in goodwill among his neighbors and friends.

The Killing Time characterized the years that followed Turner's appointment, an era of unprecedented bloodshed, as King Charles II pressed on with his campaign to bring Scotland in line with England's religious and political beliefs. The atrocities committed against the Lowland Scots were unimaginable, yet they refused to bend, which meant that the hillsides soon were littered with graves that followed the advance of the king's troops. Turner, once considered a hero to the freedom-loving Scots, was nicknamed "Bloody Byte the Sheep" by a new generation, a reference to his cruelty and predatory nature. As a result of his service he was knighted by King Charles, an honor that transformed him into Sir James Turner.

One day he led his soldiers into the town of Dalry, where it was learned that a Covenanter had refused to pay his fine for worshipping in a Presbyterian service in a nearby field. A minister who wore a hood to conceal his identity had conducted the service, but once God's message was delivered, those who had gathered to hear the Word scattered to the surrounding villages—everyone, that is, except for one strong-willed man who refused to deny his affiliation with the church. As James retired to his quarters for a midday nap, his troops took the man named Will Grier to a barn and subjected him to a torture device known as the boot.[2] The man was held down on the floor of the barn, and the boot, a wooden frame fitted with iron spikes, was attached to his feet. A soldier with a heavy mallet stood nearby.

He was ordered to pay a fine, but refused, citing his right to worship as he pleased.

The soldier with the mallet pounded it against the boot with a fierce blow that drew a scream from the prisoner as the spikes traveled two inches into his feet, dribbling blood onto the ground. Once again the soldier asked him to pay the fine. Again, he refused.

Once again the soldier pounded the mallet.

It was during the second pounding that a band of armed Covenanters rode into town and heard the man's scream. When they entered the barn, a skirmish took place, and the king's men were taken prisoner. The Covenanter leader demanded to know the location of their commander. They refused at first, but then relented when one of the Covenanters grabbed a soldier by the hand and cleanly severed his index finger with one chomp of his rather-large overbite.

They bound the soldiers to the barn's post, then demanded to know their commander's name. Replied one of the soldiers, without much prodding, "He is Sir James Turner—and he has taken quarters in yonder home."

Those words were enough to draw a smile from the Covenanter leader, for he had long wanted to meet the man who would fight for both sides in such a passionate contest. They stormed the house and found James asleep in bed, wearing only his underclothes. Before he could reach for his broadsword, the men pulled him from the bed and dragged him outside, where he was mounted on an old nag and paraded through the streets for all to see.[3] There was talk of killing him on the spot, but some of the Covenanters argued that he should be put on trial in the nearby town of Douglas.

James rode the entire way on the nag in his underclothes, with his hands tied behind his back. Once they reached Douglas, they convened the town council and asked for a vote on his guilt. The council was equally divided, with some members pointing out his previous service to the cause, and others pointing out the obvious: he had betrayed the cause and allowed his men to torture an innocent farmer. A vote was taken, and to James's considerable relief, his life was spared by one vote.

Not so charitable was Sir Thomas Dalziel, who led an army of three thousand troops in pursuit of Presbyterian Covenanters, who left Douglas in a rainstorm that quickly turned to snow, making the roads all but impassable. The outnumbered Covenanters, under the command of Colonel Wallace, a descendant of William Wallace of Braveheart fame, made a stand near Rullion Green on the southern slope of Pentland Hills.

Dalziel began the attack by sending a wave of cavalry against Wallace's left wing. Twice Dalziel's attacks were repelled. Not until the third attempt was he successful, sending the Covenanters into retreat and making vulnerable Wallace's right wing. By then, it was already nightfall, and most of the Covenanters were able to escape into the darkness, leaving behind about fifty men, who were taken prisoner. The next morning, Dalziel toured the battlefield and saw that it was littered with the bodies of one hundred men, the dead equally divided between the two sides. The prisoners were transported to Haddock's Hole, an estate in the domain of the High Church of Edinburgh. There they were taken before the council for a vote on their guilt. James was asked to attend the proceeding, but he was given no official role to play.

The king's representative argued before the council that the men had committed treason and should be put to death for their transgressions. It was also pointed out that the prisoners had humiliated Sir James Turner by parading him about town on a nag and had, therefore, humiliated the king by association. Before the vote was taken, James rose and asked to address the council.

"It is true these men dragged me from my bed and showed disrespect of the highest order," he said, addressing the assembly. "But it is equally true that my life was subsequently spared by a vote of their neighbors—and it is of interest to me that I was well treated by the men while in captivity."

The chief magistrate glared at James, his expression showing no sympathy for his argument. "Sir James," the magistrate intoned, "we think it was the king's system of equitable governance that spared your life, not the prisoners who stand now before us. Had these men had their way, they would have stretched your neck on the spot."

"Pray, then, allow me to beg for mercy for them, for most are nothing more than farmers who want to be left in peace."

The magistrate's face flushed bright red. "Sir James, your speech does these prisoners no good—and it may do harm to your own cause. Please be seated."

After a brief recess, the council returned to announce its decision. "By order of this body, ordained by His Majesty King Charles II, we hereby find the accused men guilty as charged and order that they be hanged by the neck at tomorrow's sunrise."

James was asked to be a witness at the hanging. Exhausted, he returned to his quarters, where he went to bed without dinner. The following morning, he reported to the execution site as requested. It was a sight that sickened him. The Presbyterian men, about fifty in all, were lined up in a row. One by one they were taken to a raised platform with a trapdoor, where a noose was placed around each man's neck, and the trapdoor sprung to the gasps of the gathered townspeople. Some of the prisoners stood proudly with their chests inflated, but others waited in line and sobbed, praying aloud for God's intervention in their righteous cause.

After each hanging, the lifeless body was carried from beneath the platform and dropped to the ground. Fifty bodies make for a pyramid of disturbing dimensions, and James found the executions, which took more than two hours because of the pronouncements that were made before each drop, a disturbing sight. He held his emotions in check, but they formed a powerful brew that churned relentlessly inside him and broke his spirit.

After witnessing the executions, James wrote a letter to King Charles, requesting an audience at his earliest convenience, then traveled to his home, where he awaited the king's response. Three weeks later, a squad of soldiers rode onto his property and presented him with a proclamation signed by the king. It notified James that he had been stripped of his command and was no longer in His Majesty's service: "The gratitude I feel for your splendid service has been tempered by the disgrace of your recent actions, so that, in the end, there is nothing left for us to do but to acknowledge a parting of the ways. May God be with you, Sir James." By then Turner had a wife and family, among them a kinsman named John Turner, a young man who fancied himself a Presbyterian Covenanter and thus an opponent of Sir James Turner's royal benefactor.

While in retirement, James made history in 1683 as the author of the first published book on military strategy, *Pallas Armata: Military Essayes of the Ancient Grecian, Roman, and Modern Art of War*.[4] The book was the closest thing Europe had to a bestseller. He also wrote a book titled *Memoirs of His Own Life and Times*, along with numerous instructional essays, including several with provocative titles such as "Imprisonment," "Cruelty," and "Revenge." Two years after publication of *Pallas Armata* he was granted a pension by King James II, but he died the following year at the age of seventy-one.

In 1685, one year before the death of Sir James Turner, more than one hundred Presbyterian men and women were imprisoned in Dunnottar Castle, near Stonehaven, Scotland, suspected of being Presbyterian Covenanters. They were asked to sign an oath of loyalty to the king, and those who agreed were released. Those who refused were tortured and confined to the dungeons of the castle, a seventeenth-century version of a modern-day concentration camp:

> The floor was ankle-deep with mire, and there was but one window for the admittance of air. . . . The castle stands on a steep cliff overhanging the sea, and twenty-five of the prisoners made an attempt to escape by the window of the larger vault. Ten succeeded in eluding capture, but those who failed had reason to regret their attempt. Bound and laid upon their backs for the space of three hours burning matches were placed between their fingers—one of the approved forms of torture of the time.[5]

That same year, a group of Presbyterian resisters were captured at Wigtown and loaded onto wagons and transported to the seashore, following a road that twisted down through the rocky bluffs to a sandy level area at the water's edge. Surrounding a wooden table was a troop of soldiers. Seated at the table with a large tablet was a military captain, elegantly clothed in his dress uniform. Past the table were two large posts that had been driven into the mudflats.

The prisoners were ordered out of the carts, including two women, Margaret Lachlane, age sixty-three, and Margaret Wilson, a young woman in her twenties.[6] The two women were taken before the captain, who remained seated while he spoke, demanding their allegiance to his Majesty King James II. He pointed out that two weeks earlier they had been asked to repudiate their membership in the Presbyterian Church, and both had refused. This was their final opportunity, he explained, to pledge their allegiance to His Majesty King James II.

Margaret Lachlane refused, but not without apologizing for the rude-
ness of her refusal.

Margaret Wilson reached out for Margaret Lachlane's hand and
bowed her head. The captain was certain he had never seen a more beautiful woman. Her voice was soft but filled with conviction. She assured
him that the Lord would never condone her signing any such document.

The captain nodded to his soldiers, who took the women and led
them out to the posts, which already were dampened by the incoming
tide. Margaret Lachlane was lashed to the post closest to the sea; Margaret Wilson was secured to a post about twenty yards inland on slightly
higher ground. The other prisoners, about two hundred in all, were
brought closer to the sea and warned not to avert their eyes. It was that
time of the day when the tide lifted considerably every few minutes. At
first the water covered only Margaret Lachlane's ankles and had not yet
reached Margaret Wilson, but it soon crept over the older woman's knees
and soaked the younger woman's bare feet. The ever-present roar of the
surf created an ominous sound track that dampened everyone's spirits,
soldiers included; but then, surprisingly, out of the sea rose a voice sweet
and strong, soaring to the high heavens, singing a tune they all knew and
loved, "Greensleeves."

Margaret Lachlane began the song, but Margaret Wilson joined in
soon thereafter.

It's only been an hour
Since he locked her in the tower
The time has come
He must be undone
By the morning

Many times before
The tyrant's opened up the door
Then someone cries
Still we close our eyes
Not again

As the sea crept up to Margaret Lachlane's chin, she twisted and turned her body, then tilted her head so that the water would not wash away her voice, gasping for each breath. Even as the seawater seeped into her nose and mouth, her singing voice, garbled at times, inspired them all. Then, suddenly, her voice was stilled and the water lapped over her head.

Picking up where Margaret Lachlane left off, Margaret Wilson, tears streaming down her cheeks and a look of horror in her eyes, bravely sang with a volume that surprised all who knew her, for her youthful speaking voice was so petite and unassuming.

> Meet me when the sun is in the western skies
> The fighting must begin before another someone dies
> Cross bows in the fire light
> Greensleeves waving
> Madman raving
> Through the shattered night

As the water rose to Margaret Wilson's face, the captain shouted out to her, urging her to sign the document. There is still time, he told her. He never expected her to drown; it was his hope that she would see the older woman die and then repent, thus encouraging the others to do likewise. But she did not repent—she sang until her lungs filled with seawater, and then her body hung limp beneath the surging tide.

═══════════════

When John Turner came to America from Scotland in 1688, forced into exile at the age of twenty-one after his family name had fallen into disrepute over the puzzling excesses of Sir James—and he himself had refused to denounce Presbyterianism and embrace the Church of England—he brought with him not only a desire for religious and personal freedom but also the hard-earned experience of a culture in which violence, torture, and abuse were not only commonplace but accepted as the status quo.[7]

Sir James Turner is a good example of how the abused often become the abuser, rationalizing it as being in the national interest. Thousands of Sir James Turners in search of wealth and power made their way to America, where they helped forge communities that believed that torture and detention can be rationalized as being a necessary evil in the name of a higher cause such a perpetuating power.

Likewise, thousands of John Turners, opposed to torture and detention, were banished to America or arrived of their own free will, forming communities convinced that there is no possible "higher cause" that justifies torture and detention. For those of like mind, America was a place to begin life anew, free of the constant threat of violent intolerance—a place where serious religious beliefs or fanciful dreams could be pursued without penalty of death.

As for John Turner, his arrival in America in 1688 was not the end of a journey but the beginning of an incredible adventure that literally spans the history of America itself. Not only did he find freedom, but he found the love of his life and the acceptance of a Native American culture that was destined to fall victim to the same horrors experienced by him in Scotland.

PART I

NUNNA DUAL TSUNY (THE TRAIL WHERE THEY CRIED)

My friends, circumstances render it impossible that you can flourish in the midst of a civilized community. You have but one remedy within your reach, and that is to remove to the west. And the sooner you do this, the sooner you will commence your career of improvement and prosperity.

—President Andrew Jackson

1

THE ORIGINS OF INTERNMENT IN COLONIAL AMERICA

Scotsmen began immigrating to America only four years before John Turner was exiled to the colonies. By the time of his arrival more than seven hundred Scots had settled in a colony in New Jersey. Perhaps because of his nightmarish experiences in Scotland, Turner found life in a colony under British control not to his liking, primarily because of the fierce violence inflicted on Native Americans and the subsequent retribution inflicted on the settlers by the Indians. He traveled north into the New York wilderness and found work with a rowdy band of trappers who worked the forest north into Canada, where they gathered pelts that they sold to the colonists.

For five years, John traveled with the trappers throughout New York and across the St. Lawrence River into Quebec. It was on the St. Lawrence that he met explorer Rene-Robert Cavelier, Sieur de La Salle, who told him about a paradise he had discovered on Lake Michigan, near what is now called South Bend, Indiana. In 1693, after skirmishes with the Indians in northern New York and with English soldiers who demanded his valuable trappers' pelts, John left the trappers and headed south to Maryland, a territory known for its tolerance of Presbyterians.

Living among the settlers were several tribes of Algonquin Indians, including the Conoy (also called the Piscataway), a tribe that lived on the banks of the Potomac River on land that is now Washington, D.C. They were unique in that they were the only tribe in the colonies that allowed women to serve as chiefs. A peace-loving people, they traded with the settlers and responded well to teachings about Christianity. When they went to war, it was with Indian tribes to the south, not the settlers.

The Conoy were distinguished by black hair, dark eyes, and copper skin. They were taller than the colonists, even the women, and they had stronger builds than the whites. They wore their hair long, often pulled back into locks and tied with strings of shells. Many of the men shaved their hair from half of their heads. Some of the women had colored designs on their bodies that indicated whether they were single or members of the tribal leadership council. In the summer, men and women dressed in deerskin wraps that left their chests exposed; in winter they wore long cloaks, leggings, and well-insulated moccasins.

Soon after his arrival John witnessed a ceremony during which the leader of the Conoy, a tall, beautiful woman in her early twenties, strode into the white settlement with the bearings of a queen. John had never seen a female chief, and he was struck by her great beauty. After she left the settlement, he asked about her and was told that she was a chief but didn't yet have a husband.

John trapped and hunted on the Potomac for several weeks, unable to get the Conoy chief out of his mind. He returned to the camp, determined to make her his wife. Before the year ended, John married the chief, even though it was illegal at that time for whites to marry Indians. He renamed her Jane in an effort to promote her acceptance by whites. Despite the discrimination they faced from both whites and Indians, they were determined to have the freedom that John had dreamed of finding in America; but that proved difficult because life was changing radically in the colonies.

In the beginning, white settlers were content to build isolated settlements in America that respected the boundaries declared by Native Americans. But as white settlers arrived in ever-increasing numbers, creating an insatiable demand for settlement land, peaceful coexistence was replaced by a clumsily drafted relocation strategy of pushing Native Americans farther into the interior, the forerunner of modern-day internment. Advocates of that strategy were the powerful British corporations that garnered massive profits by seizing America's vast natural resources. Throughout the 1600s and 1700s, British corporations such as East India Company, South Sea Company, and Virginia Company were as wealthy and powerful as any twenty-first-century American corporation.

Corporate economic expansion in the colonies translated into racial and ethnic cleansing—residents who did not contribute to corporate economic expansion were forced out of their homes. John and Jane Turner found life in the colonies intolerable. For love, Jane had given up her leadership role with the Conoy and John had given up any hope of advancement in white society. They truly became stateless when the corporations pressured whites to seize Conoy land, thus cleansing the colonies of landowning Indians. Unable to live among whites or Indians, John and Jane went westward, beyond the reach of nefarious corporations and racist Indian-haters.

John and Jane followed the directions that La Salle had provided and traveled west until they reached the St. Joseph River, south of Lake Michigan. It was an area that would later be named South Bend, Indiana (Indiana means *In dih an ah*, land of the Indians, so named because of the many tribes that migrated there after being pushed off their land by the colonists). Most of the indigenous Indians on the St. Joseph River belonged to the Miami tribe, a member of the Algonquin nation, which also included the Conoy. For that reason, John and Jane were allowed to settle on the river. They picked out a piece of land on a high bluff overlooking the river and built a cabin. Protected by the Miami, they hunted, trapped and fished, and traded with the French, who set up trading posts to receive furs from the Miami. They also had four children: two girls and two boys, Richard and Samuel, the latter of whom was born when John was thirty-six. Those were good years for the Turners, although they found it necessary, from time to time, to fight with the Miami against their common enemy, the Iroquois. That part of the country was so remote that the settlement of South Bend would not be established for another 120 years. For the first time in his life John found true happiness and sanctuary.

John lived to be one hundred years old, and Jane lived to be ninety-five. They remained close in their old age, always sitting near enough to each other to be able to reach out and touch. Never once did they return to the colonies. Jane often thought about her ancestral land, but she knew she would never return to lay claim to it. When the end came for John, he died with his head cradled in Jane's arms. She gave him a Presbyterian burial, courtesy of an itinerant preacher, and then prayed to the Presbyterian God that she be allowed to accompany him on his long journey. To that end, she sat for thirty days on the crest of the bluff overlooking the river, praying for death. On the final day, she slumped over, a smile on her face—and thus began the journey.

———————————————

As white settlements proliferated on the eastern seaboard during the last half of the eighteenth century, Native American settlements quietly receded into the interior, confident that a series of boundaries established between the Indians and the English meant that Indian Territory was no longer open to settlement by the colonists.[1] Indeed, in 1763 the English government, which claimed sovereignty, declared all lands beyond the Appalachian Mountains reserved for the Indians. The British were not being generous in their allocation of land, for the dominate business acumen of the day put value only on coastal land that was accessible to ocean trade routes. The British considered interior territory that was not navigable by rivers with access to the ocean as essentially worthless, certainly not worth fighting over, so they gave it to the Indians.

Up until the 1770s, white settlers experienced conflicts with various Indian tribes on a regular basis, but nothing so severe that a forced relocation of entire tribes was ever considered a rational alternative. All that changed in 1776, when the British persuaded several Indian tribes to side with them against white settlers who supported the Revolution. Three of the tribes, the Shawnees, Delawares, and Mohawks, encouraged the Cherokee to join them in hostilities against the settlers, thereby helping the British. Advised of Cherokee attacks against settlers on the frontier, Thomas Jefferson, for the first time, advocated relocation as a final solution to the hostilities: "I hope that the Cherokees will now be driven beyond the Mississippi and that this in future will be declared to the Indians the invariable consequence of their beginning a war. Our contest with Britain is too serious and too great to permit any possibility of avocation from the Indians."[2]

═══════════════════

By the time the War of Independence began, Richard and Samuel Turner were respected traders who moved safely and easily among the various Indian tribes that inhabited what later became Indiana and Ohio. By then, the Miami were governed by Chief Mechecannochqua (Little Turtle), a man who achieved fame as one of the greatest chiefs and warriors of the era. Both sons married, but Richard and his wife never had children. Samuel and his wife, a British-born woman named Asbury, had five children: three girls, whose names have not survivied, and two boys, Joseph and Thomas. Thomas married an American-born woman named Scot and had five sons.

The War of Independence was hotly debated in South Bend. Chief Little Turtle, who lived about one hundred miles southeast of South Bend in an area that was later named Fort Wayne, supported the British, primarily because the French supported the revolutionaries and he despised the French.

Joseph and Thomas felt strongly about supporting the colonists and told their father that they felt compelled to enlist in George Washington's army. Before they set off to war, Samuel talked to them about their grandfather, John Turner, and his experiences with the British. He passed on information that had been passed on to him by his father about the military tactics that James Turner had written about in his famous book, *Pallas Armata: Military Essayes of the Ancient Grecian, Roman, and Modern Art of War*. He told them how to defeat those tactics by fighting an Indian-style war.

After the war, Joseph and Thomas returned to the Indiana territory, where Chief Little Turtle, perhaps resentful of the British defeat, went on the warpath and killed settlers in some of the worst battles in the territory's history.

Congress, then meeting in Philadelphia, sought a permanent home for the federal government. Maryland offered the land it had seized from the Conoy (about sixty-nine square miles), and on July 16, 1790, Congress voted to accept it as the site of the new capital. At first, it was named the Territory of Columbia, then later it was changed to District of Columbia. The Turners knew the true name, but they did not lay claim to the land. They knew that their grandfather and grandmother would understand. It was not a time in which whites could safely lay claim to Indian heritage.

At the end of the Revolutionary War, Congress took the position that the United States was entitled, by right of conquest, to the lands owned by England's allies in the war, and entitled to sovereignty over those people who lived on the land. As a result, the new American government adopted what it called a "conquered nation" attitude toward the Indians, with the national government administering Indian policy north of the Ohio River and the individual states administering that policy south of the river.[3]

South Carolina, North Carolina, and Georgia argued that Congress had no authority to set policy in the matter. It was their position that everything controlled by England passed to the states after the war, not to Congress. It was the beginning of the states' rights argument that eventually led to the Civil War and haunts the South to the present day. North Carolina responded by granting Cherokee land in Tennessee to any whites who wanted to move there. Georgia seized Cherokee land and gave it to white citizens. Both land giveaways infuriated Cherokee leaders, who, although conceding the "spoils of war" argument made by the states, insisted that the English never owned or governed their land.

When the southern states rejected the Cherokee argument, the Indians attacked the whites who set up settlements in their territory. Likewise, the Indians north of the Ohio River, rejecting the "conquered nation" designation imposed by Congress, responded with violence against those who attempted to settle in their territory. Fearful that the Indian wars would spread throughout the country and become unmanageable, Congress negotiated peace with the Indians and signed the Treaty of Hopewell with the Cherokee in 1785, an agreement that defined their boundaries and recognized their right to protect their homeland. North Carolina and Georgia protested the treaty, but Congress insisted that the threat of war trumped the quarrelsome claims of individual states.

Three years after the Treaty of Hopewell, the U.S. Constitution was ratified, opening the door the following year for George Washington to be inaugurated in 1789 as the nation's first president. By then it was apparent that the Hopewell treaty was not being honored. White settlers in the south poured, by the thousands, onto Cherokee land and built settlements, with the tacit approval of state government.

Washington and his secretary of war, Henry Knox, set out to forge a more durable Indian policy based on the premise that Indian tribes were sovereign nations that must be dealt with by the federal government through the treaty process. Congress endorsed that policy by passing the Indian Trade and Intercourse Act, which required that all purchases of land from Indians be arranged through treaties negotiated by tribal leaders and federal commissioners appointed by the president. States were given no authority to negotiate treaties with Native Americans, which meant that they had no power to authorize land transfers from Indians to white settlers.

One problem the Indian Trade and Intercourse Act did not solve was what to do about the thousands of settlers who already had moved onto Cherokee land. Washington's solution was to negotiate a new treaty with the Cherokee that allowed the federal government to purchase the land that settlers occupied illegally. A new boundary was surveyed, and further encroachment by white settlers on Indian land was prohibited. The Treaty of Holston was concluded in 1791 and contained the following language: "That the Cherokee nations may be led to a greater degree of civilization, and to become herdsmen and cultivators, instead of remaining in a state of hunters, the United States will, from time to time, furnish gratuitously the said nation with useful implements of husbandry."[4] The Cherokee embraced the treaty with optimistic enthusiasm and began to emulate the white settlers by acquiring black slaves and establishing cotton plantations so that they could accumulate capital by selling cotton abroad.

With the Treaty of Holston, President Washington and the Cherokee thought they had arrived at a permanent solution. What Washington didn't figure into his peace equation was the determination of the southern states to subvert the peace by adopting an argument that would poison race relations in the South for over two hundred years. The basis of that argument was that Native Americans were inferior to whites because of racial differences. Washington felt that the so-called uncivilized behavior exhibited by Indians was based on cultural differences, not racial differences—and therefore could be corrected by social and educational assimilation—but southern white politicians inflamed passions with racist rhetoric insisting with moralistic fervor that bordered on fanaticism that Indians could never be absorbed into white culture because they were racially deficient.

For that reason, southern states looked the other way for three decades as new white settlers poured onto Indian lands and established settlements that they vigorously defended. As white immigrants streamed into America, the need for land increased dramatically, both north and south of the Ohio River. Between 1800 and 1830, Virginia, North Carolina, and Georgia experienced an increase of 1.2 million whites, which translates to 1,600 new whites each day, all flowing into Indian Territory in search of land to settle.

The effect of the population explosion was to push the boundaries of the frontier west to the Mississippi River. In 1803 the Louisiana Purchase added what are today Arkansas, Missouri, Oklahoma, Kansas, South Dakota, North Dakota, Iowa, parts of Texas, New Mexico, Wyoming, Colorado, and Louisiana, making it possible for settlers to rationalize pushing the Native American population west of the Mississippi River. At first the government attempted to entice Indians to move west of the Mississippi River by offering them seemingly attractive land trades. In 1817 and 1819 the Cherokee ceded territory in the East for land in the West, beginning with Arkansas. Cherokees in North Carolina who did not wish to leave the East were offered reservations outside the boundaries of their nation. The reservations were little more than internment camps without fences that greatly restricted the movement of Indians to white-owned land.

At the time of the Louisiana Purchase, Mississippi was considered the westernmost outpost of American civilization, with the state's only major city, Natchez, recognized as the most remote settlement in America. Mississippi was populated mostly by Choctaw and Chickasaw Indians, who generally sought good relations with the settlers, most of whom traveled to Mississippi to begin new lives because they did not approve of the Revolutionary War. Indeed, most supported the British.

Early on, white settlers cultivated a strong relationship with the Indians, with intermarriage a frequent occurrence, especially in view of the shortage of white women on the frontier. The relationships began to sour in 1798 with the appointment of Winthrop Sargent as Mississippi's first territorial governor. Horrified by the race mixing that he saw taking place, he limited the number of Choctaw who could enter Natchez. Sargent explained: "It will be well, I think, to be very sparing of passports for Indians to visit white people, and to confine them to chiefs and men of real consequence amongst the tribes, for the less we mix, the better the prospect of harmony."[5] Sargent's efforts to segregate the Choctaws failed because white settlers ignored his proclamations and continued to meet with their Indian friends in clearings beyond the city limits of Natchez.

Sargent's term came to an end in 1801 with the election of President Thomas Jefferson, who appointed a new territorial governor—William C. C. Claiborne, a member of a prominent Virginia family that had fought with the colonists in the Revolutionary War. Although Claiborne was not as obsessed about racial mixing as his predecessor, he did fear that the Choctaws and the black slaves who lived in the territory might join together to drive out the whites. By the time Mississippi underwent its first census in 1817, the reasons for Claiborne's concern became apparent: the census tabulated twenty-three thousand black slaves, twenty-five thousand whites, and thirty-five thousand Native Americans. If slaves entered into an alliance with the Indians, they would outnumber whites by a margin of more than two to one.

By the 1820s, Natchez had more millionaires per capita than any city in the United States. Most of that wealth was derived from land speculation and the cotton trade. Slaves were essential to a cotton economy. Indians were not. Perhaps more important, Indians blocked further land speculation because they owned most of the land in Mississippi. White settlers were never forced to choose between slaves and Indians, but they chose to do so because of fears, unfounded as it turned out, that Mississippi's Indian population was a threat to their economic and personal security.

Evidence of the peaceful intent of Mississippi's Native American population came when Choctaw chief Pushmataha received a plea from Shawnee leaders in Tennessee to join in a war against the white settlers. Rejecting the alliance, Pushmataha explained:

> These white Americans . . . have encouraged and helped us in the production of our crops. They have taken many of our wives into their homes to teach them useful things. They pay them for their work while learning. You all remember well the dreadful epidemic visited upon us last winter. During its darkest hours these neighbors whom we are now urged to attack responded generously to our needs. They doctored our sick."[6]

There was no reason to think that the Choctaw would be anything other than supportive of white Americans. After the Revolutionary War the Choctaw aligned themselves with the new government. Choctaw leaders mistakenly thought that since they had good relations with ordinary white settlers, they also had good relations with the plantation owners. That was not the case. Plantation owners wanted Choctaw land so that they could clear more forests and grow more cotton. In their minds, Indian loyalty to the American government was not necessarily a positive thing. Many Mississippi planters secretly longed for the good old days of British rule, when great wealth opened doors to unquestioned social status.

During the first three decades of the 1800s pressure increased on the government to rid the country of Native Americans. It was the result, according to University of Kentucky professors Theda Perdue and Michael D. Green, of two factors: racism based on the belief of white settlers that Indians were racially inferior and an ever-increasing demand for Indian land.[7] Advocating the argument that President Washington was wrong to consider Indian tribes sovereign nations with whom treaties could be forged was Andrew Jackson, who led the movement to seize Indian land without compensation. Jackson felt that Indians were incapable of being assimilated into American culture.

In the years following the War of 1812, government officials tried to persuade various Indian tribes to give up their ancestral land in exchange for land in the West, but only a handful of tribes accepted the offer. In 1828, Andrew Jackson ran for president, making Indian removal an important part of his campaign. Once in office he urged Congress to pass legislation that would make it possible for the government to relocate Indians east of the Mississippi River, using force if necessary. It was the first time that federal law acknowledged that white citizens had rights that could not be applied to persons of color, an argument that continues to this day with dogged insistence that American citizens have constitutional rights that cannot be claimed by noncitizens of minority races and ethnic backgrounds. It was also the first federal law to allow internment based on race or ethnic origin and the first to establish a legal basis for restrictive concentration camps.

At that time, the most contentious disagreements over Indian land occurred in Georgia, where white settlers were impatient to rid the state of all Indians. State officials used states' rights as a justification for a series of harassing actions, such as extending state jurisdiction over the Cherokee nation. Bowing to states' rights advocates, President Jackson refused to intervene, stating that Georgia's sovereignty rights superseded those claimed by the Indians.

In 1830, when Congress considered the Indian Removal Act, Georgia's unilateral actions became an issue that threatened passage of the bill. Opponents of the bill tried unsuccessfully to add language that would require the president to protect the Cherokee from Georgia law until they could be relocated. Such an amendment to the bill was rebuffed by Jackson supporters, and on May 28, 1830, the bill was passed and quickly signed into law by Jackson. Most northerners voted against the bill, while most southerners voted for the bill. One notable exception was Tennessee representative Davy Crockett, who voted in opposition to Indian removal.

In his State of the Union address, delivered six months after passage of the Indian Removal Act, President Jackson said:

> It gives me pleasure to announce to Congress that the benevolent policy of the Government, steadily pursued for nearly thirty years, in relation to the removal of the Indians beyond the white settlements is approaching to a happy consummation. . . . Humanity has often wept over the fate of the aborigines of this country, and Philanthropy has been long busily employed in devising means to avert it, but its progress has never for a moment been arrested."[8]

Native Americans were stunned by the legislation. Especially shocked were Mississippi's Choctaws, for they were chosen to be the first Indians removed from their land. How was it possible that they would lose their ancestral land? First recognized by white explorers in the 1500s, they had lived on the land for at least two thousand years, perhaps as long as four thousand years. They had supported the colonies during the Revolutionary War. They had fought alongside Jackson at the Battle of New Orleans.

Tribal leaders were coerced into signing the 1830 Treaty of Dancing Rabbit Creek, which ceded all their land east of the Mississippi River (about fifteen million acres) and required them to relocate to Oklahoma to live in internment camps called reservations. There was a provision in the treaty that allowed some Choctaw to remain in Mississippi:

> Each Choctaw head of a family being desirous to remain and become a citizen of the States, shall be permitted to do so, by signifying his intention to the Agent within six months from the ratification of this Treaty, and he or she shall thereupon be entitled to a reservation of one section of six hundred and forty acres of land, to be bounded by sectional lines of survey.[9]

In 1831, the year the treaty was ratified, thirteen thousand Choctaw made the 550-mile journey to Oklahoma, with four thousand of them dying of hunger and exposure along the way. About seven thousand

Choctaw remained in Mississippi, where they were given land for a reservation and stripped of their tribal status and forced to adhere to state and federal laws. Not until 1945 were they allowed a constitution of their own.

The relocation of the Choctaw left an Indian population of twenty-two thousand, fifteen thousand of whom were Chickasaw who lived in the northern part of the state. President Jackson attempted to strike a similar deal with the Chickasaw, but negotiations fell apart when agreement could not be reached on a relocation site. As a result, Chickasaw leaders signed the land over to the government with an understanding that it would be sold quickly and the money deposited in a Chickasaw account. Most of the Chickasaw ended up being moved to Oklahoma, where they used the money in their government account to purchase land from the Choctaw.

Over a period of two years the Mississippi Indian population was reduced from thirty-five thousand to about twelve thousand, making whites the new majority. Joining that new majority was Thomas Asbury Turner, grandson of Thomas Turner and great-great-grandson of John and Jane Turner. In 1843 he walked to northern Mississippi near Tupelo, a land grant for 640 acres tucked inside his pocket. A cabinetmaker by trade, he carried his tools with him and worked along the way. By the time he arrived, most of the Chickasaw were gone. His parcel of land was located in the hill country, not far from the Natchez Trace, one of the oldest wilderness trails in America. He built a two-story log house with a long hallway at the back to connect a separate kitchen. In the backyard he built quarters for his slave, a kind-hearted African man named Old Tom. Once the house was completed, Thomas Asbury married seventeen-year-old Mary Elizabeth Jackson, a first cousin of President Andrew Jackson (who died the year they were married). They had nine children, eight boys and one girl.

Incredibly the bloodline established by John and Jane Turner, following the general trend of the nation, mutated from one that stood for racial equality and individual freedom to one that accepted slavery and embraced the internment policies of President Jackson, a man whom wilderness explorer John Turner never would have accepted as a leader, much less embraced as an in-law.

2

WALKING THE TRAIL OF TEARS

With the success of the ethnic cleansing directed against the Mississippi Choctaws and Chickasaw, the U.S. government turned its attention to the Seminole, descendants of the Georgia-based Creeks. The Seminole had moved south into the Spanish-controlled Florida Territory during the late 1700s, where they prospered as farmers, creating a very successful plantation culture. By 1823, with the Treaty of Moultrie Creek, the Seminole were moved inland to restrictive internment camps, which prevented them from having access to the ocean. Nine years later, with the Treaty of Payne's Landing, the Seminole were ordered to leave Florida.

Unlike the Choctaw and the Chickasaw, the Seminole resisted efforts of the whites to drive them off their land. More than forty thousand American troops were sent to Florida to move more than five thousand Seminole out west, but the Indians proved to be formidable fighters, killing more than thirteen hundred soldiers. With a price tag of $120 million, it proved to be the costliest Indian war in history.[1]

The biggest obstacle was a Seminole war chief named Osceola, a charismatic, young man who felt that his people were bound spiritually to the land in ways that the white man could never understand. At one point, the Indian agent for Florida put Osceola in chains after an argument over the Treaty of Payne's Landing. The humiliation guaranteed that the Seminole would retaliate.

On December 28, 1835, Osceola ambushed the Indian agent and killed him just outside the gate of Fort King. That same day, unaware of what had happened at Fort King, Major Francis L. Dade set out from Tampa, Florida, to Ocala, a distance of about seventy-five miles, with an army of a little over one hundred soldiers. The winding trail that Dade followed was overgrown with semitropical brush that made it difficult for the men to see what was on either side of them.[2] They were near the end of their journey, marching double file, when Seminole warriors opened fire, killing Major Dade in the first volley of bullets. The second in command succeeded in turning back the attack, but only for a short time. The Seminole resumed the attack, killing all but three of the soldiers, who survived only because they pretended to be dead. Of the three survivors, only one soldier lived long enough to tell the story.

Three weeks after the attack, Major General Winfield Scott was in the office of Secretary of War Lewis Cass when he learned of the battle. A Virginian who had an imposing physical appearance—he was six feet five inches tall—Scott was a highly regarded military officer who had compiled an impressive record of success in the War of 1812 and in the Mexican-American War. To many Americans, he was a national hero.

After telling Scott about the attack, Secretary Cass asked when he could be ready to travel to Florida. Scott's rapid-fire response was, "This evening." His anticipated departure date was overly optimistic, but not by much. He left Washington the following evening, after working feverishly with Cass to devise a practical battle plan.

All during his lengthy journey to Florida—and throughout his stay in the territory—Scott, who had the nickname "Old Fuss and Feathers," fired off ill-tempered letters to both subordinates and superiors, complaining about troop and supply shortages. While in Florida, he issued an order that was made public, criticizing local whites for showing cowardice in the face of Indian attacks.[3] He characterized their panic in the face of danger as "humiliating."

Within four months of his arrival, Scott was recalled from Florida with orders to report to Savannah to assist with the removal of the Creek and Cherokee from Georgia. Few people were happier to see Scott leave than the general himself. The year after he left, Osceola was lured into peace negotiations, only to be captured and transported to South Carolina, where he died less than three months after his capture. There was an outcry over his deceitful capture, even among whites. Fighting raged for another five years, until Seminole villages were so devastated that there was no alternative but to surrender and submit to internment in Oklahoma. Almost three thousand Seminole were forced from Florida, leaving behind less than five hundred, who were required to live under close supervision in internment camps in southwest Florida.

─────────────

In future years General Scott received attention as an outstanding Civil War general and as a tenacious, though unsuccessful, presidential candidate, but in the mid- to late 1830s, his claim to fame was as an Indian fighter. When he was dispatched to Georgia in 1838 to deal with the Cherokee, it was at the request of local whites who considered him a hardliner who would cut the Indians no slack.

The last of the so-called Civilized Tribes, the Cherokee ignored orders to relocate west of the Mississippi River in Oklahoma and Arkansas.[4] Scott was ordered to round up the Indians and move them out of Georgia. He was given six weeks to complete the task. Before setting out for Georgia, Scott received a visit from Chief John Ross, who by the age of forty-eight had been a Cherokee leader for over a decade. Ross pleaded with Scott not to go to Georgia, calling the removal an illegal act. Scott listened politely but informed Ross that he had no choice but to obey his orders. Scott's plan was simple: he would use a massive number of troops to round up the Cherokee in Georgia, Alabama, North Carolina, and Tennessee, about twenty-two thousand in total, plus two thousand black slaves, and then place them into concentration camps until they could be moved to debarkation points along the major waterways of the region and then shipped by boat to Oklahoma and Arkansas.

About one month after his meeting with Chief Ross, who continued his appeal for reconsideration with the Van Buren administration, Scott gathered an army and traveled south, issuing a proclamation to the Cherokee that began, "Cherokees! The President of the United States has sent me, with a powerful army, to cause you, in obedience to the Treaty of 1835, to join that band of your people who are already established in prosperity on the other side of the Mississippi. . . . May the God of both [Cherokees and whites] preserve them long in peace and friendship with each other."[5]

After overhearing members of the Georgia Guard, a private militia organization that had the support of Georgia public officials, say they were looking forward to the day when all Cherokee were dead, Scott followed the earlier proclamation with a second one on May 17 that stated, in part: "Every possible kindness, compatible with the necessity of removal, must, therefore, be shown by the troops, and, if, in the ranks, a despicable individual should be found, capable of inflicting a wanton injury or insult on any Cherokee man, woman or child it is hereby made the special duty of the nearest good officer or man, instantly to interpose, and to seize and consign the guilty wretch to the severest penalty."[6]

Since barbed wire had not yet been invented, the concentration camps built for the Cherokees—thirty-one in all—were built like stockades. The camps, all constructed near Cherokee towns, were meant to be temporary holding facilities. Despite General Scott's admonition that the Indians be treated with respect by his troops, they often were treated harshly, with little respect for their historic devotion to land they had occupied as a people for thousands of years.

Private John G. Burnett, a witness to the abuse, wrote in 1838: "[I] witnessed the execution of the most brutal order in the history of American warfare. I saw the helpless Cherokees arrested and dragged from their homes, and driven at the bayonet point into the stockades. And in the chill of a drizzling rain on an October morning I saw them loaded like cattle or sheep six hundred and forty-five wagons and headed for the West."[7]

Evan Jones was a Baptist missionary who worked among the Cherokee in North Carolina. When the soldiers forced the Indians off their land and herded them into concentration camps, Jones accompanied them. His experiences were duly recorded in letters he sent to the *Baptist Missionary Magazine*. On June 16, 1935, he wrote that most of the Cherokee had been captured, having been dragged from their homes and transported to military posts:

> In Georgia, especially, multitudes were allowed no time to take anything with them, except the clothes they had on. Well-furnished houses were left a prey to plunderers, who, like hungry wolves, follow in the train of the captors. These wretches rifle the houses, and strip the helpless, unoffending owners of all they have on earth. Females, who have been habituated to comforts and comparative affluence, are driven on foot before the bayonets of brutal men.[8]

Rebecca Neugin was three years of age when the soldiers came to her parents' home and took them away. Her recollections of the event, cemented by the oral history of her family's memories, were recorded ninety-one years later when she was ninety-four years of age. Interviewing her was Oklahoma historian Grant Foreman, who published her memories in *Indian Removal*: "When the soldiers came to our house my father wanted to fight, but my mother told him that the soldiers would kill him if he did and we surrendered without a fight. They drove us out of our house to join other prisoners in a stockade. After they took us away my mother begged them to let her go back and get some bedding. So they let her go back and she brought what bedding and a few cooking utensils she could carry and had to leave behind all our other household possessions."[9]

The first concentration camp used to house the Cherokee was named Fort Sixes, one of twelve such camps in Georgia. Prior to receiving Cherokee families, Fort Sixes had been used to house the infamous Georgia Guard, an organization that had the same relationship to Indians that the Ku Klux Klan subsequently had with blacks. Conditions at Fort Sixes and the other fourteen camps in Georgia were deplorable. Unspeakable crimes took place behind the wooden stockade walls. Cherokee possessions were stolen and sold to local white residents. "Living areas were filled with excrement. Birth rates among the Cherokee dropped to near zero during the months of captivity. Cherokee women and children were repeatedly raped. Soldiers forced their captives to perform acts of depravation so disgusting they cannot be told here." One member of the Guard would later write, "During the Civil War I watched as hundreds of men died, including my own brother, but none of that compares to what we did to the Cherokee Indians."[10]

Conditions improved somewhat when the Cherokee were moved from Georgia to internment camps in Tennessee and Alabama, but crowding was still a problem, since each camp sometimes held several hundred Indians at one time in primitive conditions that promoted disease. Desperate for relief, one group of Cherokee leaders bravely petitioned General Winfield Scott, pointing out the seriousness of their living conditions: "We do not ask you to let us go free from being your prisoners, unless it should please yourself. But we ask that you will not send us down the river at this time of the year. If you do we shall die, our wives will die or our children will die. Sir, our hearts are heavy, very heavy. . . . We cannot make a talk, our hearts are too full of sorrow."[11]

During the summer months of 1838, disease was rampant in the concentration camps in Tennessee and Alabama. Deaths were reported every day. There were also frequent reports of suicide. When the time came to move out of the camps in August, Cherokee leader John Ross asked the government to delay their departure until cooler weather, a request that was granted. Meanwhile, as talks about the terms of the march to Oklahoma were discussed, Ross asked Washington to give the Cherokee the opportunity to travel under their own supervision, without the oversight of the U.S. Army. His request was granted, though they were required to travel unarmed, with a promise that their weapons would await them when they arrived in Oklahoma. It was a decision that made everyone happy. General Winfield Scott was pleased to be relieved of the responsibility of escorting the Indians, and the chiefs were pleased to once again be placed in a position of leadership. The Cherokee set out from Tennessee and Alabama in the dead of winter on a twelve-hundred-mile march that later would be named the "Trail of Tears."

Relying on the stories passed to her by her mother and father, Rebecca Neugin said that there was much sickness along the way, causing many children to die of whooping cough. Those who owned wagons and horses were allowed to ride for the duration of the journey. Those who did not own wagons were forced to walk: "My father had a wagon pulled by two spans of oxen to haul us in. Eight of my brothers and sisters and two or three widow women and children rode with us. . . . The people got so tired of eating salt pork on the journey that my father would walk through the woods as we traveled, hunting for turkeys and deer which he brought into camp to feed us. Camp was usually made at some place where water was to be had."[12]

A white traveler from Maine, who came across about two thousand Cherokee in Kentucky, on their way to Oklahoma, later wrote about the experience: "We found the road literally filled with the procession for about three miles in length. The sick and feeble were carried in wagons—about as comfortable for traveling as a New England ox cart with a covering over it—a great many ride on horseback and multitudes go on foot—even aged females, apparently nearly ready to drop into the grave, were traveling with heavy burdens attached to the back.[13]

Along the way, many of the victims of what scholars would describe as the largest instance of ethnic cleansing in American history turned to Christianity for solace, punctuating the brittle wilderness air with plaintive voices that, despite the hardships of the journey, rang with hope as they sang "Amazing Grace," a hymn that later would find great resonance among newly freed African American slaves. Sometimes the verses were in English. Other times they were in Cherokee. Always they made the Trail of Tears more endurable than it otherwise might have been.

When Mississippi seceded from the Union in 1861, Thomas Asbury Turner was one of eighty thousand Mississippians who enlisted in the Confederate army. Before going off to war he left his youngest children and his wife in the care of his sister Winnie and his slave, Old Tom. His two eldest sons, James and Joseph, soon followed their father into battle.

Thomas Asbury died in July 1862, while fighting in northern Mississippi; that same month his wife died of typhoid fever, and Winnie followed soon thereafter. After their deaths, the children were left in the hands of Old Tom, who cared for them as if they were his own.[14]

James died on July 28, 1864, on Macon Road in Atlanta, Georgia, defending the city from an overwhelming assault by General William Sherman, who later candidly described the battle as a slaughter. When Joseph returned home from the war, he discovered that he was fatherless and motherless. He tried to make a go of the farm with his brothers and sisters but then quickly discovered that the restrictions imposed by Reconstruction made that impossible. The land was sold off and the Turner siblings, dispossessed by the government that their ancestors had fought for and nurtured and they themselves had fought against, went their separate ways.

One of the surviving sons raised by Old Tom was Stephen Henry Turner, born in 1849. Stephen was an unusually bright man who wanted nothing so much as to inject a sense of order in the universe. In 1883, at the age of twenty-four, he married twenty-year-old Emily Bigham of Ecru, Mississippi. It is thought that the two met while he was living with his Aunt Winnie. They lived for a time on Cherry Creek, east of Ecru, but when they were ready to build a home of their own, they went to Mantachie, where the last of the Chickasaws were in the process of leaving for Oklahoma.

They built their home across the road from a log house the Chickasaws had used as a council house. On the other side of the house was an Indian cemetery. They planted an orchard there and, for years, found arrowheads, bits of pottery, and other artifacts that worked their way to the surface of the soil. On the south side of the house was an artesian spring. Stephen built a springhouse over the water and dug a deep basin that he used to refrigerate milk and meat.

In the late 1880s, Stephen was elected a delegate to the Mississippi constitutional convention of 1890. He left the yearlong convention for a while to return to his home near Tupelo after complaining that the other delegates were obsessed with race. "All they want to talk about is putting niggers in their place," he complained to family members, troubled by visions of Old Tom, who had raised him to adulthood. "We're supposed to be there to write laws." After cooling off, he returned to the convention and completed his work on what became the Constitution of 1890, a document still in use by the State of Mississippi.

Grandpa Turner, as Stephen was called by then, was a free thinker (it took courage for him to buck the racist trend at the constitutional convention; the final document was tinged with racial considerations, but it would have been much worse without his protests) and an innovator who was ahead of his time. He owned the first automobile in the community. He bought the first radio. And he was the first to pipe water into his house. He built an engine room to generate electricity, and he installed tubs for bathing and for washing clothes.

After Emily's death in 1919, Grandpa Turner seemed to those around him to have lost his will to live. On March 4, 1920, the anniversary of Emily's birth, he wrote in his journal, an obvious throwback to the sentiments once expressed by the matriarch of the Turner clan when faced with the death of a loved one: "I am very grateful that she was born into this world for she was the source of the greatest pleasure to me of any person that ever lived. Since she died I am and have been one of the most miserable men in this world. My days and nights are alike. I miss her so much. The children are good to me but not like she was. I long to be out of this, but I await God's good time."[15]

Grandpa Turner lived another twelve years, passing away in 1931 at the age of eighty-three of what the doctors called "pernicious anemia." When he wrote the family history in the early 1920s, he noted with pride that no male Turner, in over 250 years of life in America, had ever gone to jail and only one had ever separated from his wife.

Grandpa Turner's grandchildren did not have an easy time of it, coming of age as they did during the Great Depression; but it never occurred to any of them as they huddled around Grandpa Turner's gardenia-laden coffin that they someday would have to face the old issues of war, torture, and internment that had cursed their lineage, passing from generation to generation since the 1600s, their family a microcosm of the American experience, with all its achievements, disappointments, and faults. Yet as they stood at the gravesite, the blood of native America flowing through their veins and the sweet scent of gardenia wafting about them, storm clouds were already gathering on the horizon, so that in time three of those present would be summoned to step into the maelstrom of what some historians would call the Great War and those who fought in it the Greatest Generation.

PART II

CAMPS THAT WILL LIVE IN INFAMY

As we boarded the bus
bags on both sides
(I had never packed two bags before
on a vacation
lasting forever)
the Seattle Times
photographer said
Smile!
so obediently I smiled
and the caption the next day
read:
Note smiling faces
a lesson to Tokyo
                    —MITSUYE YAMADA, "EVACUATION"

3

PEARL HARBOR UNDER ATTACK

Early on the morning of December 7, 1941, eleven-year-old Doris Berg was on her parents' bed, where her father, Frederick Berg, was reading her the Sunday comics. Discussions about the funny papers were important parts of the father-daughter Sunday-morning ritual. Doris's mother, Bertha, and her nine-year-old sister, Anita, were rambling about the three-story house, carrying out their customary early morning chores. The Bergs lived on the third floor and used the lower two floors to accommodate nineteen nursing-home patients. Theirs was the first commercial residence for the elderly in Hawaii, and it had a high profile in the community.[1]

Suddenly, there was a loud explosion.

"What's that?" asked Doris.

She jumped off the bed, ran to the window, and looked down the hill toward the U.S. military base at Pearl Harbor, about fourteen miles from their Nuuanu Valley home.

"It was just totally black with smoke," she later recalled. "We had a pretty good view. There were no mountains in the way or anything like that."

She asked her father what was going on.

"I don't know." He was unconcerned, reminding her that the military base had been conducting noisy maneuvers for the past year. "One of those big cannons on the ships probably misfired."

Not satisfied with that answer, Doris ran downstairs to the kitchen, where her mother was preparing breakfast, and she turned on the radio. Neither of Honolulu's two stations, KGMB and KGU, knew what was happening.[2] At first, the announcers reported on the explosions without attributing them to an enemy attack. Honolulu was accustomed to the ships rattling china with the booms from their big guns during target practice.

But eventually, the KGMG announcer sputtered out the awful realization: "This is the real McCoy!"

The urgency of the announcer's reporting mesmerized Doris. "The Japs are attacking!" she heard him say. "Take cover! There are people up in the hills watching. This is not just another maneuver. Pack your things and be ready to head for the hills!"

"Start packing!" her mother commanded.

"For me, it was, 'Oh boy! We're going to camp out!' I was a kid, and it was really exciting. So I got out two big boxes. Into one I tossed three blankets, and into the other I threw food. While I was in the kitchen, I heard this shrieking outside—like planes diving—so I ran outside with my little sister, and we looked up and we saw the Zeros."

"Zero" was the nickname for Japan's top carrier-based fighter aircraft. It was called a Zero not because of the red circle on the wings and fuselage, the rising-sun emblem on the Japanese flag, but rather because of its designation as a Type 0 carrier fighter. The Japanese Navy used the last digits of the calendar year when naming military aircraft, and in 1940 the Japanese calendar year was 2600. Superior to aircraft used by the U.S. military, the Zero was very difficult to bring down. It would be quite some time before American pilots devised the strategy that pitted two U.S. Wildcats against each Zero so that they could attack it during a climb or dive, when it was vulnerable due to a lack of protective armor.

Standing on the front lawn, Doris and her little sister looked up into the sky, twisting and turning to see as the planes dove, swooped, and climbed, their engines whining. They watched a dogfight between a Zero and two U.S. aircraft.

"You could see the zeros on the plane because it wasn't flying very high. An American plane shot it down," Doris recalls.

At one point they heard an explosion about a block from their home, leading Doris to mistakenly conclude that a Zero had dropped a bomb on their neighborhood. In truth, only one Japanese bomb fell beyond the harbor, but forty shells from U.S. cannons missed their mark and dropped into the surrounding neighborhoods, causing civilians to mistakenly think that they had been targeted by the Zeros.[3]

Not long after they went on the air, both radio stations were silenced by the military so that their radio waves could not be used as beacons by Japanese pilots. As it turned out, that was a mistake because the silenced radio stations only contributed to the hysteria that swept through the city, fanned by shortwave broadcasts from American ships that spread false reports about enemy troops landing on the north shore.[4] The false shortwave reports, coupled with the silence of the two commercial radio stations, were particularly hard on anxious military wives and families who searched the static-riddled airwaves for any glimmer of hope.

After the skies cleared of airplanes, Doris and her family hunkered down and waited for the second wave of attacks while comforting the fearful patients and dealing with desperate inquiries from their families, who frantically made arrangements to take their relatives out of the nursing home so that they could be moved to a place of safety.

Meanwhile, as the hours wore on and it became obvious that there would be no more attacks that day, the radio barked out a constant stream of orders:

Stay off the streets!

Keep your lights out!

There is a complete blackout for all of the Territory of Hawaii. Anyone not complying will be severely punished!

Any lights showing will be shot out!

That night Doris and her family went to sleep not certain what to expect during the night. The following morning, with the skies still clear of enemy aircraft, all residents who had jobs were ordered to report to work so that they could board up windows and erect barricades around the businesses. Doris's father had a second job at Sears, and he immediately left to report to work, leaving his wife in charge of the nursing home and the evacuation of patients.

Doris stood in the front yard so that she could greet people coming to pick up their relatives. Recalls Doris: "When they arrived, I would tell them to wait, and then I'd run into the house and tell Mom that so-and-so was here."

She had repeated that routine several times when a car pulled up and two men in dark suits got out. They said they wanted to talk to her mother. Following her routine, she asked them to wait and then bounded up the back stairs to the kitchen, where her mother was busy working. On the way up the stairs, she turned and saw that the men were right behind her, their shoes slapping against the planking of the stairway.

"I was thinking, Wait a minute! Relatives are not supposed to do that! . . . What's happening here?"

Her mother was just coming into the pantry, and Doris practically ran into her. She pointed to the men, explaining that they were here to see her, her words going a mile a minute. The men introduced themselves and spoke to her mother in low voices that Doris couldn't hear. She backed away as far as she could, frightened, her back pressed against the kitchen cabinets. No one but family ever walked up the back stairs into their kitchen, and so she assumed that something was terribly wrong. Finally, she heard her mother say, "I need to put on some lipstick."

At first Doris thought she was talking to her. But she was speaking to the men, using a tone that was polite yet uncertain. The men nodded their approval, and her mother went into the bathroom, with the men right behind her, their holstered pistols in full view. Doris felt a rising panic when she saw the men enter the bathroom with her mother. No man but her father had ever gone into the bathroom with her mother. There was something so . . . well, unnatural about that. The holstered guns were almost an afterthought. She saw men with guns every day. Soldiers carrying rifles. Policemen with holsters. But this bathroom thing. It really rattled her.

Moments later they emerged from the bathroom, her mother wearing the same thin cotton dress. To Doris's surprise, she looked at her and said,

"Take care of the patients and your sister—I'll be right back." That was it. No further explanation.

Doris was confused. Her mother had never left her in charge of the patients. She followed them back down the stairs, her little legs struggling to keep up, since they seemed to be walking faster and faster, their longer legs gobbling up two steps to her one. Once they reached the lawn she stopped and watched as her mother got into the car and drove away with the men in suits.

Doris went inside and got Anita, and together they waited in front of the house, continuing to tell the people who arrived that their family members were waiting inside for them. Many of the adults advised the girls to go upstairs to wait for their parents, but they refused. Recalls Doris:

> Dad had always told me, in case of fire, you will be trapped up there. So we stayed downstairs and there were some people in a room, three or four people, and they were laughing and making toasts. Why would people be having fun at a time like this? It was very unusual. I didn't understand it. I was just sick that my mom was gone. That had never happened to me before. I was upset. It didn't make sense at all.

———

The night of the second day was almost more than Doris could bear. Neither her mother nor her father came home. Most of the nursing-home patients were gone, leaving Doris and Anita practically alone in the rambling old house without adult supervision.

Doris assumed that her father had been killed. Was there any other possibility? Death was everywhere. It was on the radio and on the lips of those who took their relatives from the house. But she held out hope that her mother was alive and would return. She spent most of her time on the front porch, waiting for her mother. She recalls:

> The fear was terrible. Because there was a blackout, no cars could have their lights on. They had to navigate the streets without lights.

There was a militia. People with guns had taken over the streets. It came over the radio that lights were being shot out. My sister, without thinking about what she was doing, went to the third floor and turned on the lights and there was yelling on the street and the lights were shot out. That was very upsetting.

The next morning, Doris made breakfast. All she knew how to cook was pancakes, so she and her sister gorged themselves on double helpings. She was in a state of shock but tried to act as if nothing were wrong. Taking care of Anita was her top priority.

Luckily, Doris and Anita's eighteen-year-old half sister, Eleanor—who had been visiting an aunt on the island of Molokai when the attack occurred—appeared at the house the following day and took charge. Eleanor had a different father, the product of Bertha's first marriage to a German national. An arranged marriage that soon ended in divorce, it had cost Bertha her U.S. citizenship, since the law at that time penalized American women who married foreign nationals. Bertha had taken Eleanor, who retained her U.S. citizenship, to Germany, where she married Frederick, a German citizen with degrees from the University of Cologne and the University of Heidelberg. In 1930, following repeal of the law that deprived her of U.S. citizenship, she denounced her German citizenship and was repatriated to the United States with full citizenship rights. Doris and Anita subsequently were born in Hawaii with full U.S. citizenship. Hawaii did not become a state until 1959, but from the time it was annexed by the United States in 1898 and became a territory in 1900, anyone born in Hawaii was automatically granted U.S. citizenship. Frederick made it unanimous in the mid-1930s when he obtained citizenship. Although their journey had been difficult, they were now an all-American family.

Eleanor released Doris and Anita from their sentry duties, although Doris remained reluctant to leave the porch for fear her parents would arrive and then disappear again without seeing the girls. Part of her wanted to believe they would come home; another part of her wrestled with the fear that they were dead. Her only source of comfort was that she had also feared Eleanor's death only to have her show up when she least expected it. Perhaps that was a good omen.

"When she came home, it was a tremendous relief. Everything was off my shoulders. We went out and got some food and came back. The next morning, when I awoke, Eleanor was already up, folding and organizing clothes because people had come and taken things from the house and there were things all over the place."

After breakfast, Doris went outside to play with her cat. To her horror, a black car drove up, and two men in dark suits got out and walked toward her. The nightmare was beginning all over again.

As the men approached, her worst fears were realized when one of the men asked if she knew where they could find Eleanor. She screamed and ran toward the house, the men right behind her, not falling behind but not overtaking her either, everyone running up the back stairs to the kitchen, their feet slapping against the wooden steps. Doris pulled ahead, bounding over two steps at a time, finally leaving the men behind as she burst in the door. Seeing Eleanor, she grabbed her by the hand and, crying and screaming, dragged her to the attic door, trying her best to push her through the opening, only to have the men overtake them and yank Eleanor away from her white-knuckled grasp. Doris fought them the entire time, tiny fists swinging.

I had to save my sister because she was going to be murdered, too. They took her downstairs, and then across the lawn, and I was biting and kicking and scratching. One of the men, who I later learned was an FBI agent, had this look in his eyes of tremendous compassion. It was to him, out of desperation, I cried out, "Please don't take my sister!" That poor guy! He couldn't do anything. He had to follow orders. But his eyes were so sad for Anita and me. When they took Eleanor to the car, I was holding on, begging him not to take her, and he had to peel my fingers away so they could take her away. It was a horrible, horrible thing for a kid to go through. My sister didn't know what in the world was happening.

Later, Eleanor called Doris and told her that she'd been taken to the FBI offices, where she was photographed and fingerprinted. When Eleanor had asked the FBI officials why, they said that she had been brought in because she was an alien. She told them they were making a mistake. She explained that she was an American citizen, but they didn't believe her. She had come to the FBI's attention because she had traveled to Germany in 1938 to visit her grandparents. While there, she fell in love with a Jewish newspaper reporter from New York and accepted his marriage proposal. The two of them escaped Nazi Germany at the beginning of 1940 and fled to New York, where she lived for about a year before returning, alone, to Hawaii early in 1941. The fact that she'd lived in Nazi Germany raised red flags with the FBI, who questioned her loyalty to the United States.

"How are you doing?" Eleanor asked.

"OK," Doris answered, uncertain whether their conversation was being monitored. That an eleven-year-old girl would worry about being spied on by the government is a good indicator of the fear that permeated the island. "Where are you?"

"I can't say."

"Have you seen Mommy and Daddy?"

"No."

"Do you know where they are?"

"No—where will you and Anita go?"

"I'm going to take her to Molokai to visit our aunt."

"I have to go," said Eleanor, who quickly hung up the phone.

The telephone gave Doris hope for the first time. If Eleanor was still alive, perhaps their mother and father were also still alive. However, Doris did not take her sister and go to Molokai, because she feared that if she left the house, her parents would return and not know where she and her sisters were.

So she and Anita stayed on, alone in the house. The next morning she telephoned another aunt, Anna, who lived in Honolulu, but she also was German and fearful of drawing attention to herself, so she didn't suggest that they come live with her. Instead, Aunt Anna told Doris she would hire a nurse to stay with her and Anita.

Had Doris and her little sister become a lightning rod for the FBI? Were they being watched day and night from behind bushes and parked cars? Although she was only eleven, Doris could see that the world was not a safe place. She must be careful at all times, she concluded, as one could never know when the government was lurking in the shadows, watching, waiting for an opportunity to do something terrible to her and her sister.

———————————

Within minutes after the attack on Pearl Harbor, the territorial governor of Hawaii suspended the writ of habeas corpus and invoked the Hawaii Defense Act, effectively turning over control of Hawaii to General Walter Short, who promptly declared the islands to be under martial law.[5] Censorship was immediate. Mail was opened and examined. Government censors listened in on all telephone calls, especially those from island to island and those with foreign callers. If conversations in any language other than English were detected, the calls were quickly terminated.

The decision for a military takeover of the islands was not made hastily. Several months before the attack, President Franklin Roosevelt, fearing trouble on the islands because of its large Asian population, had approved plans for the implementation of martial law for Hawaii. In accordance with the plan, the military declared an immediate curfew following the attack and began rounding up Americans and aliens of Japanese and German heritage so they could be imprisoned until they could prove that they were not a threat to the United States.

In the days that followed, military commissions replaced Hawaii's civil courts and did away with jury trials, grand juries, and the issuance of writs of habeas corpus. All residents over the age of six were identified and fingerprinted. Citizens were prohibited from having more than two hundred dollars in cash, and businesses were banned from holding more than five hundred dollars, except to meet payrolls. Radio scripts were censored in advance of broadcast, and film developing was allowed only for residents known to be citizens who had permits to take photographs. People of Japanese descent were targeted for even tougher restrictions than those of German ancestry. Japanese aliens were forbidden to travel by air or to relocate without the approval of the provost marshal general. They were instructed to turn in all firearms, cameras, and shortwave radios. And they were not allowed to sell or buy alcoholic beverages.

The first stop for those arrested on suspicion of being sympathetic to Japan or Germany were county jails; the immigration station, which had a lockup section; or an internment camp hastily set up in Haiku, on Maui. After processing, the internees were usually transferred to the Sand Island Detention Center across Honolulu Harbor, and from there some were sent to camps on the mainland. The following account, provided by a Japanese American who was arrested by authorities, speaks to the bewilderment felt by many detainees:

When we reached the Department of Immigration building I was put behind bars for several weeks and no questions were asked of me. We had our meals out in the yard enclosed by walls under armed guards with their rifles drawn. All the time I was there I was not told why I was being held behind bars and neither the FBI nor the Immigration officer asked me any questions. After this I was sent to Sand Island and remained there for six months. It was during my stay at Sand Island [that] the FBI [took] me to the Federal Building where the FBI and military officers questioned me. They put their guns on the table in plain view, like a threat. I felt that they were interrogating me as though I was a spy—but I was not. The FBI and military officers told me that since America was at war with Japan and because I was raised in Okinawa, Japan, and regardless that I was an American citizen, I was an internee (P.O.W.).[6]

Each internee was given a hearing, but this procedure typically consisted of a summary of FBI evidence and questions about whether the internee had ever visited Japan or Germany or had ever donated money, food, or clothing to that country's war effort. The hearings were pretty much one-sided and rarely lasted more than fifteen or twenty minutes. Internees were not allowed to have lawyers, nor were they allowed to question government witnesses or present character witnesses. The following account by a Japanese internee named Kuantoku Goya, taken in testimony by the Commission on Wartime Relocation and Internment of Civilians, is representative of the hearings that took place:

A few weeks prior to December 20, 1942, the government conducted two separate "hearings" at Wailuku, Maui, to determine the
fate of the so-called "bad Japs." The officer in charge had already
predetermined that we were not good American citizens and he
would lock us up until the war was over. The hearings were in reality, merely individual interrogation of suspected "bad Japs." The
officer asked several pointed questions which required a yes/no
answer. If I answered affirmatively when asked whether I am loyal
to the United States, they would accuse me of being a liar. But if I
had said no, then I would be thrown in jail. I felt there was no way
I could be considered a loyal American.[7]

Of the 733 people arrested in Hawaii in the immediate aftermath
of the attack, most were of Japanese ancestry. Those of German ancestry fared better, with 13 men and 12 women arrested and interned in
Hawaii.[8] Frederick and Bertha Berg and their daughter Eleanor were
unlucky enough to be among them. Doris and her sister were among the
fortunate ones.

In some instances, children were imprisoned but had advocates who
spoke up for their release. Three days after the attack, Gertrude Schroder,
a German-born girl enrolled at Sacred Hearts Academy in Honolulu, was
taken into custody by authorities and taken to the prison on Sand Island.
At the time, a concerned nun wrote in her dairy, "Great is our conster-
nation as we know full well how innocent and harmless she is. Yet nothing can be done to release her." However, after seven weeks of prayerful
negotiations with the U.S. Army's Western Defense Command, the per-
sistent nuns secured the child's release, prompting a nun to write, "Gertrude Schroder is released and arrived here today, happy, so happy! And
what a loving welcome she received."[9]

At the conclusion of her interrogation by the FBI, Eleanor was told by
the agents that they had classified her as an enemy alien. She did not
share that information with Doris, for fear of upsetting her. After their
telephone conversation, Eleanor was taken to the Fort Armstrong Immi-

gration Station, where she was turned over to a soldier who marched her up a flight of stairs with a bayonet held to her back and delivered her to a jail matron who strip-searched her, and then put her into a holding cell with about forty other women. Much to her surprise, she saw her mother among the other prisoners.

The two women were delighted to see each other, but their reunion only added to the mystery. Why had they been arrested? Neither of them had been charged with a crime. Where was Frederick, and was he all right? When would they be released? Eleanor comforted her mother somewhat by telling her that she'd spoken to Doris and given her instructions to contact her aunt, but they had no way of knowing if Doris and Anita had made it to a place of safety. And how safe would they be with the aunt? How long would it be before the aunt was arrested? If that happened, what would happen to Doris and Anita? Would they be living on the streets? Would they be subjected to abuse? Would they be kidnapped and sold to sex traders? Mother and daughter held each other as they contemplated the possibilities.

Eleanor and Bertha had a miserable existence in the lockup cell. No one in the room had a change of clothing. There was only one sink and one toilet, both of which were in open view with no privacy. The women slept on cots that were positioned only a foot or so apart. At night the cell was totally dark, except when inmates struck matches to light their cigarettes, brief flares that revealed the depressed silhouettes of women sitting on the edges of their cots, shoulders slumped, nothing to do with their hands, their emotions running wild, darting in and out of outright fear and mind-numbing despair. Visitors were not allowed, but Eleanor eventually learned from the guards that both Frederick and her birth father were being held in the same building.

Of course, Doris and Anita knew nothing about the living conditions their parents and sister were enduring. No one from the government visited them to offer assistance, comfort, or reassurance. After a week of being cared for by the nurse hired by their aunt Anna, Doris lost all hope for the return of her loved ones. She became very depressed. She stopped eating. Another week passed, and she and her sister left the family home and went to live with their aunt. It was not a happy situation. Aunt Anna was very strict and straitlaced, primarily because of the fear that she felt over her situation. Would she be next? She warned the girls not to talk to the neighbors. If someone asked their names or where they were from, they were instructed to say nothing.

My aunt told everyone that we were war refugees. I couldn't blame her for that, of course. She and her family were U.S. citizens of German descent and afraid for their own safety. . . . She told me that she had received a note from her sister, my Aunt Marie on Molokai, in which my Aunt Marie explained that she could not possibly take us in [because] she did not take in any "outsiders." I still loved her despite what I heard. I knew that there must have been a reason. . . . Of course, they were afraid for themselves also. My uncle was manager of Pu'u O Hoku Ranch. They had three sons, all three graduates of an elite private school on Oahu. One helped on the cattle ranch and the other two were in the military. If she had taken us, how in the world would she have been able to explain that her nieces' parents, her own sister and brother-in-law, had been picked up and detained. She had been questioned regarding my parents. She said that there was no way they were anti-American. That my father had an accent and a family in Europe, but that was as far as the connection with Germany went. However, fear predominated. We remained poison to stay away from.[10]

A few days before Christmas, a Mr. Reed visited Doris and Anita at their aunt's house, and he presented them with gifts that he said had been purchased by their parents. Doris later found out that Mr. Reed was not to be trusted. One gift for Doris was a jigsaw that had been on her wish list for two years. She loved to help her father in his workshop, and the saw was something that she felt would boost her importance to him. However, her aunt, who felt that gifts only spoiled children, allowed them to keep only two or three gifts. The remaining gifts were sent to the Salvation Army. The jigsaw was among the gifts that had to be declined. How could she worry about helping her father when there was no way to know, day to day, if she still had a father much longer? The saw was a luxury in more ways than one.

After the gifts were opened, Mr. Reed drove Doris and Anita back to the house so that they could recover more of their clothing. To their surprise, nothing was left. The house had been trashed, and everything of value had been taken. They were there only a few minutes when Doris felt something rubbing against her ankles. It was her cat, Kitty-Poo. The cat had emerged from the debris on the floors and found Doris, her loud purring a reminder of happier days in the once-bustling house. Doris picked up her cat and held her close, begging Mr. Reed to allow her to take her pet back to her aunt's house.

"No," he said. "Put her down."

"But there is no one here to feed her."

"I'm sorry, but we can't take her with us."

"But she'll starve."

"I said put her down."

Doris lowered her best friend to the floor, still stroking her, still talking to her, the cat leaning into her leg the way cats do. As they drove away from the house, she looked back, heartbroken. Her pet was all that Doris could think about. No food was in the house. The neighbors certainly would not feed her. She would die for certain—just as her father, mother, and sister would die. At least, that's what she believed. That night Doris did something she had done regularly since the nightmare began. She wet her bed.

━━━━━━━━━━━━━━━━

Several days later, a woman whom Doris did not know came to the house. Aunt Anna took the woman to the far end of the living room. Doris knew what that meant. They wanted to talk without the children overhearing. Doris tried to listen, but their voices were too low.

After the woman left, Aunt Anna handed Doris a note. It was written in pencil on the back of a laundry receipt, and it was very wrinkled. Doris was thrilled when she realized it was from her mother. Later, she would find out that her mother had folded the letter many times so that it could be hidden and smuggled out of the prison and also that it was not the first note that Bertha tried to have smuggled out. The first time she attempted getting a note to her daughter, she was caught and punished.

The specific contents of the note did not survive the passage of time, memory being such a fragile and whimsical traveling companion, but many years later Doris recalled that the words comforted her and her sister. Hearing from their mother was like strolling through a cemetery and being greeted by a voice from the grave of a loved one. But her mother was not a ghost. The note was real. She could hold it in her hand. Yet she could barely believe the mother she thought was gone forever was still alive and thinking of her.

In February 1942, Frederick was taken from the lockup at Sand Island; placed aboard the U.S. Army transport *Grant* with more than two hundred Japanese, German, and Italian detainees; and shipped to San Francisco. Ironically, the ship originally had been a German ocean liner named *Konig Wilhelm II*. It had been seized by the United States during World War I and renamed, first, the USS *Madawaska* and then the USS *Grant*. Bertha and the children had no idea that he had left Hawaii. The ship also contained American soldiers who were being transferred from Hawaii to the mainland, on their way to deployment on the European front, and the detainees were segregated deep within the hold and kept under heavy guard. Since they were not allowed to leave the hold, all their meals were delivered to them by soldiers.

One day Frederick heard the clank of metal food containers and recognized a familiar face in the dim light. It was his nephew, one of Aunt Marie's three sons who had joined the military. Frederick's spirits soared. The young man had been a frequent guest in their house and often stopped by for dinner when he was not on maneuvers. Frederick's elation quickly turned to dismay when the young soldier delivered the food and turned away without acknowledging him as his uncle. Frederick eventually forgave his nephew, well understanding the tremendous pressure that he was under, but he never forgot.

Once the ship docked in San Francisco, the prisoners were taken to Angel Island, where they were held for several days before being transported to Camp McCoy, a training facility for American soldiers located near Sparta, Wisconsin. There were hundreds of U.S. soldiers at the camp, and Frederick and the other detainees were segregated from them and placed under heavy guard in buildings designated for prisoners of war and enemy aliens. Frederick desperately tried to convince his captors that he was an American citizen, not an enemy alien, but no one believed him.

It was not until Bertha received a letter from Frederick that she knew he had been moved to the mainland. In his letter, he said that he was required to purchase his own toilet items—razors, combs, soap, and so on—and he had no money. It was snowing in Wisconsin, and he and the other Hawaiian detainees had only the thin summer clothes they were wearing when they were arrested. In time, Frederick received warm clothing and blankets from the army and was even treated to beer on Saturday night, a reminder that not everyone in the U.S. military felt that the prisoners held there were truly the enemy. There were many instances across the country in which lower-level officers and even elected officials sometimes refused to carry out the letter of the law against the prisoners and looked the other way when courtesies were extended to them.

During this time, while the couple was separated and isolated, a government official visited Bertha and told her that she had to do something about her property. If she did not appoint a person to administer the property, the government would confiscate it and dispose of it in a manner of its choosing. The official encouraged her to give a person of their choosing, Mr. Reed, power of attorney over her finances.

She was uncertain about that. Mr. Reed was a slight family acquaintance, a used-car dealer who dabbled in real estate, and she had little confidence in his trustworthiness, but the government official was adamant that they would lose the property if she did not turn it over to him. The home they lived in was leased, but losing it would mean closing the nursing home—and she still had hopes she would be able to return to her former life as a nursing-home owner.

But the nursing home was not the main issue. They owned a significant amount of property in upper Waikiki—two homes, which they had rented out, and two recently built homes that contained rental apartments. Reluctantly, she agreed to give Mr. Reed power of attorney, after being told by the government that Mr. Reed "would take care of everything."

However, when it became apparent that Mr. Reed was not going to provide her with a full accounting of his transactions regarding her property, Bertha wrote letters to several savings and loans, asking them to take over management of the properties so that the mortgages could be paid. To her disappointment, she was unable to find anyone willing to work with her. Recalls Doris, "As soon as they talked to Mr. Reed, they wouldn't have anything to do with it."

In April 1942, Aunt Anna had a heart attack. Her son, who was much older than Doris—and who constantly threatened his younger cousins with warnings of what would happen to them if they were sent to an orphanage—told her to get the doctor who had an office next door. Doris, panicking, did not think to counter that their neighbor was not a medical doctor but a doctor of dentistry. She rushed over, only to discover that that the dentist was not in.

Her cousin was furious with her for not returning with a doctor. He told her to pack her bags. She and her sister were both going to the orphanage. Doris and Anita threw their arms around each other, wailing in fear.

Just at that moment, there was a knock at the back door. Simultaneously, they spun to look and could not believe their eyes. Framed in the bright light of a new day was a guardian angel—their sister, Eleanor. She had been released on parole.

After much hugging, they told her about Aunt Anna, the orphanage, and their fears of being sent away. Eleanor instructed them to pack their bags so that they could go with her. This was in direct violation of her parole because she was underage and not considered an appropriate guardian.

But because the government had taken no interest in the welfare of the children, no one bothered to investigate their living conditions. As Doris recalls, "We hid our identity by lying. . . . I was petrified of being separated and sent to an orphanage. To lose my loved ones again would have been devastating. After having been split up for months, I could not go through that again."

As Doris and Anita were being reunited with Eleanor, Frederick was on his way back to Hawaii. After three months the Camp McCoy experiment fell apart. Detained U.S. citizens wrote letters to newspaper reporters and lawyers, who were stunned that the government would hold Americans of German descent without filing charges against them.

The right to petition for a writ of habeas corpus is the mainstay of the U.S. judicial system: in order to prosecute, the government must produce evidence of a crime and present it before a lawful court that has jurisdiction over the case. The government could suspend the right of habeas corpus in Hawaii because Hawaii was a territory, not a state. However, once the detainees were brought to the mainland, they possessed the same rights as any other American. The realization of that, coupled with the threat of legal action and press coverage, prompted the army to ship the detainees back to Hawaii, where they could hold them indefinitely without charging them with crimes.

Meanwhile, Bertha's world was quickly falling apart, spiraling from nightmare to nightmare. One day, after complaining that she wasn't feeling well, an army doctor examined her and found a large tumor in her abdomen that required immediate removal. She was sent to an army hospital that had been set up at St. Louis School, a Catholic educational institution that prepared high school students for college or technical schools.

Eleanor learned of the surgery from her parole officer. She, Doris, and Anita took a city bus to the school and asked for directions to the makeshift hospital. They found their mother's room, but it was guarded by a soldier who refused to allow them to see her. As they pleaded their case, growing more and more desperate, Doris peeked around the guard to look into the darkened room; she could not see her mother or anything else. It was as if her mother had been swallowed up by the darkness. Dejected, the young girls left the hospital and took the bus back home.

Bertha survived the surgery but could barely tolerate the emotional pain of her isolation and the government's refusal to allow her to communicate with her own daughters. She asked a Red Cross volunteer for paper and pencil so that she could write to them, but the woman refused, saying, "We don't give free items to Nazi spies." She must have told them a hundred times that she was not a German spy, but no one was interested in listening to her. She was German and that was all that mattered.

Subsequently, a woman from the Salvation Army stopped by to visit and was happy to provide Bertha with paper and pencil. After the woman left, Bertha wrote a letter to her daughters. She asked someone at the hospital to mail the letter, but it never reached the children. Nevertheless, she never forgot the woman's kindness, and the experience made her a supporter of the Salvation Army for the remainder of her life.

When Bertha was released from the hospital, still fragile from major surgery, she was taken back to Sand Island, where the unsympathetic matron informed her that she had no intention of allowing a Nazi to take it easy. Bertha was given a mop and bucket and told to mop the floors and carry large buckets of water. As a result of the strain, her surgical stitches tore loose, prompting a hernia. She bound the hernia with towels and safety pins, afraid to tell anyone about her condition.

Eventually, Eleanor was told that she could take her sisters to Sand Island for a visit with their mother. For Doris, the experience was stressful. As ordered, they reported to a boat launch, where they met relatives of other inmates, many of whom had brought children with them. Despite everyone's excitement about visiting loved ones, the atmosphere was subdued, with most of the people looking down, embarrassed, and ashamed, afraid to make eye contact with someone who might find reason to terminate the visit. After a short boat ride, they were deposited on white coral and provided with directions to the camp, a distance Doris later estimated to be about one mile.

As they approached, they heard a sound that gave them chills—the haunting cries of women. Before long they saw the origin of the cries: women inside the camp clung to the barbed-wire fence, their arms outstretched to loved ones, most of whom they had not seen since they were interned.

Guards led the visitors through a baffled entrance, constructed to keep light from showing to observers at night, and then herded them into a mess hall with darkened windows.

Doris remembers the visit:

There I ate the most delicious cookies and fudge that I had ever tasted. We were allowed to sit with Mom on benches at the mess tables. She introduced us to some of the other internees. It was a low key meeting, for we were watched by matrons and guards which were located at each end of the "dining room." Our visit ended too soon. Then we had to leave. . . . We waved and waved until we could not see our mother or the others anymore.[11]

Within a month of Frederick Berg's return to Hawaii in April 1942, he was reunited with Bertha at Sand Island, where the women's portion of the camp was partitioned to accommodate couples. They slept on cots in tents surrounded by barbed-wire fences. Armed guards were stationed at regular intervals around the perimeter of the camp. The floors were made of coral and sand, and whenever it rained—which was often—the tents flooded, creating swamplike conditions inside.

Frederick dug a trench around their tent to help contain the runoff water, which seemed to help. If it wasn't raining, then the sun, particularly in the summer months, raised the temperature inside the tents to unbearable levels. Of course, there was no air-conditioning or electric fans.

Eventually, Doris and Anita were permitted overnight weekend visits with their parents. No one was more perplexed by Frederick's arrest than Doris.

"Dad loved Americans," she later explained. "He was in Germany during the First World War. The Americans took over his home for headquarters, and so he got to know the American soldiers, and they were really nice, and one of the commanders gave him a pony, and he wanted to become an American."

Slowly, Doris began to accept the possibility that something terrible could happen to her parents. They could be beaten or even killed. Nonetheless, she could not intellectually understand or rationalize their confinement. They had done nothing wrong. Why were they being punished? At night during their visits, her mother and father wrapped their arms around the children and cuddled them, making them feel loved again, an emotion the children seldom felt living apart from their parents in an unfriendly world of marching soldiers and terrified neighbors.

During their weekend visits, the sisters got glimpses into day-to-day life in the camps and the relationship between the guards and the prisoners. One time, the army captain who ran the camp entered the tent for an inspection. He wore white gloves and ran his fingers over various items in the tent in search of evidence of bad housekeeping habits. If he found any dust on his gloves, there would be trouble and privileges would be suspended. What kind of country allows its citizens to be terrorized by a man with a white glove? Doris had many questions and few answers.

Toward the end of 1942, Frederick and Bertha were granted a second hearing. This time they were allowed to have a lawyer present, though he was not permitted to question the tribunal or any of the accusing witnesses. Fifteen character witnesses were presented, individuals who attested to the Bergs' loyalty to the United States, but the testimony had no effect on the tribunal, which ruled that the Bergs must be held until the war with Japan was over. Doris was devastated by the decision.

In March 1943, the Bergs and several other Germans were relocated to Camp Honouliuli in the Waianae Mountains. The government segregated the German from the Japanese detainees with fences and guards, creating a Caucasian camp and an Asian camp. The separation contributed to suspicions that continued until the end of the war and, undoubtedly, beyond. Many Japanese felt that the Germans were POWs who may have been guilty of heinous war crimes. Likewise, the Germans considered the Japanese to be spies, traitors to the United States.

Not long after they arrived at the isolated camp, which was surrounded by pineapple fields accessible only by recently bulldozed roads, Doris was permitted to visit her parents to celebrate her thirteenth birthday. A German American and, prior to his arrest, the head chef at the Royal Hawaiian Hotel, the camp's cook baked a fancy cake for Doris, and everyone sang "Happy Birthday."

While visiting the camp, Doris was allowed to explore the gulch that contained both camps. Sometimes she visited the Japanese camp because, unlike the German camp, it had a PX, where she could get food.

"In order for me to get to the Japanese side, I had to go around the outside of the compound and then go on another dirt road to the camp," Doris recalls. "The guards were really nice to me. They were just kids, eighteen and nineteen years old. To get to the PX, I had to pass a compound that contained Japanese prisoners of war. They were scary. They didn't look like they did in the movie *Tora, Tora*. They didn't look modern. They had shaved heads and they wore loincloths and they lived in little pup tents."

The accommodations at Camp Honouliuli were similar to those at Sand Island. Each couple had its own tent, but the floors were wooden rather than sand and coral. There were no bathrooms, only outhouses and communal showers.

During Doris's visits at Camp Honouliuli, her parents were "so sweet and nice." They had always been loving, but before the nightmare began, they seldom had time to spend with their children. Now time was all they had. And like all incarcerated parents and their children, they cherished every moment that authorities allowed them to spend together.

4

EXECUTIVE ORDER 9066

On December 7, 1941, the night of the Japanese attack on Pearl Harbor, President Franklin Delano Roosevelt met with his cabinet and leaders in Congress, who listened in stunned silence as the president briefed them on the surprise attack. During nearly three hours of bombing, Japanese planes killed or wounded more than 3,500 Americans, destroyed 2 battleships and numerous other ships, and wiped out 149 American airplanes. The Japanese lost only 29 planes and pilots of their own.

The next day Roosevelt addressed a joint session of Congress and requested a declaration of war against Japan, famously describing the attack as "a day which will live in infamy." He pointed out that at the time of the attack the United States was at peace with Japan and was making an effort to resolve differences between the two nations.

The resulting war resolution passed with only one dissenting vote, cast by Representative Jeannette Rankin, a pacifist congresswoman from

Montana who voted against the measure with tears streaming down her cheeks.

Although the attack was a surprise, the onset of war was not. Roosevelt considered war inevitable and had been preparing for months. To insulate him from Republican criticism, the Democrat brought Republican Frank Knox into his cabinet as secretary of the navy. The publisher of the *Chicago Daily News*, Knox had been the vice-presidential candidate on Alfred M. Landon's ticket when he ran against FDR in 1936. Roosevelt also asked Republican Henry L. Stimson to join the cabinet as secretary of war. He had served in that same position under President William Howard Taft and was well regarded in right-wing circles. He would serve as a buffer for Republican dissent. Another Republican was John J. McCloy, appointed assistant secretary for war and put in charge of formulating policy involving Japanese Americans.

In the aftermath of the attack on Pearl Harbor, President Roosevelt sent Knox to Hawaii to inspect the damage, meet with navy officials, and evaluate the success of martial law.[1] Knox stayed for only thirty-six hours. Upon his return, he submitted his findings to the president. Among his recommendations was a suggestion that all noncitizens be removed from Hawaii and sent to another island. During a cabinet meeting, he said that he thought Japanese fishing boats had passed along information about the location of warships to Japan's military leaders.

Roosevelt was wary of Knox's assessment, primarily because, as early as 1933, Knox had publicly advocated preemptive action against Japanese Americans in Hawaii. His solution was to arrest and imprison every American of Japanese heritage on the islands, regardless of whether they were U.S. citizens. In his mind, the only good Japanese was an imprisoned Japanese. A report from FBI director J. Edgar Hoover challenged Knox's conclusions and caused the president to reconsider his options.

The American public was incensed about the surprise attack. They wanted to retaliate, not just against Japanese soldiers but, irrationally, against anyone of Japanese heritage. It quickly became a racial issue. Despite an overall progressive agenda, Roosevelt himself went through periods during which he succumbed to his baser instincts. According to historian Greg Robinson, Roosevelt believed that the Japanese possessed an innate biological character. As early as 1935, he stated that aggression "was in the blood" of Japanese leaders. He also was quoted as saying that he felt the Japanese were a "treacherous people."[2]

For weeks after the Pearl Harbor attack, Roosevelt agonized over what to do about Japanese Americans not just in Hawaii but also on the mainland. There were more than one hundred thousand people of Japanese heritage on the West Coast alone. With each passing day, they were viewed with increasing suspicion by military and civilian leaders and with outright hostility by white residents who feared they would use the freedoms they had obtained in America as a nefarious cover to sabotage the war effort.

As the debate raged over what to do about Japanese Americans, distinctions were drawn over those who were born in the United States and those born in Japan. First-generation Japanese born in the United States are Nisei, while immigrants born in Japan are Issei. By definition, Nisei are American citizens by birth. Issei are citizens only after they go through the naturalization process and obtain citizenship. Both groups are Japanese Americans by virtue of their common ancestry. In 1940, three-quarters of the ethnic Japanese population in Hawaii were native born and thus citizens of the United States. By contrast, only 64 percent of the Japanese in California were native born.[3]

At the time of the Pearl Harbor attack, about two thousand Nisei were serving with two U.S. infantry regiments in Hawaii. They helped defend the island and received praise for their efforts. However, so strong was the public mistrust of anyone of Japanese heritage that the men were placed in a segregated unit called the Hawaiian Provisional Infantry Battalion. They were eventually transferred to Camp McCoy in Wisconsin, along with male prisoners arrested shortly after the invasion. Both were housed in barracks, with the prisoners held under guard and the soldiers viewed with suspicion.

Interestingly, President Roosevelt's administration did not unanimously agree on the issue of imprisoning citizens of Japanese, German, and Italian descent. Taking a cue from Abraham Lincoln, whose cabinet was staffed with rivals representing opposing viewpoints, Roosevelt blended right-wing Republicans and liberal Democrats into his administration. Attorney General Francis Biddle, a former law professor at the University of Pennsylvania, took exception to the harsh tactics favored by Secretary of War Henry L. Stimson and Lieutenant General John L. DeWitt, commanding general of the Western Defense Command.

After a series of conferences attended by representatives of the War Department and the Justice Department, first in Washington and then in San Francisco with General DeWitt, a summary of principles was approved that effectively allowed General DeWitt to set civilian policy insofar as it involved the arrest and detention of enemy aliens, identified as people of Japanese descent who did not possess citizenship. Authorized by the Departments of Justice and War were the following actions:

- Alien enemy registration: The Department of Justice is committed to an alien enemy registration with the least practicable delay. It is understood that registration will include provision for fingerprinting , photographing, and other information to be filed locally and probably with local police, as well as at a central office, such information to be compiled alphabetically, by nationality and race as well as geographical.
- Apprehension: United States Attorneys have been or will be instructed to issue apprehension warrants upon application of the FBI special agents in charge. FBI agents in charge will entertain army requests for apprehensions submitted in writing, or, if time does not permit, oral requests which shall be confirmed later in writing. In any case where an alien enemy is found in violation of any of the provisions of the proclamation or any part of the regulations of the Attorney General there under, he is subject to summary apprehension without a warrant.
- Searches and seizures: A warrant authorizing the search of the premises of an alien enemy for the presence of contraband may be obtained merely on application to the United States Attorney. It is only necessary to support the issuance of such a warrant that it be stated that the premises are those of an alien enemy. In an emergency where the time is insufficient in which to procure a warrant, such premises may be searched without a warrant.

- Mixed occupancy dwellings: The search of mixed occupancy premises or dwellings may be by warrant only. In emergencies involving contraband such as radio transmitters, it may be necessary to keep the premises under surveillance while a search warrant is procured. As previously noted, however, in such an emergency an alien enemy's premises may be searched for contraband without a warrant.
- Multiple searches: The term "mass raid" will not be employed by the Attorney General. Instruction which have been or will be issued to United States Attorneys and to FBI special agents will permit "spot raids." This is to say, if lists of known alien enemies with addresses of each are prepared by the FBI and warrants are requested to cover such lists, a search of all premises involved may be undertaken simultaneously. Thus all of the alien enemy premises in a given area can be searched at the same moment.[4]

The phrase used so liberally in the authorization, "enemy aliens," proved to be a lightning rod for abuse. "Alien," then as now, meant simply a noncitizen living in the United States, but by adding the incendiary word "enemy," the Justice and War Departments allowed General DeWitt to apply the term to any American resident of Japanese descent who had not obtained citizenship. He classified them as enemies by virtue of their ethnicity, not because of any crimes they had committed.

In January 1942, Biddle sent the president a memo to explain his views on mass evacuation: "American born Japanese, being citizens, cannot be apprehended or treated like alien enemies; probably an arrangement can be made, where necessary, to evacuate them from military zones. Study is being made as to whether, with respect to them [aliens], the writ of habeas corpus could be suspended in case of an emergency."[5]

Why would an attorney general who had opposed action against citizens and aliens of specific ethnic origins recommend the suspension of habeas corpus? The only logical explanation is that Biddle made the recommendation as a trade-off, in exchange for the government not imprisoning citizens of Japanese, German, or Italian descent. If that was his intent, his gambit failed miserably.

By February, Roosevelt was under intense public pressure and could no longer procrastinate on what to do about Japanese Americans. Although there was not a single instance of sabotage or espionage committed by Japanese Americans, the president proceeded with a directive that essentially stripped more than one hundred thousand Americans of their citizenship and constitutional rights and set in motion events that would forever leave a dark stain on the United States Constitution.

It all came to a head on February 19, 1942, when President Roosevelt signed Executive Order 9066, which gave the secretary of war and any military commanders to whom he delegated authority the power to relocate citizens and aliens from designated areas to provide protection against sabotage and espionage. The order allowed the military to determine who would be relocated and who would remain in their homes.

With the stroke of a pen, the president made it possible for American citizens of Japanese descent to be imprisoned, without explanation or due process, for an indeterminate period based solely on their ethnicity. In time, the order would be interpreted to include Americans of German or Italian descent.

Public response to the order was enthusiastic. Two days after it was signed, the *San Francisco Chronicle* spoke for many unreasoning Americans when it editorialized, in imperfect logic and flawed grammar: "This is a fight for survival. In this fight we cannot pussyfoot. We have to be tough, even if civil rights do take a beating for a time."

The justification for Executive Order 9066 was DeWitt's allegation that he saw indications that Japanese Americans on the West Coast had organized for the purpose of disrupting the U.S. war effort. The Nebraska-born general claimed—but never offered proof—that Japanese Americans were guilty of signaling from the shore to enemy submarines and were a threat to the security of military bases. DeWitt claimed that intelligence service records showed that hundreds of Japanese organizations on the West Coast and in Arizona were actively engaged in advancing Japanese war aims. He further incorrectly asserted that thousands of American-born Japanese had gone to Japan for indoctrination before returning to the United States.

Responding to those allegations, author James A. Michener later wrote: "These grave injustices were perpetrated in spite of the fact that our government had in its possession proof that not one Japanese American, citizen or not, had engaged in espionage, not one had committed any act of sabotage. This was a bleak period in the history of American freedom. A few isolated voices tried to protest . . . but our nation was bent upon revenge. The long years of propaganda were bearing fruit, and we struck out blindly, stupidly, to our eternal discredit."[6]

The "years of propaganda" to which Michener refers was a decades-long effort by white residents on the West Coast to demonize immigrants of Asian descent. In 1924, California officials were instrumental in influencing federal policy to stop immigration from Japan. Incredibly, Japanese immigrants, even parents of children born in the United States whose birthright was citizenship, were prohibited from obtaining American citizenship. Laws were passed that prohibited Japanese immigrants from owning land. By 1940, Japanese residents on the West Coast were fodder for racist demagogues, who lost no opportunity to describe them as a "yellow peril" that, if left unchecked, would destroy white culture and economic advancement. The argument is painfully familiar to African Americans in the segregationist South.

The longstanding racism prevalent on the West Coast exploded with the attack on Pearl Harbor, confirming years of "yellow peril" warnings by Japanese haters, and the hatred continued to grow in the weeks after the attack as Japanese soldiers scored victory after victory over the U.S. armed forces. Many Californians proclaimed the Japanese, whether they held citizenship or not, incapable of assimilating into the dominant white culture. As proof, they pointed to Secretary of the Navy Frank Knox's statements averring that the Pearl Harbor attack had been aided by the sabotage of ethnic Japanese in Hawaii.

President Roosevelt himself subscribed to those views, despite having received a report from a State Department official prior to the Pearl Harbor attack that rejected claims of disloyalty among Japanese Americans: "They have made this their home. They have brought up children here, their wealth accumulated by hard labor is here, and many would have become American citizens had they been allowed to do so."[7] Roosevelt remained unconvinced. His actions and words suggested he believed that Japanese Americans, whether citizens or not, remained loyal to Japan.

When Roosevelt issued Executive Order 9066, he created a situation in which Biddle was required to direct the FBI to work with Stimson on the imprisonment of American citizens and residents of Japanese, German, or Italian heritage. Biddle was not happy about his role. A little more than a week before Roosevelt signed Executive Order 9066, Biddle met with the president and again expressed his opinion that mass evacuation was inadvisable. He insisted that citizens not be arrested or apprehended unless there was probable cause to believe that a crime had been committed. Biddle subsequently attacked the news media for creating a sense of doom by suggesting that an enemy attack on the West Coast was imminent, a threat that he totally disregarded. In a memo to the president, he pointed out that more than half the Japanese targeted by the military held U.S. citizenship.[8]

Once Roosevelt signed the executive order, Biddle succumbed to the bullying of the political right and retreated from his opposition to a race-based policy of evacuation. Against his better judgment, he allowed the army and the generals to set policy on constitutional issues. It was a decision he later would regret. In his postwar memoir, *In Brief Authority*, he wrote: "American citizens of Japanese origin were not even handled like aliens of the other enemy nationalities—Germans and Italians—on a selective basis, but as untouchables, a group who could not be trusted and had to be shut up only because they were of Japanese descent."[9]

The constant policy battles between the attorney general and the secretary of war demonstrate the failure of Roosevelt's attempt to create an administration comprising political and policy rivals. Opponents within the administration did not indulge in reasoned give-and-take leading to mutually acceptable, middle-ground positions. Rather, whenever the two sides butted heads, the "compromise" was determined by which side had the most popular support. In the case of Executive Order 9066, right-wing Republicans shamelessly used racial fears to gain political leverage and prevailed, providing Roosevelt with boosted immunity against criticism from Republican Party leaders in Congress. Clearly, Roosevelt's nobler instincts did not win out.

Once authority was granted for a roundup of Japanese Americans, whether citizens or resident aliens, decisions had to be made about what to do with them. General DeWitt's solution was to ask Japanese Americans to voluntarily move inland, away from military bases and areas of strategic importance to the military. If DeWitt truly believed that Japanese Americans were a serious threat to national security, allowing them to relocate as they saw fit is a bizarre policy, to say the least. Outraged politicians in Idaho and Wyoming pointed out the obvious—if Japanese Americans were a threat to California, they must also be a threat to the inland states where DeWitt planned to allow them to live without supervision among white and Native American residents.

A civilian agency, the War Relocation Authority (WRA), was put in place to supervise the relocation of Japanese Americans, the thinking being that, contrary to what the generals told the president, they were a law-abiding people who would offer no resistance. Milton Eisenhower, the former director of information for the U.S. Department of Agriculture and the older brother of General Dwight D. Eisenhower, was named director of the WRA, primarily because he was a native of Kansas and was thought to be able to speak the language of midwesterners.[10]

On March 2, General DeWitt issued a proclamation in which he stated that he soon would be designating military areas from which it would be necessary to "exclude" certain groups of citizens. That same day, U.S. representative John H. Tolan of California, who chaired a House committee that was investigating the practical effects of Roosevelt's executive order on rounding up Americans perceived to be a threat to the war effort, revealed that he had polled the governors of fifteen states west of the Mississippi River about government proposals to send them evacuees from the Pacific Coast. Nine of the governors said that they would not accept Japanese Americans unless they were housed in concentration camps.[11] Only one governor, Ralph L. Carr of Colorado, said that his state would accept evacuated Japanese as a contribution to the war effort.

Later that month, Milton Eisenhower met with the governors of the Mountain States and listened to their opposition to being the dumping ground for people described as dangerous by military leaders. If their states were going to be used to house Japanese Americans, they wanted them herded into fenced facilities with armed guards so that white residents would feel protected. As a result of that meeting, the WRA dropped its plans to relocate Japanese Americans and find them private employment and housing. It turned to a plan calling for them to be confined forcibly in concentration camps with armed guards. Not long after the WRA was created, Representative Tolan's congressional committee issued its report, recommending many of the steps already taken by Eisenhower. However, Tolan's committee went a step further by drawing a distinction between Japanese and German and Italian aliens, stating that the latter two groups were loyal to the American war effort and thus not a threat. The report recommended that German and Italian aliens whose loyalty could be established "beyond reasonable doubt" be given special consideration to complete their citizenship papers.[12] It was a position with which General DeWitt agreed. He ordered that all the Japanese had to be evacuated before consideration could be given to doing the same thing to Germans and Italians.

———————

General DeWitt set no deadline for Japanese Americans along the coast to be moved, but he identified a group of individuals that would be affected first—more than 400 University of California students, including 315 U.S.-born Japanese, 11 alien Japanese, 75 Germans, and 6 Italians—and he confirmed that individuals suspected of sabotage and espionage already had been taken into custody by the FBI on presidential warrants accusing them of being potentially dangerous aliens. He conceded that "several thousand" people in that group already had been rounded up.

With about 120,000 people to arrest, DeWitt hoped to frighten as many people as possible into turning themselves in, thus saving the army and the FBI the logistical nightmare of processing such a mass of humanity scattered over two thousand miles of land. In many instances, DeWitt's strategy worked. The Japanese American Citizens League (JACL), an organization with a membership of 20,000, expressed understanding about the military's need for an evacuation plan and urged its membership to fully cooperate with authorities.

In mid-March the *San Francisco News* reported that the FBI and local police were rounding up what it called alien Japanese, with known associations with Japanese nationalistic groups. An Oakland man was arrested after the FBI learned that he taught the Japanese language at both the University of Southern California and the University of Pasadena. Reported the newspaper: "Persons facing evacuation were warned today against 'stalling' or unintentionally taking too much time to straighten out their affairs before leaving the military areas. The next step in operation of the Wartime Civil Control Administration (WCCA), General DeWitt said, will 'border on enforced removal.'"[13] The WCCA was the civilian branch of the Western Defense Command and operated independently of the WRA.

Two weeks later, on April 1, 1942, General DeWitt issued his first forced-evacuation order that pertained only to the city and county of San Francisco:

WESTERN DEFENSE COMMAND AND FOURTH ARMY WARTIME CIVIL CONTROL ADMINISTRATION
Presidio of San Francisco, California
April 1, 1942
INSTRUCTIONS
TO ALL PERSONS OF
JAPANESE
ANCESTRY
Living in the Following Area:

All that portion of the City and County of San Francisco, lying generally west of the north-south line established by Junipero Serra Boulevard, Worchester Avenue, and Nineteenth Avenue, and lying generally north of the east-west line established by California Street, to the intersection of Market Street, and thence on Market Street to San Francisco Bay.

All Japanese persons, both alien and non-alien, will be evacuated from the above designated area by 12:00 o'clock noon Tuesday, April 7, 1942.

No Japanese person will be permitted to enter or leave the above described area after 8:00 a.m., Thursday, April 2, 1942, without obtaining special permission from the Provost Marshal at the Civil Control Station located at:

1701 Van Ness Avenue
San Francisco, California

The Civil Control Station is equipped to assist the Japanese population affected by this evacuation in the following ways:

1. Give advice and instructions on the evacuation.
2. Provide services with respect to the management, leasing, sale, storage or other disposition of most kinds of property including real estate, business and professional equipment, household goods, boats, automobiles, livestock, etc.
3. Provide temporary residence elsewhere for all Japanese in family groups.
4. Transport persons and a limited amount of clothing and equipment to their new residence as specified below.

The Following Instruction Must Be Observed:

1. A responsible member of each family, preferably the head of the family, or the person in whose name most of the property is held, and each individual living alone must report to the Civil Control Station to receive further instructions. This must be done between 8:00 a.m. and 5:00 p.m., Thursday, April 2, 1942, or between 8:00 a.m. and 5 p.m., Friday, April 3, 1942.
2. Evacuees must carry with them on departure for the Reception Center, the following property:
   a. Bedding and linens (no mattress) for each member of the family.
   b. Toilet articles for each member of the family.
   c. Extra clothing for each member of the family.
   d. Sufficient knives, forks, spoons, plates, bowls, and cups for each member of the family.

e. Essential personal effects for each member of the family.

All items carried will be securely packaged, tied and plainly marked with the name of the owner and numbered in accordance with instruction received at the Civil Control Station.

The size and number of packages is limited to that which can be carried by the individual or family group.

No contraband items as described in paragraph 6, Public Proclamation No. 3, Headquarters Western Defense Command and Fourth Army, dated March 24, 1942, will be carried.

3. The United States Government through its agencies will provide for the storage at the sole risk of the owner of the more substantial household items, such as iceboxes, washing machines, pianos and other heavy furniture. Cooking utensils and other small items will be accepted if crated, packed and plainly marked with the name and address of the owner. Only one name and address will be used by a given family.

4. Each family, and individual living alone, will be furnished transportation to the Reception Center. Private means of transportation will not be utilized. All instructions pertaining to the movement will be obtained at the Civil Control Station.

Go to the Civil Control Station at 1701 Van Ness Avenue, San Francisco, California, between 8:00 a.m. and 5:00 p.m., Thursday, April 2, 1942, or between 8:00 a.m. and 5:00 p.m., Friday, April 3, 1942, to receive further instructions.

J. L. DeWitt
Lieutenant General, U.S. Army
Commanding

The language of DeWitt's order was insidious. It used the term "reception center" as if it were nothing more than a benign meeting place familiar to anyone who had ever visited a public park. It made reference to being transported to a "new residence," implying that they would be relocated to new homes. There was no suggestion of the primitive living conditions that lay ahead at the reception centers, nor was the language used in the order suggestive of a concentration camp destination.

The order was reminiscent of the language used in Aldous Huxley's novel *Brave New World*, with its prophetic vision of the direction civilization was taking, a world where freedom was nonexistent and morality all but forgotten. Huxley wrote his novel in the late 1930s, a reaction to Nazi Germany and Russian communism. Ten years later, in 1949, when George Orwell published his groundbreaking novel *1984*, it was with a nod to Huxley's German and Russian influences but also to the roundup in America of citizens of Japanese, German, or Italian heritage. Orwell's new world was one in which a totalitarian government survived only by the total manipulation of its subjects. That was made possible only by a type of doublespeak that concealed truth: WAR IS PEACE—FREEDOM IS SLAVERY—IGNORANCE IS STRENGTH.

On March 4, 1942, Thomas C. Clark, a civilian control coordinator for the army, told reporters he hoped that everyone of Japanese ancestry could be removed within sixty days, but he added, "We are going to give these people a fair chance to dispose of their properties at proper prices. It has come to our attention that many Japanese farmers have been stampeded into selling their properties for little or nothing."[14]

More than one thousand Japanese American farms, totaling 50,000 acres, were transferred to new operators during March, under supervision of the Farm Security Administration, with another 150,000 acres earmarked for government takeover.[15] Advertisements in newspapers solicited new operators. It was not until after the war was over that stories of land transfers surfaced.

Mary Ishizuka told of her father's efforts to dispose of one of the largest nurseries in Southern California. Among his customers were celebrities such as Will Rogers and Shirley Temple, but neither their fame nor his wealth prevented him from being arrested. Chaos ensued after he was taken away, nearly paralyzing Mary's mother with indecision. Explained Mary: "We didn't know what to do. You cannot get rid of large nurseries—nursery stock—at this short notice. So what did she do but she gave all of the nursery stock to the U.S. Government, the Veterans Hospital which was adjoining the nursery. It was written up in the local newspaper along with the story of our evacuation. Itemized piece by piece the dollar amount . . . totaled $100,000 in 1942."[16]

Shigeo Wakamatsu later recalled the experiences of Issei truck farmers in the Puyallup Valley in Washington State: "When the valley folks were sent to the assembly center, the telephone peas were waist high and strung, the pole beans were staked, early radishes and green onions were ready for the market, strawberries were starting to ripen and the lettuce had been transplanted. Not much is known how the crops fared in the harvest nor what prices were obtained." Nonetheless, Wakamatsu noted, the Issei farmers went off to prison with an inexplicable sense of pride that they were helping America during a time of crisis.[17]

Jack Fujimoto's father had just purchased a Fordson Tractor for about $750 before the crackdown began. Recalled Jack: "Imagine [my father's delight], after a lifetime of farming with nothing but a horse, plow, shovel and his bare hands, to finally be able to use such a device. He finally had begun to achieve some success. . . . Then came the notice, and his prize tractor was sold for a measly $75."[18]

When John Kimoto learned he would be sent to a prison camp, he wondered how such a thing could happen to him. His first instinct was to go to the storage shed, get the gasoline can, pour the fuel on his house and business, and watch everything go up in flames. His wife persuaded him not to do it, saying, "Maybe somebody can use this house—we are civilized people, not savages."[19]

For Roy Abbey, the white Californians who swooped down on his family were like vultures as they went through their belongings, offering them a fraction of their value: "When we complained to them of the low price they would respond by saying, 'you can't take it with you so take it or leave it.' . . . I was trying to sell a recently purchased $150 mangle [laundry wringer]. One of these people came by and offered me $10. When I complained he said he would do me a favor and give me $15."[20]

For Yasuko Ito the helplessness of their situation was almost too much to bear. He said, "It is difficult to describe the feeling of despair and humiliation experienced by all of us as we watched the Caucasians coming to look over our possessions and offering such nominal amounts knowing we had no recourse but to accept whatever they were offering because we did not know what the future held for us."[21]

═══════════════

In March, the California State Personnel Board fired 350 to 400 state employees of Japanese ancestry. Authorities said the firings were justified because some of the employees held dual citizenship in Japan and the United States and some had attended Japanese-language schools, where what was then called Nipponese ideology was taught. "Nipponese" was simply a word for the teaching of Japanese culture, hardly a subversive undertaking. As the war in the Pacific escalated, white Americans bastardized "Nipponese" into "Nips" and used that word interchangeably with "Japs" as a pejorative.

It is difficult to understand the true extent of the terror felt by many Japanese Americans, especially those who were born and educated in the United States and who knew no other life. As the threat of imprisonment loomed ever closer in the spring of 1942, suicides became all too frequent. One Issei was found with a bullet in his head, his hand clutching an Honorary Citizenship Certificate that had been awarded to him for his service in World War I, stating, in part, "Our flag was assaulted and you gallantly took up its defense."[22] Another Issei hanged himself because he feared that his imprisonment would bring shame to his sixteen-year-old daughter. In a brief note to his daughter he explained that he had taken his own life to spare her from the ridicule she would experience if he were taken to a camp. Explained a friend: "This is just one personal tragedy in many, but that was the state of mind of many people during those trying days. . . . To them their world had come to an end, and they really felt they had nothing more to live for."[23]

The true sadness of this case is that the father apparently did not understand that his daughter would be going to a prison camp with him. His suicide deprived her of the protection he could have given to her in hostile surroundings.

At the outset of the evacuation, it never occurred to some Japanese Americans that their U.S.-born children would be required to go to prison camp with them. What kind of country would imprison its children? That concept was so far removed from everything many Japanese Americans had learned about the United States that it was inconceivable that it could ever really happen.

As the countdown to the sixty-day evacuation progressed, WCCA authorities devised a scheme to reduce the logistical and economic problems involved with the construction of concentration camps by creating the Work Corps, through which they hoped to entice Japanese Americans to build and staff their own prisons. In mid-March, sixty Japanese clerks, nurses, stenographers, and other specialists, the first enlistees in the Work Corps, were persuaded to leave Los Angeles for Manzanar, one of sixteen assembly center camps designated to imprison Japanese American refugees. An abandoned mining site, Manzanar was situated about 230 miles northeast of Los Angeles in the high desert, at the foot of the snowcapped Sierra Nevada.

Originally, Manzanar was built as an assembly center to be used to process prisoners on their way to concentration camps, but it later was converted to an actual concentration camp. All but three of the assembly centers—Puyallup in Washington, Portland in Oregon, and Mayer in Arizona—were in California. The complete list, with each assembly center's maximum population, is as follows:

Fresno 5,120
Manzanar 9,837
Marysville 2,451
Mayer 245
Merced 4,508
Pinedale 4,792
Pomona 5,434
Portland 3,676
Puyallup 7,390
Sacramento 4,739
Salinas 3,586
Santa Anita 18,719
Stockton 4,271

Tanforan 7,816
Tulare 4,978
Turlock 3,661[24]

—————————————————————

The evacuations began on March 27, 1942, with assurances to Japanese Americans from authorities that life in the assembly centers would only be temporary and that they were being relocated for their own protection. German and Italian aliens were exempted from reporting to the assembly centers. Instead, they were instructed to remain in their homes from 8:00 P.M. to 6:00 A.M. and to travel no more than five miles from their homes during the day. General John L. DeWitt told reporters that there would be no exceptions to the rules for Japanese Americans, but exceptions for certain classes of Germans and Italians were a separate matter: "You needn't worry about the Italians at all except in certain cases. Also, the same for the Germans except in individual cases. But we must worry about the Japanese all the time until he is wiped off the map."[25]

On the first day, nearly seven hundred Japanese Americans reported to the WCCA control station in San Francisco for processing and transfer to the assembly center at Santa Anita Racetrack. Following the government's instructions, they brought with them blankets, bed linens, towels, soap, clothing, and dinnerware. From the WCCA center, they were bused to a railway station, where they boarded a train that took them to the racetrack.

Most of the assembly centers were situated on racetracks or fairgrounds. Everyone could be housed under one roof at the Pacific International Livestock Center in Portland, Oregon, where the pavilion covered eleven acres. Of the four areas at Puyallup, south of Seattle and east of Tacoma, near Mount Rainier, three were parking lots and one was the fairgrounds that annually hosted one of the ten largest fairs in the world.

In some instances, tar paper barracks were constructed for the prisoners. In other situations, families were forced to live in primitive conditions in animal stalls that had asphalt floors. For mattresses, they were given cotton ticking in which they were told to stuff straw. Some prisoners were housed in the same area where the famous racehorse Seabiscuit lived.

As it did in prisoner-of-war camps, the Red Cross checked on the prisoners. One report stated: "Generally, the sites selected were satisfactory with the possible exception of Puyallup, where lack of adequate drainage and sewage disposal facilities created a serious problem."[26]

Bath and toilet facilities in the camps were communal, the showers partitioned for males and females, though the women complained that the men often climbed to the top of the partition to watch them bathe. Meals were served in mess halls, where prisoners stood in line with tin cups, plates, and buckets. The menu varied from prison to prison. Cold cuts, sardines, and salted liver were commonly served with stale bread and rice. Occasionally, canned pears or peaches were offered.

Medical care, which was under the supervision of the Public Health Service, was inadequate. No Public Health Service physicians or nurses were sent to the assembly centers. Instead, medical personnel were drafted from the prison population, a decision based on the premise that Japanese Americans should take care of themselves. Dental chairs were fashioned out of crates. Medical supplies typically consisted of mineral oil, iodine, aspirin, alcohol, sulfa ointment, and Kaopectate.

Yoshiye Togasaki, a San Francisco physician, was sent to Manzanar, where she found the facilities greatly lacking in the basics. "In three weeks time we were faced with children ill with measles, chickenpox, whooping cough, diarrhea," she later offered in written testimony to the Commission on Wartime Relocation and Internment of Civilians. "The only place we had for care were barracks without heat, no stove, no water. In due time the Military Emergency Hospital Unit arrived as did medical staff among the evacuees. For me, it was a matter of 14 to 16 hours per day of struggle and frustration."

The evacuation of San Diego began in early April 1942. As white, Hispanic, and African American Californians went about their business as usual, reporting to work, school, and a thousand other places, fifteen hundred Japanese American men, women, and children were rounded up and driven to the assembly center at Santa Anita. Each person was allowed to pack only what he or she could carry. They were given no explanation, nor were they told where they were being taken.

Posted bulletins informed potential prisoners that they would be moved from assembly centers to relocation centers and would be able to leave the compounds at the relocation centers to take a job or to establish a "normal" residence, provided the following conditions were met:

1. A careful check is made of the evacuee's behavior. If there is any evidence from any source that the evacuee might endanger the security of the nation, permission for indefinite leave is denied.
2. There must be reasonable assurance from responsible officials or citizens regarding local sentiment in the community where the evacuee plans to settle. If community sentiment appears so hostile to all persons of Japanese descent that the presence of the evacuee seems likely to cause trouble, the evacuee is so advised and discouraged from relocating in that particular area.
3. Indefinite leave is granted only to evacuees who have a definite place to go and some means of support.
4. Each evacuee going out on indefinite leave must agree to keep the WRA informed of any change of job or address.[27]

Hysteria and abject fear were sweeping through Japanese American communities, and such postings comforted many evacuees and lessened their anxiety about reporting to the assembly centers. No one felt he or she would be affected by item 1; the evacuees knew they were not any danger to the nation. Item 2 seemed harmless enough, because words such as "advised" and "encouraged" indicated friendly assistance rather than loss of freedom. Few evacuees would have been bothered by number 3—most people felt they had places to go and were unconcerned about supporting themselves. And number 4 was reasonable enough and offered no red flags.

Unfortunately, government press releases about the centers were all a lie, an expression of Orwellian doublespeak in which passionate art had become sinister life. "Evacuation" was just another word for "freedom," or so the government would have them believe. Whoever said the government didn't have a sense of literary style? Contrary to what the government said, relocation centers were not benign campgrounds built for the security and safety of the residents. Once the prisoners were secured in the camps, the government had no intention of allowing them to come and go as they pleased, regardless of what was posted. On the contrary, they would be held behind fences patrolled by armed guards. By then freedom would be a distant memory.

━━━━━━━━━━━━━━━━

After living for four months in makeshift shelters at the assembly centers, the prisoners were loaded onto trucks and buses and driven back to the train station in San Francisco, still without explanation. Waiting at the train station to see them off on their journey to the camps was Clara Breed, the supervising librarian at the San Diego Public Library. In her capacity as a librarian, she had gotten to know many of the young people subject to imprisonment, and when they gathered with their parents at the train station, she handed out stamped, self-addressed postcards so that they could write to her about their experiences. Over the years, she heard from more than 250 people. The postcards were later donated to the Japanese American National Museum, an affiliate of the Smithsonian National Museum of American History.

When sixteen-year-old Louise Ogawa arrived at the camp, she sent Clara Breed a postcard expressing her thoughts on the departure: "I shall never forget how I spent that night of April 7 sleeping on the train. My sister and I stuck our heads out the window never peeling our eyes off the direction of our home. We filled our eyes with the sight of San Diego to the limit until my pupils gave in and I dozed off."[28]

Breed's correspondents were all Nisei, and their writing often dealt with the cultural differences between themselves and their Issei elders. Fusa Tsumagari wrote of going to a talent show that left her and her Nisei friends "disgusted" over a program that was "half American" and "half Japanese." She explained: "We had been expecting all American songs and dances and skits. We expected them to save all the Japanese songs and dances for the Issei Night."[29]

While her correspondents were imprisoned, the doe-eyed, mild-mannered Clara Breed spoke out about the injustice of the concentration camps, firmly taking the position that democracy begins at home. In an article for *Library Journal*, published in 1943, she noted that the children and young people of Japanese ancestry, all born and educated in this country, had their security swept away by a war that overtook them like a hurricane. She wrote: "One day they were living in a democracy, as good as anyone or almost, and the next they were 'Japs' aware of hate and potential violence which might strike with lightning swiftness."[30]

There was no shortage of opposing views. An editorial that appeared in the February 23, 1942, issue of the *Sacramento Bee* was indicative of the rabid jingoism prevalent in American newspapers at that time. In part, the editorial said:

> Californians never can feel reasonably secure until all enemy aliens—and fifth column citizens, too—are put in a place and surrounded with conditions which will make it utterly impossible for them to serve their superiors in any totalitarian capital whose deadly purpose is to destroy the United States of America.

Like other Americans who felt safer with all Japanese imprisoned, the editorial writer for the *Bee* wrongly equated the Japanese bomber pilots who destroyed Pearl Harbor with Japanese American citizens, seeing anyone of Japanese ancestry, even the children, as the enemy.

Clara Breed was not the only teacher remaining in contact with former students who made the transition from assembly center to concentration camp. Claire Sprague, a teacher at French Camp School in San Joaquin County, California, corresponded with her Japanese American students as well. Sprague had a different take on the camps, which she described in a 1942 letter to the editor of the *Saturday Evening Post*. Expressing the cultural naivete of the era, she cheerfully wrote that her "American" pupils deserved praise for the way they tolerated their "Japanese" classmates: "Today they are spending all their spare time in the fields, doing their best to help salvage this year's crops. And oddly enough, they have been using a small part of their earnings to send candy, gum, and so forth to their Japanese classmates at Assembly Centers. Yes! All this could only happen in America!"[31]

In her letter, Sprague reflects a belief prevalent among white citizens of that era that efforts by white Americans to show generosity toward Japanese Americans is somehow indicative of their capacity for "tolerance" of their cultural differences. That she cared about the children is undeniable, but her inability to understand the suffering that the children went through in the camps is disturbing in the sense that it totally overlooks the importance of the children's human and constitutional rights, an oversight that makes her statement that it "could only happen in America" more chilling than celebratory.

Such views were fueled by news coverage that depicted Japanese Americans as the "yellow peril" and newspaper photographers who persistently asked victims of the roundup to smile, providing the public with "proof" that the Japanese were not unhappy about being sent to a concentration camp.

━━━━━━━━━━━━━━━

Noted American poet Mitsuye Yamada wrote "Evacuation" in response to a single photograph depicting her Japanese American family members smiling broadly as they are loaded on a bus to be transferred from the assembly center in Puyallup to a concentration camp in Minidoka, Idaho. The photograph, taken by a staff photographer, was published in the *Seattle Times* with the caption "Note smiling faces. A lesson to Tokyo." In the photograph, seventeen-year-old Mitsuye is wearing the largest smile; as she told the author many years later, "When someone points a camera at you and says, 'smile,' of course you smile." When she saw the photograph in the newspaper, she was horrified because it did not depict the situation as it really was. She felt tricked by the photographer who asked her to smile.[32]

She was born Mitsuye Yasutake; she and her three siblings lived with their father and mother, Jack and Hide, in Beacon Hill, an affluent neighborhood in Seattle now known as the world headquarters of Amazon.com. Jack, a 1919 graduate of Stanford University, was a successful insurance agent and an interpreter for the U.S. Department of Immigration, which at that time was under the supervision of the Department of Commerce. They lived in a two-story house in a mostly white section of town, and because of Jack's social skills they had many friends, including many white friends. Both Jack and Hide were born in America, thus American citizens, but Mitsuye was born in Japan during her mother's visit to see a sick relative. She was thus a Japanese citizen, unable to become an American citizen because of then-existing law that prohibited Japanese-born Americans from becoming citizens. The Immigration Act of 1924, which was in effect until 1952, specifically prohibited Japanese immigrants from entering the country or obtaining citizenship.

"I think my father had a[n insurance] territory among Japanese immigrants," says Mitsuye. "Because he was so active socially, he knew everybody, and because he was an interpreter, he went to Vancouver to meet all the incoming ships that came from Japan. He did that for almost twenty-five years, so he met every Japanese person who came to Seattle."

On the afternoon of December 7, 1941, within hours after the attack on Pearl Harbor, FBI agents appeared at their home. Jack, who was president of a local poetry society, was at a restaurant where he was meeting with fellow poets. In his absence, FBI agents searched the home for about three hours, paying close attention to Japanese-language books and letters that they found in Jack's desk. Most of the letters were from relatives in Japan. As the search continued, Jack was picked up by agents at the restaurant. Recalls Mitsuye: "He was among the first to be arrested. They arrested every man who was socially active, the cream of the crop. I imagine they had a whole list of names. There was no way they could compile a list on that day."

Jack was taken to the FBI headquarters in Seattle for questioning. Then he was taken under armed guard to various prisoner-of-war camps. He was in Montana at one point, then was moved to a camp in San Antonio, Texas, where he was housed with Italian and German sailors picked up at sea. He was also imprisoned in New Mexico.

As Jack was disappearing into the system, Hide and her children were arrested and taken to the Puyallup assembly center. "We were lucky," says Mitsuye. "My dad had many white American friends, and his boss at the Seattle Immigration Service was very helpful. When we were about to leave, they came to our house and took some of our furniture and stored it in their basements."

Unlike many Japanese Americans, who were subjected to jeers, taunts, and the occasional violence as they were taken into custody, Mitsuye's family experienced little hostility from whites. Explains Mitsuye: "Most of our neighbors were white Americans, and many of them were sympathetic and very helpful."

After Mitsuye and her family were taken into custody and sent to the racetrack at Puyallup, they did their best to find out what had happened to Jack. They were extremely concerned about his safety. Had he been killed? Had he been taken out of the country? Rumors abounded that people who had been arrested would be deported, with no notice given to the families. Mitsuye's brother wrote letters to the FBI asking about their father, but there was no response. What the Yasutakes did not know was that the FBI suspected Jack of being a spy because he had attended college, an extreme rarity at that time for Japanese Americans. The agency was also suspicious because of his many white friends. In the minds of the FBI agents, he was at the center of a great conspiracy to spy on white Americans. But they never found anything even remotely incriminating.

When the Yasutakes were sent to the assembly center, they were told by authorities that it was for their own good. Eager to believe their government, the family accepted that as the truth. However, as the weeks passed, the reality sank in: they had been arrested to protect whites from imaginary threats. Mitsuye's memories of the assembly center are still vivid, nearly seven decades later: "The fairgrounds had a fence around it. We were housed in animal stalls. There were grandstand seats there, and that created a shelter. Some of the people lived under the grandstand to protect themselves from the rain."

In addition to the animal stalls that housed horses, cattle, goats, and pigs during the annual fair, authorities built temporary shelters for the prisoners. These buildings were loosely constructed clapboard shanties, flimsy frames onto which tar paper was slapped without regard to aesthetics. The buildings looked as if they would collapse if a sudden wind gust were to whip through the fairgrounds. "My family lived in one of those," says Mitsuye. "We had a room that was about ten feet by ten feet. We had one window."

So that she wouldn't have to interact with people during the day (she felt overwhelmed by the great mass of people, all of whom were strangers to her), Mitsuye got a job in the makeshift hospital, where she was assigned to the outpatient ward as a nurse's aide, working from midnight to 8 A.M. The hospital had examining rooms and emergency rooms, but little else. Soldiers stood guard outside the doors.

Armed guards also surrounded the compound. Were they there to protect Japanese Americans from angry whites? Were they there so that they could torture the prisoners? Or were they there to kill Japanese Americans the way they killed Native Americans in a previous century? It was all very confusing to the prisoners.

Recalls Mitsuye, a slight shift in her voice foretelling the irony that was to come: "I was babysitting this four-year-old girl one day, and she said, "Let's go talk to the soldiers at the gate." When we walked away after visiting with them, she asked why they were in a cage like that. She thought *they* were the prisoners."

5

MANZANAR'S GATEWAY TO HELL

At the time of the roundup, Aiko Yoshinaga was seventeen and in love. Born in Sacramento, she lived in Los Angeles, in the Westside, with her mother, father, two brothers, and two older sisters. A third older sister lived in New York. Her boyfriend, a Japanese American named Jacob, lived in Los Angeles's Eastside with his family. That geographic fact assumed great significance, at least for Aiko and Jacob.

When the government ordered Americans of Japanese heritage to report to assembly centers, it specified that families living in Westside should report to the Santa Anita Racetrack, and families in Eastside should report to designated churches and schools for transport to Manzanar. Rather than go with her family, Aiko eloped with Jacob and rode with Jacob and his siblings to Union Station and then traveled by train to Manzanar.

"We were filled with fear," Aiko recalls. "We weren't sure that they weren't going to just take us out into the desert and shoot us. We had no idea what to expect. They didn't tell us where we would be going. We didn't know how to pack. Some of the clothes we had were inadequate for the cold winters there."[1]

The buildings at Manzanar were fragile structures built of planks nailed to studs and covered with tar paper. There were no inside walls, nor were there any indoor toilets. Prisoners ate in mess halls and used communal baths and toilets. In contrast, the buildings constructed for administrative personnel and the military police were spacious and better furnished, and they were painted and fitted with indoor toilets and baths, refrigerators, and cooling systems.

"The first thing I missed was privacy, and then freedom," recalls Aiko. "I couldn't go to the corner drugstore to get a soda when I wanted to. There was a lack of privacy in sharing that one small room. The only thing that was there when we arrived was an army cot, and we had to fill canvas bags with straw to make mattresses."

In all, there were seven of them in that one room—Aiko and Jacob, his brother and wife, and his sister and her husband and their eighteen-month-old child. The camp was divided into evenly spaced blocks, with an average of 250 people in each block. They were prohibited from having cooking utensils in their quarters, which meant that they could not prepare their own meals. Three times a day they stood in long lines for their meals.

At home, Aiko was accustomed to a Japanese diet of fish, rice, and vegetables. At the camp they were fed apple butter, potatoes, and Spam. They requested canned milk, but they were told that it was being saved for American soldiers.

"We were deprived of good food until our men started to create gardens," she says. "We grew a lot of our own produce, but that took a while to take place. After that, our people were given jobs as cooks and waiters, and we started to get more of our type of food."

The communal bathroom facilities were segregated by sex, with separate buildings for men and women; but privacy was not a concern within the buildings. "It was difficult for the women, since women are more shy about sharing their bodies, I think," Aiko states. "We didn't even have separate toilets. We had a long row of holes, and it was very difficult. The showers were not separated either. The men didn't seem to mind as much, but the women had a terrible time adjusting. Most of us waited until the wee hours to go to the bathroom to do bowel movements, because we didn't want to just be sitting there to the whole world. It was humiliating."

Aiko and Jacob married before they reported to the assembly center, but she lied abut her age, so when she turned eighteen in the camp, they had a second ceremony. Despite the lack of privacy, she and Jacob conceived a daughter, who was born in December, nine months after their arrival at the camp. Their child was an American citizen, as was Aiko. Her parents and three of her older siblings were born in Japan—and therefore not American citizens, since, at that time, it was against the law for anyone born in Japan to become a citizen. As a result, her father, mother, older brother, and two sisters were considered aliens. After their separation from Aiko, they were kept at the Santa Anita Racetrack until October 1942, when they were transported by train to a concentration camp in Jerome, Arkansas.

───────────────

Manzanar was the only assembly center to morph into a concentration camp, euphemistically called a relocation camp by the government. The other assembly centers were meant to serve as temporary detention facilities until enough concentration camps could be constructed to house about 120,000 prisoners. The camps, all under the oversight of the War Relocation Authority, included:

Tule Lake, California (capacity 16,000)
Poston, Arizona (capacity 20,000, in 3 units)
Gila River, Arizona (capacity 15,000 in 2 units)
Heart Mountain, Wyoming (capacity 12,000)
Amache, Colorado (capacity 8,000)
Jerome, Arkansas (capacity 10,000)
Manzanar, California (capacity 10,000)
Minidoka, Idaho (capacity 10,000)
Rohwer, Arkansas (capacity 10,000)
Topaz, Utah (capacity 10,000)[2]

For the most part, the camps were in barren locations that had been passed over for generations by settlers and developers. Manzanar and Poston were in the desert. Minidoka and Heart Mountain were known for dust storms and harsh winters. Gila River was known for its severe heat. Rohwer and Jerome were in heavily wooded and snake-infested swampland, not far from the Mississippi River. Only the Tule Lake camp, in a dry lake bed, offered potential for planting crops.

One of the important voices in the selection of sites for the camps was a U.S. Department of Agriculture engineer named Thomas D. Campbell, who was an expert on federally owned land. It was his idea that Japanese Americans be sent to wilderness areas where they would pose no threat, and it was his idea that Native American land be used as the campsite at Poston. After a dinner meeting with Roosevelt, during which he expressed his views, he sent the president a letter explaining his position in more detail. Accompanying the letter was a copy of a memo he'd sent to Assistant Secretary of War John McCloy. If there was any doubt about the paranoid nature of Campbell's racism, it was expressed clearly in the memo: "We probably can place the men in camps or at gainful jobs, but how about the wives and children? It is better for us to err on the safe side and place many foreigners in camps, some of which foreigners may be loyal, than to be less careful and let just one remain free who might do great damage."[3]

When the time came to leave the assembly centers for the camps, the prisoners were herded into the wilderness at a rate of about five hundred a day. Not until they arrived did they understand how desperate their situation had become. Most of the assembly centers were in urban areas, where the sound of traffic and human activity were part of the rhythms of daily life. The concentration camps were wrapped in stony silence—dreary, inhospitable moonscapes that presented a vaguely threatening visage. Not until their arrival at the camps did the prisoners realize that they had been duped. They had been assured that they were being sent to resettlement communities where they would be free to travel to neighboring areas to shop and mingle with local residents.

In the beginning, the WRA stated that the prisoners would be entitled to the same treatment as other American citizens. However, as the months went by—and public hostility toward Japanese Americans increased—the agency reversed its position, especially when it came to how the prisoners were fed. Under pressure, the WRA felt compelled to announce that "at no time would evacuees' food have higher specifications than or exceed in quantity what the civil population may obtain in the open market."[4] To prove that it wasn't coddling Japanese Americans, the WRA sent its monthly menus to Washington in advance for approval.

———————

There was nothing about the exodus from the West Coast that inspired confidence among the prisoners. Public officials often seemed confused about the undertaking, and the facilities used to house the prisoners were substandard, only a notch above those used for family pets.

In her memoir, *Farewell to Manzanar*, Jeanne Wakatsuki Houston wrote movingly about her experience as a prisoner at the desert camp:

> The truth is that the camp was no more ready for us when we got there than we were ready for it. We had only the dimmest ideas of what to expect.... Some old men left Los Angeles wearing Hawaiian shirts and Panama hats and stepped off the bus at an altitude of four thousand feet, with nothing available but sagebrush and tar paper to stop the April winds pouring off the back side of the Sierras.[5]

The evacuation was so hurriedly planned that nothing was completed when the prisoners arrived. Everything was under construction. The camps were noisy and dusty, and the best that one could hope for was a roof, because the walls were slow to take shape, with windows and doors nonexistent.

Sue Kunitomi Embrey was a teenager when she arrived at Manzanar. Before the roundup, she lived with her two sisters, four brothers, and mother in downtown Los Angeles. Her father had died four years earlier in an automobile accident; a fifth brother had voluntarily gone to Manzanar earlier as a laborer.

When she arrived at Manzanar, it was already dark, and she was escorted to the barracks by her brother, who led the way with a flashlight. "It was cold and dark and very quiet except for the shuffling of our feet on the uneven ground," she explained. "We were pretty shocked at the bare room—no insulation, no linoleum, planks with knotholes, and the wind blowing through the top where the roof peaked . . . it was cold and bleak."[6]

Diarrhea was the most pressing problem after arrival at the camp, due first from the many shots that caused aches and pains and upset their stomachs and then from the undercooked and unrefrigerated food that often made them ill. "The Manzanar runs" became a condition of life, and inmates only hoped that when they rushed to the latrine, one toilet would be in working order.

One of the doctors at the camp was Yoshiye Togasaki, a 1935 graduate of Johns Hopkins University School of Medicine, the first graduate-level medical school in America to admit women on an equal basis with men. It was remarkable for a woman to receive a medical degree at that time, and by all indications Togasaki was a remarkable woman. She was born in 1904 in San Francisco, where her father owned a grocery store, but she lived the first six years of her life with her grandmother in Japan because her mother had four older children and felt overwhelmed by a fifth. Upon her return to the United States, she was enrolled in Hearst Grammar School and progressed through the public school system before receiving a degree from the University of California. After graduation from Johns Hopkins, she returned to Los Angeles, did her residency in communicable diseases, and then worked as a bacteriologist for the city of Berkeley before setting up a private practice in September 1941, just weeks before the attack on Pearl Harbor. When it became obvious that Japanese Americans with city jobs would be fired, she went to the president of the California Council of Churches and asked for his help in protecting their jobs. Togasaki was stunned by his response. She later recalled that he "said to me the filthiest darn things like, 'you're a traitor,' and 'how do I know how to trust you? I don't know you from anything—you're Japanese, so you're not trustworthy.'"[7]

Shortly after President Roosevelt signed Executive Order 9066, the thirty-eight-year-old physician volunteered to go to Manzanar so that she could help supervise the young girls who had been recruited to do clerical work at the camp. If she had not volunteered, she knew she would have been caught in the dragnet and would have little control over where she went.

The first thing that Dr. Togasaki did at Manzanar was set up a medical unit. Three weeks later, convoys started dumping hundreds of new arrivals into the camp each day. She tried to anticipate problems before they became unmanageable: "I knew that we were going to have problems with tuberculosis, and I also knew that we would have problems with typhoid because a lot of people had already had typhoid in their youth out in the country or back in Japan. They were still carriers. So these were two illnesses I felt were preventable, and this could be done in part by vaccination."[8] Preventing such diseases required very careful food handling, and Togasaki made few friends when she insisted that the eating utensils be sterilized after each meal.

William Minoru Hohri was fifteen when Pearl Harbor went up in smoke. Of Japanese ancestry—born in the United States with Japanese-born older siblings—he had graduated the previous year from Ralph Waldo Emerson Junior High in Westwood, California.

On the night of the attack, FBI agents showed up at his family's storefront home in North Hollywood, California, and arrested his father, a Christian minister whose tiny congregation met weekly at a rented American Legion hall. Without being charged with a crime, he was whisked away to a U.S. Army detention camp at Fort Missoula, Montana, where a hearing was held—in English, a language in which Hohri's father was not fluent.

Hohri's father was not detained there for long. Americans who were born in Japan were taken to Fort Missoula and interrogated to determine if they were dangerous enemy aliens. Only a handful of Japanese Americans met the criteria, and of the few held there for an extended time, none was ever proved to have engaged in sabotage or espionage.

Once Hohri's father was released, he and his entire family were sent by bus to Manzanar. "[The] camp was mostly desert, in the middle of nowhere, in a valley that had the highest winds I've ever seen," William

Hohri later wrote. "When we arrived, the barracks were still under construction. Ours lacked windows . . . We had to drink from water barrels. There was no sewage system so we had to use small outhouses which afforded neither privacy nor comfort."

Hohri and his family were given ill-fitting war-surplus clothing left over from World War I—khakis for the summer and woolens for the fall and winter. The only item of clothing that the prisoners considered as decent was the navy pea coat.

As the months went by, showers and latrines were installed at the camp, inoculations were given against typhoid and other diseases, food safety improved, and drinkable water was provided out of the tap, but those amenities hardly compensated for the loss of freedom felt by the prisoners. Hohri recalls: "We could never escape the oppressive reality of incarceration. We were prisoners. Not prisoners of war, for we were not from the enemy nation. We felt more like criminals. Our crime was genetic and cultural. It was not what we had done, but what we might be planning to do . . . we were such a feared species we were imprisoned in a concentration camp, surrounded by a barbed wire fence and guard towers."[9]

One of the saving graces of Manzanar was that the land formerly had been used for commercial apple orchards. In fact, *manzanar* is Spanish for "apple orchard." The apple trees had been abandoned several years prior to the start of World War II, but prisoners with a background in agriculture were able to fertilize, prune, and water the trees, in effect bringing them back to life. The trees provided fresh fruit for the camp and enabled prisoners to earn small amounts of spending money by working in the orchards. Prisoners at all the camps were encouraged to work, with the pay scale set at $12 to $19 a month. Those who could not find work were provided unemployment compensation payments, at rates from $1.50 to $4.75 a month.[10] Even at those low rates, there was public outrage that the government would pay them anything.

Manzanar was unique among the camps in that it had an orphanage, called Children's Village. It was the only child-welfare unit in the nationwide camp system. The orphanage, which was supervised by a Japanese American couple, was housed in three one-story buildings located near the hospital. The children lived in dormitories and were expected to perform housekeeping duties in the barracks. More than one hundred children, ranging in age from infancy to adolescence, were sent to the camp.

While Children's Village was a noteworthy addition to Manzanar, it raises questions about how children without parents were cared for in the other camps—and it raises even bigger questions about why authorities would see fit to send orphaned Japanese American children to concentration camps instead of providing for them in existing civilian child welfare agencies. As benign as the name Children's Village sounds, the place represents one of the more incomprehensible horror stories of that era. The children were rounded up by the army from three orphanages in California—the Maryknoll Home for Japanese Children, the Shonien (Japanese Children's Home of Los Angeles), and the Salvation Army's Japanese Children's Home in San Francisco—despite pleas from orphanage personnel that the children be allowed to stay. At orphanage after orphanage nuns and employees tearfully chased the trucks that carted away the children, their arms outstretched.

Francis L. Honda was seven when he was yanked from one of the orphanages. "It was a very lonely place and sad, too, with babies crying and nothing to do. It was like the end of the world for me."[11] In one instance, Dennis Bambauer, a blond, fair-skinned child, was taken from a white orphanage and sent to the camp when army investigators learned, after a check of all confidential orphanage records, that his mother was of Japanese ancestry. That was enough to brand him a "Jap."

Father Hugh Lavery of the Maryknoll Home was so disturbed by the roundup that he bravely pressed the army for an explanation.[12] The answer came from Colonel Karl R. Bendetsen in Washington, D.C., who had given the coldhearted order to take the children: "I am determined that if they have one drop of Japanese blood in them, they must all go to an internment camp."[13]

Foster homes also came under attack by military authorities. Children of mixed Japanese heritage also were uprooted, separated from their foster parents, and sent to Manzanar. Once the children in Los Angeles were gathered, they boarded an army bus for the trip to Manzanar. A social worker named Matsumoto did her best to keep the children entertained, but it was not easy because most of them were afraid. As the bus made its way through the city, she persuaded a four-year-old girl to sing, which settled the children for a time. When the little girl, her young voice soaring with blind optimism over the grinding road noise, sang "God Bless America," a military policeman on the bus openly wept.[14]

Jeanne Wakatsuki, seven at the time, recalls a hierarchy among children in the camp; children treated the orphans "as if a lack of parents put them somehow beneath everyone else."[15] When the camp director, Ralph P. Merritt, visited the orphanage on Thanksgiving Day 1942, he was touched by what he saw. Later, he wrote in his notes: "The morning was spent at the Children's Village with the ninety orphans [more were on the way] who had been evacuated from Alaska to San Diego and sent to Manzanar because they might be a threat to national security. What a travesty of justice!"[16] Merritt was correct about the "travesty of justice," but he was incorrect about the orphans being Alaskan. They were mostly from the Los Angeles area, though some were born to unmarried teenage mothers who had arrived from other camps.

How much racial hatred must have existed among white Californians for them to consider orphaned Japanese American children not worthy of the same level of services provided to children of other races and ethnic backgrounds? The existence of orphanages at any of the camps is a sobering indictment of society as a whole at that troubled time in American history.

━━━━━━━━━━━━

Orphanage and apple trees aside, Manzanar was a prison camp surrounded by barbed wire and guard towers. More than five hundred military police officers were assigned to the camp, making it difficult for inmates to feel that they were anything other than prisoners of war. Inevitably, tensions arose.

Perhaps with those tensions in mind, authorities allowed prisoners to publish a twice-weekly newspaper, the *Manzanar Free Press*. Edited by inmates, the mimeographed newspaper, which originally was published only in English, reported local news, announced upcoming events, and voiced opinions that did not put the newspaper in opposition to authorities. In the first issue of the newspaper, editors pledged to be "as informative and as entertaining as any of the big dailies" and editorialized: "We don't have a 'policy' ... politics are out! We don't have to worry about what our advertisers think! We will have no circulation department worries."[17]

Nisei prisoners could not benefit from the newspaper, since they did not speak English, so authorities decided to allow a Japanese-language supplement but with a requirement that both original and translated stories had to be reviewed by a three-member government board. When it became obvious that rising tensions were going to result in problems at the camp, the *Manzanar Free Press* published an editorial addressing that issue under the headline "Back to Barbarism":

The thrill of pride that surges down our spine when we view the miracles wrought in a few months' time is dampened when we hear of increasing cases of vandalism and mob rule here.

Ruffians who have taken the law into their own clenched fists have escaped with a reprimand from the police who were powerless to do more than maintain surveillance. This was due to the lack of any recognized court of law that could enforce order.

Now the situation has changed. Even though it is temporary, we have a judicial committee empowered to pass judgment. Every case of gang warfare and unrefereed fisticuffs should be severely punished. The Manzanar Free Press promises full publicity in these cases.

If the prospects of cooling their heels in the iron cage will not deter these hotheads, perhaps the threat of having their names smeared on the pages of a documentary newspaper will make them hold back that punch.

We cannot revert to barbarism![18]

In summer 1942, the WRA investigated security arrangements at Manzanar and reported that guards had been instructed to shoot anyone who attempted to leave the camp without a permit or who refused to halt when ordered to do so. Noting that guards were armed with guns that had an effective range of up to five hundred yards, a WRA official asked a supervisor what would happen if a prisoner did not halt when ordered. The supervisor replied that he only hoped the guard would bother to ask.

"He explained that the guards were finding guard service very monotonous, and that nothing would suit them better than to have a little excitement, such as shooting a Jap," noted the official in a report. "Some time ago, a Japanese [he happened to be a Nisei] was shot for being outside of a [camp]. . . . The guard said that he ordered the Japanese to halt—that the Japanese started to run away from him, so he shot him. The Japanese was seriously injured, but recovered. . . . The guard's story does not appear to be accurate, inasmuch as the Japanese was wounded in the front and not in the back."[19]

On December 7, 1942, the first anniversary of the attack on Pearl Harbor, there were two riots at Manzanar. The first took place in the northern part of the camp, where some prisoners gathered to denounce members of the Japanese American Citizens League for being apologists for American authorities. Paranoia was the dominant emotion of the day. Frank Chuman, a prisoner at the camp, recalls a group of men roaming about the camp, angrily looking for JACL members, saying, "Well, let's go out and kill these guys."[20]

Aiko Yoshinaga recalls a second riot that day, when a kitchen worker discovered that sugar and other staples were being stolen by white administrative employees and sold on the black market. Recalls Aiko: "When that was exposed, the man was jailed and the people responded and gathered in front of the camp jail and demanded his release. The military police were called in and one fellow was shot running away because the MPs were threatening him. I didn't go to the scene because I was pregnant and scared."

Among the prisoners who met with officials to request the man's release was the father of John Y. Tateishi, who was only a young child at the time. Years later, Tateishi recalled the terror he felt as he watched the whistle-blower and his father taken away in handcuffs and shackles:

All night long, the searchlights swept the camp, and bands of men could be heard running past our barracks, shouting angrily. We had no idea what had happened to my father, and at one point in the night I sneaked out to try to find him. I can recall running from building to building, avoiding the searchlights and the bands of men and, most fearfully, hiding from the soldiers as they swept through the camp. . . . At some point, the guards opened fire on the crowd."[21]

Tateishi's biggest concern was his father. He told his mother that he feared guards would shoot him. She tried to reassure him, but he was unconvinced. As the days went by and he heard nothing more about his father, the silence fed his fears. Christmas came and went, the first Christmas he and his brothers ever spent without their father. As time went by, adults told him that the riot was his father's fault. Their stern looks seemed to blame the child for what they wrongly perceived to be the sins of the father. Tateishi would not see his father for one year. It was a year that had a profound effect on him. "What I did not understand for some years was that my father refused to accept that there could be any justification at all for our imprisonment and suffering," he wrote. "Live by your principles, he always told me: if you believe in them, always stand by them, even die for them if you must. It was the price he paid for what he believed in. And so he was taken away by the soldiers."[22]

On another occasion, a suspected informer, a member of a secret group that was cooperating with camp administrators—providing them with information—was beaten up by six masked men, one of whom he identified. The assailant was arrested and removed from the camp. The following day, there was a mass demonstration at the camp to protest the arrest. As tensions rose, the prisoners selected a committee of five and offered to negotiate with the camp director.[23]

At first the camp director refused, but eventually he agreed, and the result was an agreement whereby the suspect was returned to the camp for a trial, with the understanding that the prisoners would cooperate with the director in the event of future disturbances. However, on the day the suspect was returned, a crowd assembled inside the camp, demanding his release. The director responded by calling in the military police. The demonstrators were ordered to disperse. When they refused, the military police tossed tear-gas grenades into the crowd, which quickly broke up as the prisoners ran to the far corners of the compound. Once the gas dissipated, the demonstrators returned, started a car, and drove it toward a machine-gun placement, prompting the military police to open fire with their rifles. Two prisoners were killed, and nine were wounded. Years later, in testimony before the Commission on Wartime Relocation and Internment of Civilians, Grace Nakamura recalled, "I ran and became one of the curious spectators. The MP fired shots into the defenseless crowd. A classmate, Jimmy Ito, was shot and killed. It was a terrifying experience."[24] After the disturbance, all the informers who had cooperated with WRA administrators were gathered up and taken to the military police barracks outside the compound. Later, for their own safety, they were relocated to another concentration camp. The demonstrators who could be identified were sent to a Justice Department camp used to isolate prisoners that the government considered troublemakers.

Four and one half months later, the *Manzanar Free Press*, in its one-year anniversary edition, looked back on the riots with forced optimism, noting that for two weeks all activity at the camp ceased: "Slowly, return to normal life was brought about. Greater understanding between the residents and the administration was gained through the efforts of both sides. So now Manzanar stands, a year from inception, an isolated barrack town behind the high Sierras, housing ten thousand orphans of the war whose lives are controlled and limited by confining barbed-wire fences."[25]

Riots at Manzanar and other camps might have offered safety values for escalating tensions, but the quietness that always followed the disturbances was misleading because the reasons for the tensions were never fully vented. Manzanar had all the political and social dynamics of any city of ten thousand people. The Nisei and the Issei were continuously at odds. The Nisei aligned themselves with the JACL, which the Issei felt was favored by camp officials, primarily because it granted privileges to JACL officers that were not extended to others in the camp.

Within those two primary groups at Manzanar, a much smaller group emerged called the Black Dragons, a secret, right-wing organization that supported Imperial Japan, the political entity that governed the country for more than seventy years, ending in 1945 with the defeat of its leaders. The Black Dragons rebelled against both camp officials and the JACL by instigating rock-throwing incidents against prisoners who worked at industries within the camp. Those who voiced opposition to the Black Dragons could expect a sound beating. Although Manzanar was located in a near-wilderness setting, where there was little contact with outsiders, the dynamics of camp life were as complicated and diverse as could be found in any urban area in which there are power struggles based on generational and cultural differences.

6

LIFE IN AN ARKANSAS SWAMP

In December 1943, Aiko Yoshinaga learned that her father, who was imprisoned at the concentration camp in Jerome, Arkansas, was deathly ill. So that she could join her family and help care for her father, she requested a transfer from Manzanar to Jerome for herself; her husband, Jacob; and their daughter, Gerrie. To her disappointment, a bureaucrat for the War Relocation Authority approved family transfers for Aiko and Gerrie but not for Jacob, since he was related to the ailing father only by marriage and was therefore not "family." She was told to choose between her father and her husband.[1]

Anxious about her father's health and fearful of a journey to an unknown place while pregnant with her second child, Aiko left Jacob behind and set out for Arkansas with Gerrie, first on a train that took the better part of a week to get there and then by bus through countryside that was entirely foreign to her. Jerome is located in a rural, hardscrabble part of southeast Arkansas, only a few miles from the Mississippi River, in the alluvial plain better known to blues fans as the Mississippi and Arkansas Deltas.[2]

When Aiko stepped off the train at Jerome, she was greeted by terrain that had not changed much over the centuries, other than levees built in the late 1920s and early 1930s to control the river. The Arkansas Delta was swampy and sweltering in the summer, economically depressed, and rife with racism, notably evident in the strength of the Bayou Knights, a virulent, Louisiana-based franchise of the Ku Klux Klan.

Arkansas was the site of two concentration camps, one at Jerome and the other in the small community of Rohwer. The two camps, which were designated ten thousand prisoners each, were about forty miles apart. For easy access, the camps were built along the tracks of the Missouri Pacific Railway. Arkansas was chosen as a site for the camps because of the state's sparse population and because of its geographic isolation, away from large cities and seaports. Before construction on the camps began, the federal government conducted a public opinion poll that revealed that more than 90 percent of the Arkansans surveyed supported the government's policy of interning Japanese Americans who were not citizens and nearly 60 percent supported interning Japanese American citizens. Most Arkansans of that era had never met a person of Japanese heritage, and, other than the Chinese Americans who lived across the river in Mississippi, they had little experience with Asians.

Aiko arrived at the camp barely in time to help. She was there long enough to speak to her father again, long enough to do what she could to make him comfortable, but he passed away shortly after she got there on Christmas morning. The time was one of sorrow mixed with joy: although grief-stricken from her father's death, she was glad to be reunited with other family members.

One of her first priorities after she arrived was to find work. She received a monthly clothing allowance of $2.95 for Gerrie and $3.95 for herself, hardly enough to purchase the things that she needed to provide for her child. There were plenty of jobs within the camp, ranging from positions in the laundry and kitchen to professional positions such as nurses and physicians. Unskilled workers were paid $12 a month, skilled workers were paid $16 a month, and physicians were paid $19 a month.

"They provided us with food," she later recalled. "But we had to buy toothpaste, baby diapers, and things like that. The mail-order houses that sent out catalogs made out like bandits—Sears and Roebuck, Montgomery Ward, Spencer's—we studied those books like they were bibles."

Aiko recalls that they chose the least expensive items in the catalogs. Adding to her troubles was her ailing daughter, who could not drink the canned milk offered in the camp or the powdered milk that camp officials offered as a substitute. As a result, Aiko's daughter was in and out of the hospital for treatment of digestive disorders.

Since she needed milk and diapers on a regular basis for Gerrie, Aiko was allowed to leave the camp to go shopping in nearby communities, though the word "shopping" implies a choice, and there was very little choice when it came to consumer goods, since it was rare for a community in that part of Arkansas to have more than one grocery store or drugstore. It was not all that unusual for officials at some camps to allow prisoners to leave to go into nearby towns. Their attitudes are reminiscent of the U.S. soldiers in the Vietnam War who refused to obey orders to kill civilians. Some camp officials stood on principle, and that was the case, from time to time, in Arkansas.

One hot summer day, while nearing the final stages of her pregnancy, Aiko took the bus to a nearby town to purchase supplies for Gerrie, a journey of about thirty minutes. When it was time to return to the camp, she boarded the bus, and as it drove away, she walked to the rear and sat in the backseat.

Suddenly, the bus screeched to a halt.

"Lady, you get up—or you get out!" screamed the bus driver.

She looked at him, not moving, not understanding why he would scream at her in such a manner. She knew she had done nothing wrong.

"You either stand in the front, or you get out!"

She stared at the driver, not believing that he was talking to her. No one had ever shouted at her about her choice of seats on a bus. It was such a surreal experience that she sat frozen in her seat, her feet incapable of movement.

"Get up front!" he insisted.

Finally, understanding the extent of his anger, she responded with the truth. "I'm tired and I want to sit down." There was standing room only at the front of the bus. The only empty seats were in the back.

Unbeknownst to Aiko, the back of the bus was reserved for African Americans. At that time of racial segregation, it was illegal for blacks to sit in the front of the bus. For a white or an Asian to sit in the back of the bus was a serious violation of both law and social custom.

As the debate between Aiko and the bus driver raged, other white passengers urged her to move to the front. The bus was not air-conditioned, and exhaust fumes and sweltering gusts of air wafted through the open windows, putting everyone on edge.

"Come stand with us," urged two white missionary ladies.

Aiko stayed put. She could be stubborn that way.

Again, the driver insisted, "Either get up—or get out."

Without another word, she got up and left the bus, standing in the wake of the gas fumes as the bus drove out of sight. As she walked back to the camp, a distance of several miles, she thought: This is really strange that here I have to go back behind barbed wire and I don't have my freedom and I'm not free enough to be able to sit where I want and the blacks have to sit in the back. What's happening here? I was really puzzled. I was totally apolitical at that time. Much later, after my kids started growing up, I became political. I thought, "We'll have to fight a little harder for equality."

Not long after Mary Tsukamoto arrived at Jerome in October 1942 with her four-year-old daughter, Marielle, a cold snap settled upon the camp, sending temperatures near freezing. Cold weather in the Arkansas and Mississippi Deltas is different than it is in other parts of the country. Because of the extreme humidity and the sudden temperature changes that sometimes see differences of forty or more degrees in a twenty-four-hour period, the coldness has a penetrating quality to it that usually comes as a surprise to residents of drier climates. One of the first chores faced by Mary's family was to venture into the frigid swampland to gather and cut wood for the heating stoves. Recalls Mary: "All the men stopped everything; school, everything was closed and the young people were told to go out and work. They brought the wood in, and the women helped to saw it."[3]

With their feelings made raw by the damp, bone-piercing cold that frequently dropped below freezing, the inmates began to hoard wood. Tempers flared. Harsh words were spoken. It was neighbor against neighbor and friend against friend. The situation got so bad that block managers were asked to search every apartment for excess firewood.

One of the things that Marielle remembers most is the wooden woodpecker that her father made for the door to their barracks so that she would know where they lived when she left to go to the latrine, since she couldn't read and all the doors looked alike to her.[4] Another of her strong memories is the day that they had to leave their farm in Florin, California, where her father raised strawberries and grapes, to be driven to the railway station. She was sad because she could not take her dog and because her grandmother was weeping in the garden. Her mother and father "had no idea where we would be sent," Marielle explained to interviewers. "People were all crying and many families were upset. Some believed we would not be treated well, and maybe killed. There were disturbing rumors."

━━━━━━━━━━

When twenty-two-year-old Miyo Senzaki arrived at Rohwer, it was late at night and she was pretty discouraged. She was born in Seattle, where her parents owned an import business. When that business didn't pan out as expected, the entire family moved to California, where Miyo's parents opened a produce market that quickly expanded to five markets. Life was good, up until the attack on Pearl Harbor and the subsequent evacuation that resulted in her father losing all his businesses. She went through numerous life-changing events, including a rushed marriage to keep from being separated from her boyfriend, until, finally, they were rounded up and sent first to an assembly center and then loaded on a train to be sent to Arkansas. On the way, they were instructed to pull down the shades each time they neared a town.

After a lifetime in urban areas, Miyo found herself in what seemed the middle of nowhere. One day she ventured away from the camp in search of wood only to be confronted by men on horseback, who warned her that she would be shot on sight if caught stealing lumber. She recalls:

Being at Rohwer was just a lonely feeling that I can't explain. I thought to myself, I never ever dreamed that I would come to live here. I had this really sad feeling. . . . You couldn't run anywhere. It was scary because there was no end to it. You could run and run and run but where are you to go? It was just nothing but water and then there were rattlesnakes.[5]

Rohwer and Jerome were twins in most respects. There was little to distinguish one from the other, other than location. Local residents did not appreciate the nuances between Nisei and Issei. To most Arkansans, all Japanese were potential enemy agents, regardless of their citizenship status.

Almost twenty thousand Japanese Americans were transported into the state from September 1942 until the end of the war, creating the largest migration in Arkansas history. As more inmates arrived, the combined number of imprisoned Japanese Americans and the state's resident African American population soon outnumbered white residents. Conflict was inevitable, as white Arkansans had never before experienced themselves as a racial minority.

There were instances at other camps where military police shot prisoners for various reasons, but only at the camp in Jerome was a prisoner shot by civilians. It happened while three prisoners were out on work detail. Two of the men were shot and wounded by a vigilante tenant farmer on horseback who mistakenly identified them as escapees. Apparently, no charges were filed against the farmer, even though there was a white supervisor present when the shooting occurred, which made the escape story difficult to believe.[6]

In January 1943, the *Commercial Appeal*, an influential Memphis newspaper, published a story that reported that the camp at Jerome had become a "nest of sabotage and unrest" and was plagued by slowdown strikes and misappropriation of food.[7] The article created a public stir, prompting an investigation by the War Relocation Authority, which concluded that the news story was "largely untrue."

The WRA investigator attributed the story to a disgruntled reporter:

It should be noted that the writer of this article was alleged to have written a scathing article regarding the Farm Security Administration after [he] had been dismissed from a position with the Administration. [The reporter] is also said to have been rejected for employment at the Jerome Relocation Center where he had applied for the position of News Director previous to the time the article had been written.

There may have been truth to that, but several weeks after the article ran, there was a major disturbance at the camp following introduction of the WRA's loyalty questionnaire, which was designed to reveal tendencies of disloyalty to the United States—and a voluntary registration for the military draft. Apparently, it never occurred to camp officials that some people born and educated in the United Stated might be outraged and insulted to be asked to sign a loyalty oath. The trouble began in mid-February, when an inmate who volunteered to assist the army with the registration process was threatened by other inmates. Three weeks later, a committee of six inmates met with the camp director and voiced their opposition to the questionnaire. While the protest meeting was taking place, about one hundred inmates gathered outside the building to protest. Many protesters, insulted by the loyalty requirement, said they preferred to be repatriated to Japan.

While the protest was taking place at the camp director's office, a group of inmates went to the hospital and assaulted a physician, then continued to a minister's residence and assaulted him. Both victims were active members of the Japanese American Citizens League, which some inmates felt had sold them out by making deals with the government that benefited one segment of the inmate population over the other. The men who were attacked were not seriously injured, but they were taken to the camp hospital, where they were held under military protection.

Despite the protest, the registration process continued, resulting in only 33 out of a possible 1,296 eligible persons enlisting for military service. By contrast, 781 inmates eligible for military service asked to be repatriated to Japan. That left 482 inmates who refused to answer yes or no on the questionnaire. The WRA concluded that the low registration rate was due to an organized group of individuals inside the camp who campaigned against registration, noting that "the Department of Justice has not yet rendered an opinion as to whether prosecution will be instituted under the sedition statutes."[8]

Interestingly, there were no reports of organized political disturbances at nearby Camp Rohwer.[9] By April 1943, the only incidence of violence reported to the WRA involved two Hawaiian-born Japanese Americans who, according to camp officials, entered one of the mess halls in a "slightly drunken" condition and objected to the type of meat being served on that particular day. The cook took exception to criticism of his meat, and an altercation took place that involved more than fifteen inmates, eleven of them from Hawaii. Assault-and-battery charges were filed against the Hawaiians, and they were taken to the county jail in Arkansas City. None of the men was ever prosecuted. Instead, in a revealing decision indicating that some WRA officials had misgivings about the justification of its mission, camp officials granted the men leave to accept employment with the Santa Fe Railroad Company in Kansas City, Kansas. When the WRA was created, its leadership, especially Milton Eisenhower, the first director, wanted to allow Japanese Americans as much freedom as possible, the purpose of the camp being to isolate them from white Americans. The WRA was opposed to concentration camps, preferring the placement of Japanese Americans in new homes from which they could travel to civilian jobs. According to the report of the Commission on Wartime Relocation and Internment of Civilians, "They [WRA] believed that the vast majority of evacuees were law-abiding and loyal and that, once out of the combat zone, they should be returned quickly to conditions approximating normal life."[10] Although the WRA lost the argument to right-wing voices in the president's cabinet, individual WRA members occasionally made compassionate decisions about individual prisoners on a selective basis, hoping that their actions would not be noticed by the army.

At Camp Rohwer during this time was the Takei family, composed of the father, Takekuma; the mother, American-born Fumiko; and their American-born children: four-year-old Henry, three-year-old Nancy, and five-year-old George, who went on to achieve fame as the popular *Star Trek* character Mr. Sulu. Takekuma had come to America from Japan at the age of thirteen with his older brother and his widower father. Together they sought the American Dream. Takekuma attended public school in San Francisco and later graduated from Hills Business College. He started up a successful cleaning business in Wilshire and met Fumiko, eventually marrying her on the twenty-seventh floor of the Los Angeles City Hall. Their first child died at the age of three months. When their second child was born, they named him George (after England's George VI). Henry was named for Henry VIII. Nancy was named after a family friend, but her middle name, Reiko, means "gracious child" in Japanese. After the attack on Pearl Harbor, they were rounded up with everyone else and placed aboard a slow train bound for Rohwer, for them an exotic land that they had never heard much about, much less expected ever to visit.

Once they arrived, each family member was tagged with a card that read 6-2-F, their new address—block 6, barrack 2, unit F—and herded into the back of a flatbed truck and driven to their new home. "Beyond the fence we could see a forest of tall trees with thick, shrubby underbrush," recalls George. "It was dense with dark shadows. From the distant depths of the woods, we occasionally hear eerie "caw-cawing" sounds. The forest looked and sounded like a scary place beyond the barbed wire fence."[11]

Although all the prisoners were Japanese Americans, it was a diverse population. Some inmates were U.S. citizens (Nisei). Some inmates had lived in America for many years but were deprived of citizenship under law (Issei). Some were wealthy. Some were poor. Conflicts were inevitable.

George recalls that privacy was a major issue with women, since here, as in other camps, they had to use toilets that were built in long rows, with no partitions between the toilets. Food was a frequent source of discord. One of the Takei family's first meals was beef brains, a dish that most people of Japanese ancestry found unpalatable. Native southerners in the region, who might eat the occasional raccoon or opossum, were repulsed by beef brains, one reason that the dish was fed to the "Japs," since it meant that officials could make economical use of leftover slaughterhouse products.

Because he was outspoken on those issues, and because he was fluent in both Japanese and English, Takekuma was elected by the other inmates to serve as block manager. It was a job that kept him busy, sort of like being the mayor of a small town. People came to him when they had problems, whether with camp officials, one another, or their spouses. Takekuma did what he could to help.

As camp life dissolved into a monotonous series of chores and accommodations to family life, five-year-old George spent his free time exploring the compound. One day he was approached by two Japanese American brothers, both in their teens, who went through the motions of befriending him. The brothers were named Ford and Chevy, and when George asked his father why the brothers had such funny names, he explained that their father had owned a Ford when one was born and a Chevy when the other was born.

The brothers told George they wanted to teach him a magic word that exerted a mysterious power over the camp guards. George was game for that. The term they gave him was "Sakana Beach." Even at that young age, he thought it was an odd mixture of words. *Sakana* means "fish" in Japanese. "Beach" is obviously English. He did not see anything magical about "Sakana Beach," and they told him it was magical only if he spoke the words very quickly. After he practiced saying the phrase several times, the brothers took him to one of the guard towers. They arrived during a shift change, so both guards were at the base of the tower, talking.[12]

George walked close to the tower and shouted, "Bubble gum!" He hoped they would have some in their pockets and would toss it to him. There was no reason for him to think so, since the guards did not have a history of tossing candy to children, but he figured he had nothing to lose.

The guards ignored him.

George responded with another request that he hoped would bear returns: "Popsicle!"[13]

No chance. The guards shrugged and looked away.

By then, George was getting desperate. In his mind, guards were rich and had everything in life they wanted. He called out for something more substantial: "Tricycle!"

Again, the guards ignored him.

It was then that George reached for the magic phrase.

"*Sakana Beach!*"

The guards gave him a dirty look.

Encouraged by the attention, he said it again, saying it just the way the brothers taught him. This time one of the soldiers picked up a stone and tossed it at him, calling out, "You little snot!"

George ran back to the barracks, past the brothers who were hiding behind a building, hysterical with laughter. When he got home, he told his father about what had happened and asked him what "Sakana Beach" meant. There was no quick answer. His father toyed with the phrase, saying it over and over, sometimes fast, sometimes slow. Finally, he figured it out and told George never to use that phrase again, since it was a dirty word. It was not until George was much older that he understood. "Sakana Beach," when spoken a certain way, sounds like "son of a bitch."

Childhood adventures aside, the defining moment for the Takei family at Camp Rohwer came with the arrival of the questionnaires that asked inmates if they would serve in the military and pledge their loyalty to the United States.

"My father had no particular allegiance to the Emperor, but Japan was the country where he was born," writes George. "It was the place where he still had relatives and memories. . . . For my father, this was ultimately the point where he had to say enough—no more! It was now no longer a question of any citizenship but of simple dignity. He answered "no-no."[14]

George's mother had much the same reaction, though she was an American-born citizen and it was unthinkable that she could be sent to Japan simply because her parents were born there. George awoke one night to see his mother and father engaged in deep conversation, illuminated by a kerosene lamp that had been placed on a chair his father had built for his little sister, their voices intense, but hushed. He gazed through the night at the flickering light and saw tears on his mother's cheeks. His eyes filled with sleep, he called out, "Mama, don't cry!" She wiped her tears and told him that everything was all right; he should go back to sleep. He wouldn't know until much later, but in the light of the kerosene lamp his mother decided to answer no to the two questions, sealing their fate to be shipped to the concentration camp at Lake

Tule, where all the protesters and others who fought for their rights were sent.[15]

=========

Also at Rohwer during that time was sixteen-year-old Ruth Asawa, whose family had been uprooted from Norwalk, a farming community south of Los Angeles, where the family worked a truck farm. Ruth was American born and attended public schools, but on Saturday she and her brothers and sisters attended a Japanese school, where they learned the language and the art of calligraphy.

The Asawa family's journey to an Arkansas concentration camp began with the FBI's arrest of the sixty-year-old father, Umakichi Asawa, Without explanation, he was taken to a detention center in New Mexico. Several months later, the mother and children were rounded up and sent to the assembly center at the Santa Anita Racetrack, where some inmates were housed in animal stalls. Commenting on the racetrack experience, Ruth once told an interviewer, "The stench was horrible. The smell of horse dung never left the place the entire time we were there."[16]

Before her arrest, Ruth's life had revolved around school. Since there were no schools at the assembly center, she spent her time focusing on her passion—drawing and art. Some of the prisoners had been animators at Walt Disney Studios, and they taught art classes in the racetrack's grandstand. Ruth learned a great deal from those classes and realized that she could pursue drawing as a career.

In September 1942, Ruth, her mother, and her siblings were unceremoniously put on a train for Arkansas. They had no idea where Umakichi was being held, and if they had known, it would have done them no good. They would not see him again for two years. Once they were assigned quarters at Rohwer, Ruth was delighted to learn that she could continue her art studies, although at a fairly primitive level. Paint was available, but students were limited to painting rocks and fashioning sculptures out of tin cans.

The tar paper barracks were an improvement over the horse stalls that they had lived in at Santa Anita, but it was still a primitive existence in a forced society in which one had to wait in line for meals, bathroom privileges, medical treatment, and employment consideration. In later years, what she remembered the most was the water, which she described as having an odor like "rotten eggs."[17] It was a common complaint about the water supplies on both sides of the river. The water was drawn from wells in which the water level was close to the surface, resulting in a great deal of organic materials filtering into the water supplies and injecting the water with a high bacteria contact and a nauseating sulfurous odor.

Unlike the assembly centers such as Santa Anita, the relocation centers provided schools for the children prisoners. Ruth did well at the school at Rohwer, so well that when she was graduated from high school, she was given permission to leave the camp to continue her education at a college in Milwaukee, Wisconsin. When the time came for her to leave Rohwer, she was driven to the train station by her white English teacher, a resident of the community, who told her: "This is a terrible thing my government has done to your people. Don't look back on your life here. You must go on."[18]

Ruth never visited Rohwer again and did not see her parents for five years. She finished her course requirements at Milwaukee State Teacher's College, with the goal of becoming an art teacher, but because of discrimination she was unable to get a job to fulfill the requirement of practice teaching and so was unable to obtain a degree. Still eager to have a career involving art, she went to North Carolina and enrolled in the well-regarded Black Mountain College, where she studied under Josef Albers. By the 1950s, she had achieved prominence as an artist who specialized in wire sculpture and public fountains.

———————

Almost directly across the river from the Arkansas camps is Greenville, Mississippi, a city that was destined to become instrumental in America's coming to terms with the discrimination it inflicted on Japanese Americans. The city is unique in many respects, the most enduring being its reputation as a literary oasis that, over the years, provided fertile intellectual soil for the only pocket of liberalism in a state known more for its lynchings than for its enlightened thought.

That tradition began with Harvard-educated William Alexander Percy, a wealthy planter who believed in the importance of public service—and who published a memoir, *Lanterns on the Levee*, that argued for the assimilation of blacks into white society at a time when any kind of social or educational contact was against the law. Because he felt strongly that the existing newspaper, the *Democrat-Times*, in Greenville, was incapable of providing the type of enlightened leadership the city needed, he persuaded a Hammond, Louisiana, editor named Hodding Carter and his wife, Betty, to move to Greenville and establish a competing newspaper, the *Delta Star*. One of his reporters and copyeditors was Shelby Foote, who went on to become an award-winning historian who focused on the Civil War.

Together, Percy and Carter changed the social landscape of Greenville and the surrounding counties by standing up for racial equality at a time when the Ku Klux Klan had a powerful influence on white residents in the Mississippi Delta. One result of their efforts was that the Greenville Country Club had a Jewish president at a time when Jews were banned from country clubs elsewhere in the United States.

Perhaps because of that tolerance, Greenville was chosen for a World War II prisoner-of-war camp for German and Italian soldiers shipped back to the United States from the European war theater, along with eighteen other locations in Mississippi. Four of the Mississippi camps were large camps, with the remaining fifteen camps given a branch camp designation. The four large camps were Camp Clinton, in the small town of Clinton just outside Jackson, the state capital; Camp Como, situated in the northern part of the Delta; Camp Shelby, in the southern part of the state; and Camp McCain (named after Major General Henry McCain, an uncle of 2008 presidential candidate Senator John McCain) located near Grenada, not far from where the Delta meets the hills.

Altogether the camps housed twenty thousand German and Italian prisoners from Nazi Germany's Afrika Korps in North Africa. The large camps, which consisted of tar paper–covered barracks, mess halls, an administration building, a chapel, and a recreation building, were surrounded by double barbed-wire fences and guarded by armed soldiers who overlooked the camps from guard towers. The camps were almost identical to those housing Japanese American, German American, and Italian American citizens who had been rounded up by the army.

Unlike the U.S. citizens held prisoner in the concentration camps, the German and Italian prisoners were treated under the provisions of the Geneva convention, which required that officers receive special, preferential treatment, according to their rank. Special treatment was something that Mississippians understood. For decades, in the segregated South, whites received special treatment over citizens of color.

As a result, amazingly, Camp Clinton allowed thirty-one German generals to live in a hilltop village of individual houses shaded by trees and furnished with chairs and sofas upholstered in red leather. Their orderlies also were provided special housing. As a show of respect, camp officials allowed the generals to don their dress uniforms and occasionally leave the camp to stroll, unguarded, in downtown Jackson, among local residents who no doubt were shocked to encounter a German general in full-dress uniform outside the Piggly Wiggly or the snow-cone concession.[19]

German and Italian POWs were especially popular in the Delta, where they were much in demand for plantation labor. There were few citizens of German ancestry in the Delta, so they were considered something of a novelty. Not so with the Italians. Because many Italians had dark features, white Mississippians were never fully convinced that they were white, although the Italians were allowed to attend white schools.

When the United States entered World War II, local citizens of Italian ancestry were treated much like Japanese Americans were treated in California. In his history of Italians in the Delta, Paul V. Canonici wrote that although most of the Italian American men of draft age were in the armed forces, Delta Italians were looked upon with suspicion because of Italy's alliance with Germany: "Italians were required to remove pictures of Mussolini from display in their homes. U.S. officials went to Italian homes and collected guns and shortwave radios. Josephine Pandolfi Belenchia said they even took an Italian version of *Romeo and Juliet* from their home."[20]

In October 1943, a squadron of 250 German war prisoners arrived in Greenville, the first of 1,000 scheduled for imprisonment in that area. The men, dressed in blue overalls with the letters WP in bold yellow on the seats of their pants, were housed in tents at Recreation Park, just outside the city. The park was encircled by barbed wire and guarded by uniformed soldiers armed with machine guns.[21]

POW branch camps in the Delta were operated more like Boy Scout camps, where crafts were encouraged and inmates were allowed to form orchestras and produce plays. Prisoners were paid only eighty cents a day to work in the cotton fields, but security was minimal, and they were free to mingle among local residents.

On occasion, the prisoners mingled a little too much. At one of the branch camps north of Greenville, near Beulah, Mississippi, a German prisoner named Helmut von der Aue became romantically involved with a planter's wife while working on the plantation. One day Aue and several other prisoners had lunch at the plantation house while the woman's husband was away. After lunch, Aue stayed behind when the other prisoners left and had a few drinks with the thirty-seven-year-old lady of the house. Smitten, the woman provided the prisoner with some of her husband's clothes and drove with him to Memphis, leaving her befuddled husband behind to explain her behavior to authorities. From Memphis, the fugitive couple headed to Winchester, Tennessee, and then on to Nashville, where they checked into a hotel. The Nazi aviator and the lovesick plantation belle were captured in Nashville as they were checking out of the hotel.[22]

It was not the Nazi aviator's first escape attempt. After a previous attempt, he confessed to authorities that he planned to steal a P-38 plane and fly to Greenland. Aue was turned over to military authorities in Tennessee, and the planter's wife was sent back to the Delta, where she was prosecuted for aiding in the escape of a fugitive. There is no record of what happened upon her return to the plantation, but it probably did not involve a warm reception from her husband, whose name was published on the front page of the newspaper under the headline "Delta Planter's Wife Held After Flight with German POW."

Other escapes were less dramatic. At the branch camp in Belzoni, thirty-one German prisoners walked away from their facility and disappeared into the night, prompting a frantic convergence of sheriff deputies, FBI agents, and military police onto the camp. Heavily armed, they fanned out across the countryside in search of the missing POWs. Meanwhile, local residents locked their doors and bolted their windows shut, fearful of a confrontation with Nazi storm troopers. Finally, weary from searching the dense woods and swamps surrounding the camp, authorities returned to town and stumbled across the prisoners as they strolled about in small groups, meandering up and down the streets while window-shopping at local businesses.

In the Delta, German POWs received a high degree of acceptance among white Mississippians, who afforded them considerations and privileges that were unthinkable to the Japanese American prisoners across the river at Jerome and Rohwer. The German POWs looked like the people who owned the plantations and the Japanese Americans did not. Besides, most Mississippi white residents didn't have a big problem with the social theories associated with Nazism. They believed in the concept of a master race, and they weren't all that opposed to placing restriction on Jews. However, the Japanese were an entirely different story. They attacked Pearl Harbor, killing many southerners. They were not Caucasian. They were perceived to be subhuman, even if they were American citizens.

If the prisoners at the concentration camps at Jerome and Rohwer were aware of the warm reception that German and Italian POWs received from Mississippians almost directly across the Mississippi River from their camps, it must have baffled and infuriated them that soldiers who had killed Americans were so well treated, while they—and most of them were loyal American citizens—were looked upon as dangerous animals that could be shot down in cold blood if they ventured beyond the barbed-wire enclosure of their camps.

All of this would have been fodder for stinging editorial comment by Hodding Carter at the *Delta Democrat-Times*, except for the fact that he was not there. A little more than a year before Pearl Harbor, Carter's National Guard unit was called up for active duty. His entry into service was unremarkable except for his refusal to wear the regulation combat boots expected of him. Instead, he wore his favorite tennis shoes throughout the war, more of a comfort statement than a protest.[23]

In the weeks leading up to the attack on Pearl Harbor, Carter decided to leave the army and return to Greenville. However, America's entry into the war changed everything and he decided to stay in uniform, vowing that he would not leave the army until the enemy had been defeated. He asked for a transfer to the intelligence division and was quickly promoted to first lieutenant and then to captain. Betty turned the newspaper over to an acting editor and moved to Washington to be with Hodding. Since they still had payments to make on their loan to purchase the newspaper, she got a job in the Office of Facts and Figures, which she described to friends as the propaganda wing of the government. She also helped Hodding finish his book, *Lower Mississippi*, which was published in the fall of 1942. By the time Hodding and Betty returned to Greenville in the summer of 1945, the concentration camps in Jerome and Rohwer had been vacated and closed. Hodding had missed one of the biggest stories of the decade.

What he found was controversy over the admission of Chinese American children to Greenville's white public schools (he opposed an American Legion resolution condemning the admission of the children) and reports of the mistreatment of German POWs in the Delta (he wrote an editorial condemning their mistreatment). As the weeks went by, he learned more about Japanese American internment in concentration camps and more about Japanese Americans who served in the U.S. Army, so much so that by the end of the summer he was prompted to write an editorial that would leave an indelible imprint on the history of that era.

7

EASTWARD HO TO THE WILD, WILD WEST

In August 1942, when Mitsuye Yamada and her family arrived at the concentration camp in Minidoka County, Idaho, they were greeted by her brother, who had volunteered to go early to help construct the buildings. The first thing that Mitsuye noticed when she stepped off the bus was that the barracks were still under construction. That's not much work for almost five months, she thought.[1]

When completed, the camp comprised thirty-six tar paper barracks, with each building divided into six or eight units, some separated by six-foot-high partitions that did not reach the ceiling, making it possible for an intrusive neighbor to stand on a chair and peer over into the next unit. Prisoners who lived in units without partitions were allowed to hang privacy sheets from the ceiling. Each building had one coal-fired potbellied stove for heat and a single lightbulb that dangled from the ceiling. One stove, one light for six to eight families, all herded together like livestock at a state fair, though most barns for cattle and horses of that era were better ventilated and offered greater protection from the cold.

Minidoka, which is part of the Magic Valley region of the Snake River Plain in south-central Idaho, takes its name from the Dakota Sioux and translates as "spring of water." The Japanese Americans who were bused there did not know what to expect, but since Idaho is adjacent to their home state of Washington, they did not expect much of a change in climate. That expectation seemed justified when they arrived, because the mean temperature of Seattle and Minidoka County in August are quite similar, falling in to the midsixties. However, once the seasons changed, they were subjected to radical changes in temperature. During the winter of 1942 the snowfall was significant, and the temperature dropped to twenty-one degrees below zero. The following spring, the camp went from a muddy quagmire of melted snow to a hellhole buffeted by blistering dust storms and temperatures well over one hundred degrees. Since most of the prisoners were from the Seattle area, where extreme shifts in weather were rare, the misery index was off the charts.

"It was desolate," Mitsuye recalls. "But at the time, if the government told you to do something, you just did it. I think part of it may have been guilt [over Pearl Harbor]. One of the reasons we were given was that we were being rounded up for our own protection. At the time Japanese American businesses were being attacked. It made Japanese Americans feel like they would be safer in a camp. Then we got there and found out it was like a prison."

Among those who arrived around the same time as Mitsuye was Jim Akutsu, a Japanese American who had been born and raised in Seattle. "It was my understanding that we were to get the same kind of food as served in the army base mess hall, the same type of living quarters as in an army base, and clothing to suit the climate," he says. "After months of enduring poor food and primitive living conditions, I felt someone had to speak out. My complaints were [first] addressed at the block level. But without any response, I elevated it to the administration level. For this, I was placed on a stop list and also [placed] under surveillance as a possible agitator."[2]

Perhaps because of his protest, Akutsu soon received a letter from the War Relocation Authority, giving him the option of either enlisting in the army or being deported to Japan. The letter sent a chill over Akutsu. Was it possible for an American citizen to be deported to a foreign country? How could that be possible? Not long after receiving the letter, he was notified that his father had been sent to a maximum-security prisoner-of-war facility in Louisiana and was very ill. Akutsu's mother fell apart emotionally when she learned of her husband's arrest and illness.

Several months later, Akutsu's mother unexpectedly received a wire to meet her husband at the gate on a certain day. On his way to the gate to meet his father at the appointed time, Akutsu encountered an old man who asked where the Akutsu family lived. He pointed in the general direction of their barracks, thinking nothing of the request. People were always asking for directions. After waiting three hours at the gate, without finding his father, he returned to the barrack and was shocked to discover that the old man to whom he had given directions was actually his father. Recalls Akutsu:

I couldn't believe my eyes. . . . We hadn't recognized each other. Although my mother felt relieved that my father was back, it was a shock to see him in such emaciated condition. Shortly thereafter, she started to get weaker and finally succumbed to a total physical breakdown. She was under emergency care for many days, hovering between life and death. My mother's death, a few years later, was directly attributed to the evacuation.[3]

After seeing his father, Akutsu complained to the camp administration and threatened to contact the news media to expose what he considered abuses at their camp. Not long after his complaint was lodged, a letter was slipped under his door containing a copy of a letter sent to the draft board by a WRA official. The letter asked the selective service board to draft Akutsu. Not long after that he received an induction notice that instructed him to report to the camp hospital. It was dated *three weeks before he received the notice*, so it was impossible for him to keep the appointment. It was all a setup calculated to frame him. As a result, he was prosecuted for draft evasion and for stealing government documents [the copy of the letter that was mailed to him]. He was convicted and sent to the federal penitentiary at McNeil Island in Washington State, where he served two years in the maximum security wing with hardened criminals.[4]

━━━━━━━━━━━━

Ruby Inouye was a twenty-one-year-old premed student at the University of Washington when the roundups began. "We were embarrassed that Japan would have the nerve to attack America," she later recalled. "And the other students were looking at us as though we were a part of the enemy, so we didn't know how to feel, because we were Americans and yet we had the Japanese face. So we tried to go to classes and go home as soon as possible."[5] That attempt to keep a low profile failed. She was arrested and taken to Minidoka, one of 440 Japanese American students at the university who were rounded up and sent to the camp. She says, "In those days, we didn't have that mindset of rebelling. We were very obedient with family values and sticking together. Mainly we were incensed that we, as Americans, were treated as Japanese aliens . . . as though we were enemies and we were growing horns and claws and stuff like that."

━━━━━━━━━━━━

There were several things about Amache, a concentration camp located near Granada, Colorado, probably best known as the Gateway to Colorado, that made it unique among the other camps. The first was that its location on the Santa Fe Trail imbued the camp with a sense of history. Since the late 1800s, until the camp was constructed, Granada had been a ghost town. As white workers flocked to the area to help construct and maintain the camp, Granada became a boomtown again.

Amache was not an ideal place to live, especially for people who had lived their entire lives on the West Coast, where life was defined by urban sensibilities and a temperate coastal climate in which snow was an extreme rarity. In the winter months the temperature at Amache often hovered in the teens or low twenties, and in the summer months it soared to the low nineties. At its peak, Amache had a population of seventy-five hundred inmates, making it the tenth-largest city in Colorado. Most of the buildings at Amache were primitive wood-frame structures built on concrete slabs. The barracks were not insulated, nor were inmates given furniture. Heat was provided by coal-burning stoves. Barbed wire surrounded the compound, and the guard towers were equipped with machine guns.

About the only thing that gave distinction to the camp was Colorado governor Ralph L. Carr, one of the few governors who did not surrender to the war hysteria sweeping across the West and Midwest. A Republican, he favored a war declaration against Japan because of the attack on Pearl Harbor, but he went against the right-wing elements in his own political party to oppose the internment of Japanese Americans. After receiving a supportive letter from the Ministers Association of Boulder, Carr responded with a letter of his own:

> I am speaking my feelings all over Colorado, and up until now I have been met with sympathy and understanding. I believe that if we will continue to carry the banner and try to show the people the true philosophy of this situation, we shall convince them and turn this apparent difficulty into a benefit for all of our people.[6]

A few months later, Carr wrote to the U.S. attorney for Colorado, Thomas J. Morrissey, to request clarification of the government's position on the construction of concentration camps in his state. At that time, Japanese Americans already had been rounded up on the West Coast and sent to assembly centers. Carr had read news stories that the prisoners would be sent west, and he was concerned because he had received no communication from the government, and Japanese Americans already were showing up in Colorado in the belief that a self-imposed exile would satisfy government demands that they leave the West Coast.

Carr was also concerned because some Colorado landowners had received letters from Japanese Americans inquiring about renting farmland, and the landowners had notified the governor's office that they were prepared to rent or donate their land to people they saw as refugees. Taking the opposite position were many conservative Colorado residents who demanded the internment of all Japanese Americans relocating in the state. Wrote Carr: "At least one mass meeting has been held. Loose talk and wild threats are made by others which imperil our own citizens."[7]

Fearful that a situation was developing that quickly could get out of hand, Carr, a lawyer and former newspaper editor, pleaded with the U.S. attorney to pass his concerns along to Washington so that the federal government could intervene and take charge of the situation. The government needed either to protect the landowners' rights to do business with anyone of their choosing or to establish a facility to care for and protect incoming Japanese Americans. In his letter, Carr expressed his own thoughts about the rights of Japanese Americans, using language that brought honor to his office:

> This state bows to those principles of American government which give to American citizens the right to move freely from place to place, to earn a living as they deem fit or as circumstances allow, unhampered in their movements as individuals. The suggestion that an American citizen should be seized, deprived of his liberty, or otherwise placed under restraint without charge of misconduct and a hearing is unthinkable.[8]

Carr's vocal support of Japanese Americans' rights was supported by religious leaders, some newspapers, and a cross section of residents, but some newspapers and residents were vehemently opposed to his position. Their strength was sufficient to end his political career. One of his last acts as governor was to address a joint session of the Colorado legislature. He used the occasion to comment on the attitudes of those who had attacked him:

> Have we come to the point in this country where it is necessary, in order for us to live, that we must modify and control the attitudes and thoughts and actions of every human being in America according to a chart developed by some group which would make us conform to a national scheme?[9]

Despite the primitive conditions at the camp, many inmates had good things to say about the facility. Primarily because of Governor Carr's support of their rights, inmates were allowed monthly leave to shop in nearby towns and granted seasonal permits to take temporary agricultural and industrial employment outside the camp. Sometimes indefinite leave was granted to inmates to attend colleges or even to settle elsewhere in the United States, with the government picking up shipping expenses for their personal property.

When the day finally came for the camp to be closed, no one was in a hurry to leave. The day after the announcement not a single inmate had left. They felt safe at Amache, thanks to the protective environment created by Governor Carr. His contribution to their well-being was later acknowledged with a plaque placed outside the governor's office, a gift of the Japanese community and the Oriental Culture Society of Colorado. The inscription reads:

> Dedicated to Governor Carr: a wise, humane man, not influenced by the hysteria and bigotry directed against the Japanese Americans during World War II. By his humanitarian efforts no Colorado resident of Japanese ancestry was deprived of his basic freedoms, and when no others would accept the evacuated West Coast Japanese, except for confinement in internment camps, Governor Carr opened the doors and welcomed them to Colorado. The spirit of his deeds will live in the hearts of all true Americans.[10]

Named after the nearby limestone fault that rises more than eight thousand feet against the horizon, Heart Mountain Relocation Center was in northwest Wyoming, not far from Cody and fewer than one hundred miles east of Yellowstone National Park. A familiar profile in Hollywood westerns, the mountain seems an unlikely place for a concentration camp. Wyoming is probably best known for its beautiful vistas; its climate, which can vary from the low eighties in the summer to the high teens in the winter; its cowboy legends; and its notorious outlaws, like Butch Cassidy and the Sundance Kid, whose Hole in the Wall Gang made Wyoming a home away from home. Add to that historic profile more than ten thousand Japanese Americans, whose arrival forever changed the racial history of the state and made Heart Mountain, at least for the duration of the war, the state's third-largest city. Heart Mountain had a profound influence on both local residents and Japanese American prisoners, who felt that they had entered a foreign country when they left the West Coast.

One of the most interesting residents at Heart Mountain was Estelle Ishigo, the only known white woman to be interned with Japanese Americans. Her journey began at the Otis Art School in Los Angeles, where she met Arthur Ishigo, a San Francisco–born Nisei. She was intent on becoming an artist. He wanted to become an actor. They fell in love and married in 1928. Shortly after the attack on Pearl Harbor, they both were fired from their jobs. By the time the roundup began, she was forty-three and he was forty.

Estelle and Arthur gathered at a church with other evacuees, where they waited to be picked up by soldiers. As they were being loaded into the buses, she wrote movingly in her memoir, *Lone Heart Mountain*, a young girl became hysterical and suffered a heart attack. Her parents were allowed to take her back into the city for medical treatment. Unfortunately, the girl died, and the grieving parents were ordered to the nearest assembly center wondering, What next?

Estelle and Arthur were first sent to the Pomona Assembly Center, where they lived in sheds until they could be moved to Heart Mountain on a train that took four days to reach its destination. When they stepped off the train onto what, for them, seemed like foreign soil, they were exhausted from the constant movement of the railcars and ashen from the stress of confinement. "We began marching into a health inspection barn and were examined," Estelle recalls. "The wind seemed to find barren deserted places where it tore away at earth and life, leaving naked skeletons of rocks and shrubs for only those whose toughness and insensibility to pain might find existence endurable."[11]

The living conditions were primitive. Entire families were forced to live in a single room—mothers, fathers, babies, the elderly—all crammed together. Babies were born inside the barracks, new Americans birthed in captivity, and the elderly died inside the barracks. Birth and death sometimes coexisted within the same space. On any given day, crying, laughter, anger, and hushed conversations wafted through the barracks, commingled into a hivelike hum.

Amid the hardships and chaos, Estelle came to terms with the fact that she was the only white prisoner among twelve thousand Asians—the only prisoner who could leave if she demanded her freedom—delicately balancing competing emotions of bewilderment, love, anger, and compassion, writing: "Gathered close into ourselves and imprisoned at the foot of the mountain as it towered in silence over the barren waste, we searched its gaunt face for the mysteries of our destiny: and some spoke its name with the same ancient reverence, felt for their own mountains in Japan."[12]

An accomplished artist who also played violin and helped publish the camp newspaper, Estelle was commissioned by the War Relocation Authority to paint while at Heart Mountain. Her watercolor paintings, sketches, and pencil drawings are a haunting portrait of the camp experience.

━━━━━━━━

The Gila River concentration camp, located on a fifteen-thousand-acre tract leased from the Pima Indian Agency, was one of two camps in Arizona, the second being Poston. Named after Charles Poston, often called the Father of Arizona, the camp was situated twelve miles south of Parker in the Sonoran Desert, on land owned by the Colorado River Indian Tribes Reservation. Gila River was further divided into two camps about four miles apart, and Poston comprised three camps. An interesting footnote about the Arizona camps is that they were constructed by Del Webb, an Arizona contractor who shortly thereafter became notorious for building gangster Bugsy Siegel's Las Vegas hotel and casino, the Flamingo.

The Gila River camp had a project director and 150 white employees, most of whom worked in security. The hospital was under the direction of a white physician and eight white nurses assisted by ten inmate physicians and six inmate nurses. The police and fire departments were staffed by inmates, but they were under the direction of white advisers.

When the roundups began, Nao Takasugi was nineteen, enrolled at the University of California in Los Angeles, where he was studying business. First, he was placed on curfew and ordered off the streets from 6:00 P.M. to 6:00 A.M. Then he was told he could not venture more than five miles from his family home. Since the university was fifty miles away, it meant he could not attend classes.

Each day brought a new restriction. Then came the posting of Executive Order 9066. Takasugi's entire family, including his parents and four sisters, were instructed to report to the railroad station in Ventura. They were driven to the station by a family friend, a branch manager for the Bank of America. At the station they were confronted by soldiers with their weapons on display. Once they boarded the train, they noticed that all the blinds were drawn. Their first stop was the Tulare County Fairgrounds, where they were assigned a horse stall to live in. Within weeks they were again on the move. Another train with drawn blinds. When the train stopped at Gila River, and they stepped into sunlight for the first time in days, they saw that they were in the middle of a desert. The land was barren and inhospitable. The sun was hot.

The Takasugi family was represented in greater numbers at Gila River than Nao initially realized. The camp's inmates included four of Nao's cousins—brothers who soon volunteered for the 442nd Regimental Combat Team, an army unit composed entirely of Japanese Americans. After the brothers went through basic training, one of them returned to the camp to visit his family. Recalls Nao: "Here was my American-born cousin, in his army uniform, leaving to fight for his country, yet he had to wait at the barbed-wire fence to get a security clearance to see his family."[13] He wondered why, if his cousin and his brothers were good enough to fight for America, they could not be trusted to visit their family in a prison camp. As it turned out, that visiting cousin in uniform, Leonard Takasugi, was killed in action in Italy during the final year of the war.

George Aratani was named after George Washington by his Issei parents as a respectful nod to their adopted country. However, as a young man, George was sent to Keio University in Tokyo to study because his parents wanted him to improve his Japanese and learn about Japanese culture. After four years of study, he returned home for summer break. His father said his Japanese had improved so much that he wanted his son to stay in the United States and resume his education at Stanford University.

George dutifully enrolled at Stanford in 1940, only to be called back home three weeks into the semester because his father had become ill. He died ten days later, making it necessary for George to withdraw from school so that he could help run the family farm and the family business, the Guadalupe Produce Company, in San Fernando Valley, California.

Shortly after the attack on Pearl Harbor, FBI agents showed up at the Guadalupe Produce Company and asked for George. The workers were shocked. George was American born. It never occurred to them that Nisei would be arrested. They told the agents that he was working in the fields and would return later that afternoon. When George came back from the fields, the workers told him what had happened, but George was not concerned, since he felt the agents had made a mistake. Before the day ended, the FBI appeared once again and questioned him about his activities and then left. The visits went back and forth this way for several weeks, until President Roosevelt signed Executive Order 9066, which made it clear that all Japanese Americans, whether citizens or not, would be rounded up and sent to concentration camps. George was devastated by that news because he knew that he would have to leave the farm.

There wasn't much time, so he had to scurry to do what he could with his family's businesses. He and seven other partners were forced to unload their inventory and property leases for $8,000, a loss of more than $165,000. He couldn't find anyone to operate the hog farm, so he sold it at a loss for $13,500. He pooled his other resources with two other agricultural companies and established a trust called the California Vegetable Growers that would be operated by trustees until the war was over.[14]

When George's time came to report to an assembly center, he rode the bus to Tulare, California, where he was greeted by more than five thousand fellow prisoners milling about under armed guard. He was assigned a horse stall to live in until he received word of his next destination. It was a very hot spring and summer, with the temperature sometimes exceeding one hundred degrees. It was not until late August 1942 that George and about five hundred other prisoners were put on a train that they thought was traveling north to Colorado. Instead, they went to Casa Grande, Arizona, a small town southeast of Phoenix. Waiting for them at the train station were hot, dusty buses into which they were loaded for the forty-mile trip to a concentration camp on the Pima Indian reservation at Gila River.

George fell into an easy rhythm of living at the camp, adjusting well enough to the hardships, trying to do what he could to oversee what was left of his family's business interests, while waiting for the inevitable second shoe to drop. His first real test of conviction and character occurred when he was asked to sign the loyalty questionnaire. After a great deal of thought he answered "yes-yes" because he did not feel there was a real alternative. Above all else, George was a practical man. From what he knew about Japan, he knew he didn't belong there. Besides, he was pretty sure that Japan would be defeated by America. Later, when the opportunity came to volunteer for the all-Japanese 442nd Regimental Combat Team, he attended camp meetings where it was discussed. There was a lot of hostility toward the formation of an all-Nisei military unit, because it was argued that Nisei who volunteered should not be required to fight in a segregated unit. Others thought it would be a good opportunity for Japanese Americans to demonstrate their patriotism. George was still debating what he wanted to do, when one of his former employees and his wife came to him for advice about their military-age son. Actually, they wanted his help in dissuading their son from enlisting. "Why should he fight for America, when America would not fight for him?"

George agreed to meet with the parents and their son, with each side hoping he would support their point of few. The son came with a bundle of letters from his former high school friends. "They're in training camp," he said. "So they're in one kind of camp, and I'm in another. Why should they risk their lives and not me?"[15]

The father shook his head, telling his son that he simply didn't understand.

George intervened, with what he hoped would be words of wisdom. As the employer, certain things were expected of him. "You're right," he said to the father. "But your son's right, too. If the Nisei don't register or accept the call to duty, I'm sure they are going to be picked up by the United States military police. That means that you all might have to go to Japan, and what will happen to your children there? They have a Japanese face, but they cannot speak the language. So what's their future going to be?"[16]

That wasn't the advice the parents wanted to hear.

In May 1943 more than one hundred Gila River prisoners volunteered for military service, including the son who had put George on the spot with his former employees. Some camp members refused to register for the draft or take the loyalty oath. More than two thousand men, women and children from Gila River who answered "no-no" were transferred to the Tule Lake camp, where the dissidents were kept. Nearly eighty prisoners at Gila River applied for repatriation to Japan, and they were shipped to Japan on the *Gripsholm*, a prisoner-of-war exchange ship.

George held out to the bitter end. He answered "yes-yes," but he declined to volunteer for military service. Instead he bided his time until the draft was reinstituted for the Nisei in January 1944. He was among the last of his friends to leave Gila River. On May 1, 1944, he loaded up the car that a WRA employee had retrieved for him from storage in Guadalupe, and he drove to Camp Savage in Minneapolis, where he reported for service at the Military Intelligence Service Language School.

Among Gila River's more illustrious visitors was Eleanor Roosevelt, who traveled to the camp in April 1943 with WRA director Dillon S. Myer. The publicity flacks for the agency described her visit as one in which she was "greeted by crowds of enthusiastic evacuees" and they distributed photographs of her surrounded by grinning children. By then it was no secret that prisoners would smile for the camera, a natural reflex, especially among the young, who associated the word "smile" as a friendly command that was usually uttered by family members.

Several months later Mrs. Roosevelt wrote about her visit to the camp in an article for *Collier's* magazine. She did so in the context of explaining a new government policy that required all Japanese Americans over the age of seventeen to complete a questionnaire meant to assess their loyalty to the United States:

> I can well understand the bitterness of people who have lost loved ones at the hands of the Japanese military authorities, and we know that the totalitarian philosophy, whether it is in Nazi Germany or

in Japan, is one of cruelty and brutality. It is not hard to understand why people living here in hourly anxiety for those they love have difficulty in viewing our Japanese problem objectively, but for the honor of our country, the rest of us must do so.[17]

She explained that disloyal Japanese Americans would be moved to a heavily guarded camp where they would face more restrictions than previously had been imposed on prisoners. The information used to determine an individual's loyalty would be gathered by camp officials, the FBI, the Office of Naval Intelligence, and army investigators.

"We have no common race in this country, but we have an ideal to which all of us are loyal," she wrote. "It is our ideal which we want to have live. . . . Every citizen in this country has a right to our basic freedoms, to justice, and to equality of opportunity, and we retain the right to lead our individual lives as we please, but we can only do so if we grant to others the freedoms that we wish for ourselves."[18]

For some reason, Poston lagged behind Gila River in providing necessities to prisoners. By fall 1942, there were food shortages, warm clothing still had not arrived, and the barracks were still without heating stoves. To keep warm, prisoners huddled outside around bonfires. Under such primitive conditions, it is not surprising that passions bubbled over.

On November 1, 1942, camp officials arrested two male prisoners after an informant was beaten for spying on his neighbors and reporting to the WRA. When word got out that the two men were going to be tried in a civilian court outside the compound, an Issei delegation met with the project director to request the men's release, but they were turned down. After a second meeting ended in failure, camp workers went on strike, shutting down all services at the camp except those related to the police, fire department, and hospital. The strike led to a picket line outside the police station and a demonstration of about one thousand persons, during which strike leaders raised the Japanese flag and played military music on a phonograph, the volume turned up as high as possible. By the end of the third week of turmoil, a compromise was reached, whereby one man, who was cleared by an FBI investigation, was freed and the second man was released to the custody of two prisoner lawyers. After the U.S. attorney refused to prosecute the man, the prisoners returned to work and camp leaders agreed to help stop the beatings.[19]

Isamu Noguchi was unique among Japanese Americans of that era. The son of a Japanese poet and a white American writer, he was an accomplished sculptor whose work drew from the surrealist movement. He was spending some time in California when the attack on Pearl Harbor occurred. It was then that he realized he was Nisei in addition to being American. In order to demonstrate Nisei loyalty to America and the war effort, he organized a group of Nisei into a group he named the Nisei Writers and Artists Mobilization for Democracy.

Weeks before Executive Order 9066 was issued, Noguchi and his Nisei friends foresaw the coming of evacuation and took a strong position against it; but they quickly realized that it was a losing battle, and Noguchi decided to return to the East Coast so that he could escape arrest. As a resident of New York, he was not subject to arrest or imprisonment. En route to New York he stopped in Washington, D.C., with the intention of lobbying against evacuation. While there he met with John Collier, the commissioner of Indian Affairs, who persuaded him to voluntarily enter the camp at Poston so that he could work for change from the inside. Not long after Noguchi entered the prison camp, where he worked in the carpentry shop, Collier visited the camp and gave a speech in which he urged the prisoners to nurture the seeds of democracy within the camp despite the beating that democracy was taking outside the camp. Observed Noguchi: "It soon became apparent, however that the purpose of the War Relocation Authority was hopelessly at odds with that ideal cooperative community pictured by Mr. Collier. They wanted nothing permanent nor pleasant."[20]

About two months after Collier's visit, Noguchi wrote him a letter in which he asked him to do whatever was necessary to secure his release from the prison camp. "I am extremely despondent for lack of companionship," he wrote. "The Nisei here are not of my age [he was thirty-seven] and of an entirely different background and interest. . . . As it is I become embittered. I came here voluntarily. I trust that you will not have difficulty in securing this request."[21]

Collier spoke to Dillon Myer about his case and obtained his release, not because he had volunteered for camp, but rather because authorities considered him to be of "mixed blood." Noguchi's experience led him to later conclude that Nisei lived in a no-man's-land, neither American nor Japanese. After leaving the camp, he went on to nurture an accomplished, award-winning career as a sculptor and landscape artist, prompting the *New York Times* to write a story upon his death in 1988, describing him as "a versatile and prolific sculptor whose earthy stones and meditative gardens bridging East and West have become landmarks of 20th-century art."[22]

The loyalty questionnaire that prompted Eleanor Roosevelt's article was viewed by the government as a way to separate disloyal Japanese Americans from those they suspected were a threat to national security. Its origins can be traced to an earlier debate about whether Nisei should be allowed to serve in the armed forces. At the time of the attack on Pearl Harbor, there were over five thousand Japanese Americans in military service, most of them drafted by their local draft boards. After the attack, most local draft boards stopped drafting Japanese Americans by classifying them as IV-F (unsuitable for military service), although the armed forces still accepted them as volunteers.

The fate of Japanese Americans already in service was left to the discretion of their commanders. Some soldiers were allowed to remain in service. Others were abruptly discharged without explanation. The confusion was eliminated in June 1942, when the War Department declared that it would not accept for service, except in special circumstances, persons of Japanese heritage. Three months later, the Selective Service System, which supervised local draft boards, announced that it would no longer allow the induction of Nisei and it would require that American citizens of Japanese ancestry be given an enemy alien classification (IV-C).

Taking exception to that was Assistant Secretary of War John J. McCloy, who, impressed by the performance of the all-Nisei Hawaii National Guard unit, looked for ways to reverse the policy. Bolstering his argument were reports that large numbers of Nisei were displaying bitterness that they were not being allowed to serve in the armed forces—and a resolution from the JACL requesting that selective service be reinstated for Japanese Americans. However, the biggest roadblock to changing policy was the fundamental argument in favor of the concentration camps, namely that all Japanese Americans must be considered disloyal by virtue of their Japanese heritage. If the government changed policy and allowed Japanese Americans to serve in the military, that would undercut the government's justification for the concentration camps. At the same time, it would raise questions about whether the government intended to use Japanese Americans as cannon fodder. On the surface, it looked like a no-win situation.

At the end of September the Pentagon issued a report claiming that "the military potential of the United States citizens of Japanese ancestry be considered as negative because of the universal distrust in which they are held."[23] The report put career military officers in stark opposition to McCloy and other civilians who were having second thoughts about the internment policy. Aside from the military issue, McCloy had concerns about what should be done with the prisoners. He knew that they couldn't be kept penned up forever. There would come a time when they would have to be released.

In early October, Elmer Davis, director of the Office of War Information (OWI), and his deputy, Milton Eisenhower, former head of the War Relocation Authority, broached the subject in a memorandum to President Roosevelt. Their position was that current policy was a propaganda bonanza to the Japanese government. The best way to fight the propaganda, argued the memorandum, was to allow Japanese Americans to enlist in the army and navy: "Moreover, as citizens ourselves who believe deeply in the things for which we fight, we cannot help but be disturbed by the insistent public misunderstanding of the Nisei."[24]

The memorandum ended up on the desk of McCloy, who wasted no time in using it to convince his boss, Secretary Stimson, that the time had come for a policy change. McCloy argued three points: that citizens have a right to serve their country; that there was widespread agreement that most Nisei were loyal; and that enlistment would have a significant psychological effect overseas and would make the Office of War Information's work much easier. Stimson readily agreed and sent Chief of Staff General George Marshall a handwritten note that expressed his agree-

ment with McCloy and Davis: "I don't think you can permanently pro-
scribe a lot of American citizens because of their racial origin. We have
gone to the full limit in evacuating them. That's enough."[25]

Marshall responded by ordering the creation of an all-Nisei combat
team. In order to accomplish that a committee was assembled to determine the means by which Nisei, in general, could be released from the
concentration camps. Within one week, the committee recommended
that a questionnaire be used to assess loyalty. The questionnaire asked
questions about the applicant's background and solicited a pledge of loyalty to the United States. It was a ludicrous solution, since a true Japanese
American spy would lie to obtain release from the camp, whether to join
the military or to return to civilian life.

On February 6, 1943, teams of army officers, bearing government-
issue questionnaires, fanned out across the West to visit the concentration camps. Most of the questions solicited background information.
Only two questions dealt with the issue at hand: 1) "Are you willing to
serve in the armed forces of the United States on combat duty, wherever
ordered?" and 2) "Will you swear unqualified allegiance to the United
States of America and faithfully defend the United States from any or all
attack by foreign or domestic forces, and forswear any form of allegiance
or obedience to the Japanese emperor, or any other foreign government,
power or organization?"[26]

To their surprise, the army officers were greeted with hostility. Both
Nisei and Issei were suspicious of the government's intentions. They wondered if the questionnaire was part of a nefarious scheme, using trick
questions, to send them to an even darker fate. Was America toying with
the idea of using death camps to solve its Japanese American "problem"?
To a people who had been stripped of their freedoms and imprisoned in
camps just a notch above dog kennels, anything was possible.

The Issei were especially disturbed by the loyalty question because
it required them to renounce their Japanese nationality, even though
they were prohibited by law from becoming American citizens. If they
signed the loyalty oath, they would lose their Japanese citizenship and
thus become men and women without a country, subject to deportation. If they refused to sign the oath, they feared it could result in hus-

bands being separated from wives and parents being separated from their children. According to a report issued years later by the Commission on Wartime Relocation and Internment of Civilians, "The Issei were also bitter about their own treatment and that of their citizen children. As a Naval Intelligence report stated, Issei opposition to enlistment was based less on reluctance to see their sons fighting Japan than on losing faith in America. [They] made quite an issue of the fact that the citizen Japanese and the alien Japanese received identical treatment. This indicates, they say, the American Government does not recognize the Nisei as full citizens."[27]

Nisei opposition was based on the wording of the loyalty question, which required they "forswear" their allegiance to the Japanese emperor. If they signed the oath as written, it was an admission that they previously had sworn allegiance to the emperor. That suggestion infuriated many Nisei, who considered themselves good American citizens. In the end most Nisei and Issei signed the oaths after resigning themselves to their hopeless situation. If they wanted to leave the camps or enlist in the army, they knew they had no choice but to trust the government.

Of the approximately 120,000 Japanese Americans interned in the camps, 42,000 were children and thus ineligible to complete and sign the questionnaire. Of the nearly 78,000 who were eligible, 68,000 signed the loyalty oath. Of the remaining 10,000, 5,300 answered no, and the remainder refused to complete the questionnaire.[28] Of the 5,000 or so who refused, more than 3,000 were at one camp—Tule Lake, located in north-central California. It was the largest of the camps, with a population of almost 20,000.

Authorities were surprised that such a large number of prisoners refused to answer the loyalty oath question or answered with a no. Some said it was because they were disloyal. Others said that their reasons had nothing to do with loyalty.

One prisoner who signed no to the loyalty oath explained it this way: "I answered both questions, numbers 27 and 28, in the negative, not because of disloyalty but due to the disgusting and shabby treatment given us." Another prisoner who signed "no" said he did it because he wanted to fight back: "I didn't want to take this sitting down. I was really angry. . . . Whatever we do, there was no help from outside, and it seems to me that we are a race that doesn't count."[29]

Once all the questionnaires were gathered, government officials had to decide how to process those who refused to complete the documents and those who answered no to the loyalty oath question. They decided to send officers to each camp to interview those who had either refused to answer the question or who had answered no. If the interviewees stuck by their decisions, they asked those who had American citizenship if they were prepared to renounce that citizenship. If they received a yes answer, the interviewee would shortly thereafter receive a form letter from the Immigration and Naturalization Service asking them to sign a document relinquishing their citizenship. If they received a no, they were told to pack their bags so that they could be relocated to a maximum security facility.

Tule Lake was the natural choice for a maximum security facility because it had the largest percentage of prisoners who answered no to the loyalty oath and because it was the largest facility in the system. Several criteria were used to determine who would be relocated to the camp, including: those who answered no to the loyalty question or to military service or refused to answer the question; those who previously had applied for expatriation or repatriation to Japan; those who were denied leave clearance due to some accumulation of adverse evidence in their records; and aliens from Department of Justice camps who were earmarked for relocation by the Justice Department for various reasons.

The transfers took place in 1943, from mid-September to mid-October. About eight thousand prisoners were moved from Tule Lake to make room for about ten thousand dissidents culled from the other camps. The transformation of the camp itself was startling. Six tanks were lined up in a threatening way. A double barbed-wire fence was built around the camp. And the guard was increased to more than one thousand armed soldiers. Not only was the atmosphere more threatening than at the other camps, but also the accommodations were inferior and there simply was not enough room for the new arrivals, making it necessary for them to be assigned cramped quarters with few amenities. No effort was made to communicate good intentions to the new prisoners. They were left hanging in the wind, so to speak. Most felt they soon would be deported, if not executed on the spot or sent to a death camp.

Morgan Yamanaka and his older brother, Al, were among the "no-no boys" sent to Tule Lake. They had a brother and a younger sister who lived in Japan. They didn't want to go into the army and perhaps fight against their brother or other family members. "Up to the issue of loyalty, my plans, my ideas, were you must be a good citizen," he explains, and continues:

> But you see being a good citizen for me didn't involve fighting against Japan. You do whatever you can to be a good American citizen, but it never occurred to [us] you might have to fight your brother or uncles . . . so when I answered no-no on the questionnaire, the basic reason was that Al and I would not want to fight our brother.[30]

For George Takei's family, Tule Lake was a vastly different world from what they had experienced at Rohwer, Arkansas. They went from a sultry, hot climate, where honeysuckle hung in the air and time sometimes stood still, to one where everyone was either angry or in a hurry and the air always seemed cool and brittle. Rohwer was laid back, a reflection of slow-paced southern culture. Tule Lake was a powder keg of pent-up emotions, a place where anything could happen at any time.[31]

Sometimes George was awakened at daybreak by the sound of young men jogging around the blocks in unison, white headbands called *hachimaki* around their heads. Some of the headbands bore the image of the rising sun, an in-your-face challenge to their white captors. As the men shouted out cadence—*wah shoi, wah shoi, wah shoi*—it generated hypnotic ripples throughout the camp, delighting some, frightening others. Recalls George:

> There were the young men who had turned radical in their disillusion and their sense of betrayal by America. If America was going to treat them like enemies, then they resolved to give America adversaries it would have to take seriously. They would become

the enemies that America would be forced to reckon with from within. . . . They would prepare to rise up when the Japanese military landed on the West Coast."[32]

=======

November was a contentious month at Tule Lake. On November 1, Dillon Myer, head of the WRA, visited the camp, prompting a large group of inmates, estimated at five to ten thousand, to gather near the administration buildings in an attempt to speak to him about inadequate medical care, squalid housing, and food shortages. Illnesses were ignored in the camp. Food was rationed, and some prisoners went hungry. While Myer was meeting with them, another group of frustrated inmates went to the hospital and assaulted the chief medical officer.

Myer ended up meeting with both groups, a gesture that resulted in them returning to their barracks. However, three days later a group of inmates got into a fight with guards while trying to prevent food from being removed from the warehouse by white workers they thought were stealing inmates' food to sell on the black market. According to inmate Tokio Yamane, he and a camp leader, Koji Todorogi, rushed to the scene to restore order and were brutally attacked by guards and taken into custody.

A third camp leader, a Mr. Kibayashi, also was taken into custody. During his interrogation, soldiers repeatedly swung the baseball bat against his head, blood gushing out everywhere, the blows continuing with such force that the bat broke in two. Later, in testimony, Yamane recalled the incident: "I was a witness to this brutal attack and remember it very vividly. From about 9 p.m. that evening until daybreak, we were forced to stand with our backs against the office wall with our hands over our heads and we were continuously kicked and abused as we were ordered to confess being the instigators of the disturbance."[33]

What began as an attempt by inmates to improve medical care and protect food supplies escalated into a full-fledged riot. Martial law was declared, and soldiers filled the compound, backed up with tanks, machine guns, and tear gas. Military police officers searched the quarters of all twenty thousand inmates, causing one inmate to later observe: "To be forced to let the MPs in our small humble quarters seemed like such invasion of personal privacy that the emotional effect of that search still haunts me."[34] During one midnight raid, Morgan Yamanaka recalls, he and others were ordered outside in the snow. Soon an armored personnel carrier with a machine gun pulled up. In actions chillingly reminiscent of newsreels from Nazi Germany, soldiers aimed the machine gun at the unarmed prisoners and forced them to stand in the snow for hours in their underwear and zoris [a thonged sandal]. "What the hell could we do? I don't know whether they would have shot us if we had gone back [inside]."[35]

In the wake of the disturbance, Attorney General Biddle sent President Roosevelt a memorandum that seemed out of touch with the facts: "Five hundred Japanese internees armed with knives and clubs shut up Dillon Myer and some of his administrative officers in the administration building for several days. The army went in to restore order. The feeling on the West Coast is bitter against the administration for what they think is its weak policy towards the Japanese."[36] Influenced by inflammatory right-wing newspaper editorials that viewed all Japanese citizens as enemies, Biddle urged the president to intervene and order an FBI investigation about the incident. Roosevelt left the matter in the hands of the War Relocation Authority, which depended on the army to restore and maintain order at the camp. About seven months after the disturbance, on July 1, 1944, Congress passed and Roosevelt signed a law that permitted American citizens to renounce their citizenship in wartime. Clearly, the law was directed at the prisoners at Tule Lake.

After the war, under pressure from both the American government and camp dissidents, 5,461 prisoners from Tule Lake surrendered their U.S. citizenship.[37] Of that group, 1,327 were expatriated to Japan, many of them children.[38] To some non-Asian Americans, the banishment was proof of Japanese American disloyalty, which many Americans desperately wanted to believe was pervasive. To other Americans, who believed that otherwise loyal Japanese Americans had been manipulated, insulted, and sometimes driven to the point of believing that their freedom depended on a renunciation of their citizenship, it was one of the saddest chapters in U.S. history.

8

THE KONZENTRATIONSLAGER BLUES

Max Ebel's American nightmare began innocently enough. The son of a German sculptor and master carver who had abandoned his wife and children to forge a new life as a stoneworker at the National Cathedral in Washington, D.C., Max left Hamburg, Germany, in May 1937 at age seventeen and headed to Boston to join his father. Before he left Germany, he was stabbed in a knife fight with another boy, a member of the Hitler Youth, an organization that Max refused to join.

Max's father had fought in World War I and had killed a man in hand-to-hand combat while serving in France. The experience haunted him, causing him to become depressed on the anniversary of the killing. The emotional suffering he saw in his father each year influenced Max to become a pacifist, a decision that was not appreciated by his peers, almost all of whom were enamored of the Nazi movement.

Max stepped onto American soil in New York with a suitcase filled with woodworking tools and a single change of clothing. The nickel in his pocket was German and therefore worthless, so in effect he was penniless. His father greeted him at the dock, and they walked to the train station to catch a train to Boston. Max later recalled: "I was an American right from the beginning, and I always will be. I think I appreciated my freedom as much as a fish let out of a bowl to swim in a river."[1]

Four days after he arrived, he turned eighteen and celebrated his birthday with his father and his father's new wife. His father owned a woodworking shop, where Max was expected to work. He befriended an African American coworker who taught him English, and in return, he taught his friend German.

Max was not in America long when he received a letter from Germany that demanded he return to serve in Adolf Hitler's army. He burned the letter. Then a second letter arrived. He burned it as well. When he received a third letter, Max's father went with him to the German consulate and asked officials to strike his name from the list of persons declared eligible to serve in the military. Germany was gearing up for war, and Max, a confirmed pacifist, wanted no part of that. His request was granted.

Fewer than two years after Max arrived in America, Germany invaded Poland, an action that led to American officials impounding a German freighter, *Pauline Frederich*, in Boston Harbor. One day Max and his father visited the ship, and the first mate, an old friend of Max's father in Germany, took them on a tour. Max's father invited several of the seamen to dinner. Unknown to Max or his father, their interactions with the German seamen were being watched by FBI agents who had been assigned to keep an eye on the ship. The FBI knew about the tour, the dinner, and the visit to the consulate, and a photo of them leaving the consulate ended up in Max's FBI file.

Long before America's entry into World War II, the FBI began tracking German nationals once they entered the United States, primarily because of news reports that chronicled Adolf Hitler's rise to power. A tremendous knowledge of European history was not required to understand that Nazi Germany's goal was world domination. As a step toward preparation for a possible war with Germany, in 1940 Congress enacted the Alien

Registration Act, which required all aliens fourteen and older to register with the government. The new legislation was based on the authority of the Alien Enemies Act of 1798, which gave the president extraordinary powers during a time of war. Section 1 of the Alien Enemies Act proclaimed that in the event of war or threatened invasion of the United States, the president has the authority to apprehend as enemy aliens any and all males of the age of fourteen years and older who are native to the offending country.

In the eyes of many Americans, the Alien Registration Act was not unreasonable in view of German political activity in the United States. Months before the act was approved by Congress, the Deutschamerikanische Volksbund, an organization of German Americans that claimed membership of two hundred thousand throughout the United States, held a rally at Madison Square Garden in New York to praise Hitler and denounce Roosevelt. The louder that groups such as the Volksbund became, the more American public opinion demanded that the government take action to protect the homeland against possible German saboteurs.[2]

In March 1941, agents for the Immigration and Naturalization Service (INS) seized sixty-five German, Italian, and Danish ships docked in American ports for the declared purpose of preventing them from being used in acts of sabotage. Nazi Germany protested vociferously and demanded the release of the ships and their crews, but American officials stood their ground. There had, in fact, been instances in which sabotage efforts had been blocked by authorities. For instance, the captain of the Italian freighter *Mongolia* admitted to coast guard officers that he had been ordered to sabotage his ship's engines in an effort to block the harbor, telling the coast guard: "We tried to carry out those orders completely. I presume we will be interned now for the duration of the war."[3]

By April, the U.S. government had arrested nearly nine hundred crew members from the ships they had seized, imprisoning them at Ellis Island and prompting a new wave of protests from Germany and Italy. The situation escalated that month when a federal grand jury in Boston indicted the captain and four officers of the *Pauline Frederich* on charges of sabotaging the freighter before it could be seized.[4]

On December 5, 1941, two days before the attack on Pearl Harbor, Max filed a signed declaration to become a U.S. citizen. Shortly after the attack, President Roosevelt issued Proclamation 2525, based on his powers under the Alien Enemies Act of 1798, which authorized the government to detain enemy aliens considered dangerous to the public safety. The following day, he issued similar proclamations that authorized the Justice Department to apprehend anyone of German or Italian descent suspected of crimes. In the days and weeks that followed, Max's hopes for citizenship took a backseat to the realities of the times. Instead of being asked to take an oath of citizenship, he was required to register at the post office, submit to fingerprinting, and be photographed for an identification card that described him as an "enemy alien," a label that was only partially correct. He was an alien but not an enemy. Under the law, all noncitizens of German, Italian, or Japanese birth were classified as enemy aliens.

Germans presented a problem for the Roosevelt administration. In 1940 there were about 1.3 million people of German birth in the United States, making Germans the second-largest foreign-born ethnic group, just behind Italians. When the families of that 1.3 million were added, the number rose to more than 5 million. Unlike Japanese Americans, German Americans had considerable political and social clout, particularly on the East Coast.

Not sharing Roosevelt's political concerns, General DeWitt asked for approval to round up West Coast German and Italian aliens en masse, and Eighth Army general Hugh A. Drum asked for permission to round up Germans and Italians on the East Coast on the grounds that it was the most logical place for a roundup to take place in view of the ships being disabled off the East Coast with the help of saboteurs. By the end of March 1941, the United States had seized sixty-five ships, twenty of which had been sabotaged by their crews.[5]

Roosevelt considered roundups on the East Coast of the type used to arrest Japanese Americans on the West Coast, but he quickly rejected that option because of the nightmarish logistics of arresting and relocating such a large number of politically connected people. The decision was made instead to put so-called enemy aliens under the jurisdiction of the U.S. Justice Department, since Roosevelt could not assign that duty

Anita (left) and Doris Berg in Hawaii, one year before the attack on Pearl Harbor. COURTESY OF DORIS BERG NYE

Frederick Berg in 1945.
COURTESY OF DORIS BERG NYE

Bertha Berg in better days before the war. COURTESY OF DORIS BERG NYE

Doris Berg surfing off the coast of Hawaii. COURTESY OF DORIS BERG NYE

The concentration camp on Sand Island, Hawaii, one of the first built in the wake of the Japanese attack. COURTESY OF U.S. ARMY MUSEUM OF HAWAII

Evacuation photo, April 1942, San Pedro, California.
COURTESY OF NATIONAL ARCHIVES

Japanese Americans arriving at the Santa Anita assembly center in April 1942. COURTESY OF NATIONAL ARCHIVES

This store in Oakland, California, was closed after evacuation orders were issued by the U.S. Army.
COURTESY OF NATIONAL ARCHIVES

Photo taken by a *Seattle Times* photographer in 1942 of Mitsuye Yamada and her family as they were being moved from the assembly center in Puyallup, Washington, to a concentration camp in Minidoka, Idaho. COURTESY OF MITSUYE YAMADA

Newcomers arriving at Manzanar relocation camp in Manzanar, California.
COURTESY OF NATIONAL ARCHIVES

A young prisoner at Manzanar in 1942.
COURTESY OF NATIONAL ARCHIVES

Barracks at the Rohwer Relocation Center in Arkansas, 1943. COURTESY OF NATIONAL ARCHIVES

Barracks at the camp in Jerome, Arkansas. COURTESY OF UNIVERSITY OF CENTRAL ARKANSAS ARCHIVES

Baton twirlers at Jerome, Arkansas.
COURTESY OF UNIVERSITY OF CENTRAL ARKANSAS ARCHIVES

Children's pageant at Jerome, Arkansas. COURTESY OF UNIVERSITY OF CENTRAL ARKANSAS ARCHIVES

Japanese Americans at
Rohwer, Arkansas.
COURTESY OF UNIVERSITY OF
CENTRAL ARKANSAS ARCHIVES

Camp store at Rohwer, Arkansas.
COURTESY OF UNIVERSITY OF CENTRAL ARKANSAS ARCHIVES

Japanese American prisoners working in
the fields near Rohwer, Arkansas.
COURTESY OF CENTRAL ARKANSAS ARCHIVES

Japanese American artist at work at Rohwer.
COURTESY OF UNIVERSITY OF CENTRAL ARKANSAS ARCHIVES

Heart Mountain can be seen in the distance at the concentration camp at Heart Mountain, Wyoming. COURTESY OF NATIONAL ARCHIVES

Mrs. Eleanor Roosevelt visits the concentration camp at Gila River, Arizona. COURTESY OF NATIONAL ARCHIVES

An aerial view of the concentration camp at Minidoka, near Eden, Idaho. COURTESY OF NATIONAL ARCHIVES

Japanese American prisoner bathes in a homemade tub at Heart Mountain, Wyoming. COURTESY OF NATIONAL ARCHIVES

above: Max Ebel works under the watchful eye of a guard alongside other prisoners from Fort Lincoln, North Dakota. COURTESY OF KAREN EBEL

left: Mitsuye Yamada (left) and her mother, Hide Yasutake, at Minidoka, Idaho. COURTESY OF MITSUYE YAMADA

Max Ebel and his wife, Doris, on their wedding day in Boston in 1948.
COURTESY OF KAREN EBEL

In 1949, at the age of nineteen, Doris Berg was selected as Hawaii's Pineapple Bowl Queen.
COURTESY OF DORIS BERG NYE

After years of imprisonment, Japanese American prisoners board a train at Heart Mountain, Wyoming, to return to what was left of their former lives.
COURTESY OF NATIONAL ARCHIVES

Karen Ebel with her father, Max.
COURTESY OF KAREN EBEL

A more recent photo of Mitsuye Yamada.
COURTESY OF MITSUYE YAMADA

to the army without declaring martial law for the entire country, something he was not willing to do. The army was given jurisdiction over Japanese Americans, Germans, and Italians, both citizens and noncitizens, on the West Coast and within the territories of Hawaii and Alaska, and the Justice Department was given jurisdiction over noncitizens, or "enemy aliens," of Japanese, German, or Italian heritage outside the army's area of jurisdiction. The Justice Department, however, could take anyone into custody within or outside the army's jurisdiction if it was felt that sabotage or espionage was at issue. Justification for that approach was based on credible information about German spy rings operating inside the United States. Months before Pearl Harbor, the FBI uncovered a major German spy ring that the bureau infiltrated and watched for nearly two years, finally garnering thirty-three espionage arrests and convictions.[6]

The FBI wasted no time rounding up individuals who fit its profile of an enemy alien. The agency already had spent months drawing up secret lists of people to be arrested. Each person was classified according to a rating system: *A* was assigned to noncitizens who headed up cultural or assistance organizations; *B* was given to slightly less suspicious aliens; and *C* was reserved for those who either contributed to or belonged to ethnic organizations (included were Japanese-language teachers and Buddhist priests).[7]

Individuals on those lists were all arrested in early December and sent to detention camps. When the roundups made news, Attorney General Biddle issued press releases to dampen criticism of the government's actions. He insisted that no one would be arrested without probable cause. Clearly, the government treated Japanese Americans with less consideration than they did German Americans and Italian Americans, as was evident in the arrest figures released by FBI director J. Edgar Hoover on December 10, 1941, an accounting that he said represented "all" those he planned to arrest: 1,291 people of Japanese descent, 857 people of German descent, and 147 people of Italian descent. Two months later, Hoover was proved to be inaccurate. By February, the totals had escalated to: 2,192 Japanese, 1,393 Germans, and 264 Italians.

For much of 1942, it appeared that Max and his father would not be caught up in the roundup. Things took a turn for the worse in August, when the Ebel home, where Max still lived with his father, was twice searched by FBI agents who had presidential warrants permitting them to search homes in which an alien from an enemy country resided. Max fell into that classification, but his father did not, because he had become a citizen long before the war began. According to Max's daughter, Karen Ebel, during one search Max told agents about a secret compartment in a nightstand that he'd designed. He had nothing to hide, so he offered to show it to them. As he unlatched the compartment, agents drew their pistols. Satisfied that the nightstand was not a threat to national security, the agents left the home, but not before gathering up a radio, camera, and several German-language books that they took with them for further study.[8]

The following week, Max was arrested at work and questioned about his activities. Perhaps because of his visit to the *Pauline Frederich*, he was sent to the Boston immigration station, where he remained for three months with no explanation of why he was being held. Eventually, he was allowed a hearing before a civilian board composed of three local appointees. He was without counsel, which probably did not affect the proceedings, because he was not allowed to question witnesses or ask questions. The evidence against Max was presented by a district attorney, who mainly argued that when Max registered with selective service, he declared that he did not want to fight against Germany, since that would put him in opposition to family members living there. To Max, the reasoning seemed logical. As a result, he was classified IV-C (enemy alien).

He felt good about his classification: it meant that he would not be drafted. Not until his hearing did he realize that such a classification was not so good after all.

The district attorney made a point of saying that if his own son could fight in the war, Max could fight as well. What Max didn't understand was that although the Selective Service System offered alternative classifications, including various limited-service options for conscientious objectors, that did not mean that the options were acceptable to authorities. Conscientious objectors and those classified IV-C were subject to reprisals of various kinds by authorities. Max's lack of understanding of the law set him up for persecution, which is what happened at the hearing, when he was depicted as a coward who was unwilling to serve the country that had provided him refuge. In other words, they offered him a IV-C classification and then prosecuted him for accepting it, a common practice used by authorities in the 1940s, 1950s, and 1960s.

On January 20, 1943, Max learned that the civilian board that had conducted his hearing recommended that he be released on parole, but that recommendation was rejected by the Justice Department, which ordered him sent to Ellis Island for internment. It was certainly an ironic choice for a concentration camp. Located in the upper part of New York Bay, next to the Statue of Liberty, it was the portal through which millions of immigrants entered America. For many, Ellis Island was a powerful symbol of freedom.

Max Ebel's stay at Ellis Island was anything but a symbol of freedom. In an interview with the author, Max's daughter, Karen, who has established a Web site to present the stories of her father and other German Americans, said that her father's stay at Ellis Island was a dark period in his life. "As he conveyed it to me, people stayed in the big building on Ellis Island," she says. "It was really dirty. The food was really bad. When they were taken outside for exercise by the army guys, it was always at gunpoint and the men screamed out at them, something like, "I don't care what happens to you. I'm taking you out either head first or feet first."

═══════════════════════════

Other prisoners at the facility had similar stories. One of the prisoners, Emma Neupert, was sent to Ellis Island because, unlike her German-born husband, George, she failed to become an American citizen after she emigrated from Germany. The FBI visited their home on several occasions, sometimes in the middle of the night. Each time they searched the house and went through their belongings. After several such visits, the FBI arrested Emma and took her to Manhattan, where she was locked up at a police station until she could be moved to Ellis Island.

For Rose Marie, their ten-year-old daughter, it was a traumatic experience. After her mother was taken away, her father lost his job and was blacklisted from finding new employment. He'd escaped imprisonment solely by the technicality of citizenship. Unable to properly care for Rose Marie, he asked friends to care for her. One day social workers from the Child Welfare Department came to Rose Marie's school to question her. Fearful that Rose Marie would be sent to a concentration camp—by then it was common knowledge that the orphanages in California were being raided by the army—George worked it out with officials so that she would be able to join her mother at Ellis Island. Many years later, Rose Marie's memories of Ellis Island are still vivid. "The building was alive with roaches; every time anything would be moved, the roaches would scurry about," she recalls. "I remember a woman complaining because I had nightmares and woke her up."[9]

The visits continued until the summer of 1943, when George's citizenship was revoked and he was arrested by the FBI and sent to Ellis Island. There he was housed in the men's section, away from his wife and daughter. He was interrogated on a regular basis but never informed of the charges against him. When it became obvious that they were going to be there for a long time, George and Emma asked officials if they could be sent to the internment camp at Crystal City, Texas, a facility that accepted families. Permission was granted in October 1943, and George, Emma, and Rose Marie were put on a train bound for Texas, confident that they would fare better as a family.

Crystal City was originally a migrant labor camp under the supervision of the INS. With the entry of America into World War II, a decision was made to convert the one-hundred-acre camp into a facility capable of housing interned families. At the time the decision was made, there were forty-one three-room cottages and more than one hundred one-room cottages, all surrounded by high fences with barbed wire and guard towers fitted with spotlights. To accommodate internment prisoners, numerous one-room shelters were added for couples and small families, and apartments were built for larger families. A seventy-bed hospital was also equipped to care for the prisoners.

One of the prisoners at Camp Crystal was eight-year-old Ted Eckardt, who was there with his mother, Ruth, and his younger sister. The story of how they came to be imprisoned at the camp is incredible, to say the least. Ted's father, Albert, was a German-born immigrant who entered America in 1909 at the age of fifteen through the facility at Ellis Island. He settled in Brooklyn, New York, and became a naturalized American citizen as soon as he was old enough to do so.

Albert worked as a seaman and traveled a great deal in Latin America. During one of his trips he met a woman in Panama named Ruth Jankwitz. They were married and made their home in Limon, Panama, an isolated village with dirt roads and thatched-roof houses. Albert died in 1938, and Ruth raised their two children as a single mother. They lived a fairly mundane existence until June 16, 1942, when they were summoned to Panama City, where they were arrested and locked up in cells.

"I recall having to wear a three-inch ID button with a number," says Ted. "There was no explanation—just a letter that we must report to the Panamanian police. My sis and I were held there overnight while our mother went back to our home to pack a few things. The day we left Limon was the last time we ever saw our home."[10]

Because Ruth and her children were American citizens by virtue of her marriage to Albert, they were handed over, without explanation, to the INS and interned in Balboa, Panama, for a while before being deported and shipped to New Orleans on a U.S. troop transport. From New Orleans they were transported to Crystal City and housed in a one-story duplex.

Ted recalls that the food was good and that there were playgrounds for the children and schools that offered lessons taught in German.

The Eckardts were held at the camp for two years and then sent to Toledo, Ohio, after the superintendent at the Lutheran orphanage in Toledo agreed to be the children's guardian. Ruth was given shelter at the orphanage and helped provide for her children by working at the nearby senior citizens' home. Ted recalls "going to parochial school and working on the farm. My chores were to keep the floors clean and scrubbed and to feed the chickens and pigs, plus hoeing and weeding in the fields."

Ted grew into adulthood without ever understanding why the government felt it was necessary to arrest a widow and her two children. "We were just German Americans who have been a part of our country's history since it began," he says. "Personally, I believe the Panamanian government went along with the deportation so that they could then confiscate our property."

Approximately three thousand Americans of German, Italian, or Japanese descent were arrested in Latin America and deported to the United States during the war. The rationale at the time was that it had to be done out of what authorities called "military necessity." American military strategists were fearful that the Japanese would either attack the Panama Canal to destroy its usefulness or invade the country to control the waterway, interrupting U.S. shipping from the Atlantic to the Pacific.

The reality was that there were only a handful of German, Italian, and Japanese diplomats and business executives who could even be remotely considered a threat. The majority of those deported were like the Eckardts. They were innocent bystanders who were targeted because of prejudice or because they owned land that was desired by individuals with the power to take it away from them. A widow and her two children were an easy target. The Eckardts were never compensated for their home and belongings, a travesty that, to this day, still haunts Ted Eckardt, who now resides in Hot Springs, Arkansas. Says Ted:

> We were devastated to have lost all and to have been taken out of the mainstream of life for those years and away from close friends we had in Panama. I still am bothered that my country doesn't seem to care that we lost all that we had, everything that my mom and dad worked for all their lives to provide us with a stable family life., Ironically, I thank God for the opportunities I had in America.

Another survivor of Camp Crystal and Ellis Island was twelve-year-old Arthur Jacobs, the American-born son of German immigrants who were caught up in the hysteria of the times. In 1944 his father, Lambert, was at work at his factory job when the FBI arrived unannounced and took him away in handcuffs. Arthur, his brother, and his mother, Paulina, were beside themselves with worry for three days, waiting for word of his fate. Then on the third day an Immigration and Naturalization Service officer visited their Brooklyn home and told them that he had been arrested and interned at Ellis Island.

Unable to support herself and her two sons, Arthur's mother took them to Ellis Island and told officials that she wanted to join her husband, since she was now homeless. Authorities were not accustomed to accepting volunteers, but they took her and her two sons into custody and assigned her to the women's barracks and her sons to the men's barracks. Two months later the family was transferred to Camp Crystal. Recalls Arthur, "We were quite disappointed and appalled when we first saw the living quarters. The duplex to which we were assigned had been shut up for a long time, and as we opened the door several wasps and other flying insects flew out in front of our faces."[11]

They were there only eight months when they were pulled out of Camp Crystal and sent back to Ellis Island, where they were told that they would be deported to Germany. After they arrived in Germany, the family was split up and sent to different locations. Despite his young age, Arthur was transported in a frigid boxcar with armed guards to a prison at Hohenasperg, which at that point was under the control of the U.S. Army. "I was just a kid," he later wrote in his memoir, *The Prison Called Hohenasperg*. "Why did they call me a 'little Nazi'? It was cold, wet, and dreary in my cell—it was stark. It was beyond scary. It was frightening. It was madness."

It took weeks for Arthur to convince authorities that he and his brother, Lambert, were American citizens—he often wondered why the government had shipped them to Germany without asking for proof of their American citizenship—but once they were released, it was not an easy matter to convince the American consulate that they were eligible for American passports. Finally, they arrived back in the United States in November 1947 without their parents. Fortunately, they were taken in by a Kansas family and raised until Arthur came of age and joined the U.S. Air Force. It was not until 1958 that the brothers were reunited with their mother and father, who had elected to stay in Germany after their release from prison in 1946. It is a measure of the passions and complexities of the times that Arthur and his brother chose America over living with his parents in Germany, and that his parents chose Germany over a life with their two sons.

During his stay at Ellis Island, Max Ebel became ill with one of the worst sore throats he'd ever had. He asked for treatment, but prison officials declined to treat him, because he was going to be transferred the next day to a U.S. Army installation at Fort Meade, Maryland. True enough, he was shipped out the following day with a group of prisoners. Once they reached the New Jersey shore, they were put on a train that had all the shades drawn. In each railcar were soldiers with rifles. Other railcars contained prisoners of war. It perplexed Max that the German Americans in his railcar were prohibited from raising the shades but the POWs were allowed to raise theirs and look out the windows at the passing countryside.

Fort Meade was an improvement. Max received medical treatment for his sore throat, and he was fed hearty meals that had been prepared by interned German cooks. He was given a physical and several vaccinations, and, after a two-week stay, he was put on another train with shaded windows and transported to Camp Forrest, at Tullahoma, Tennessee. Camp Forrest, which was named after Confederate general Nathan Bedford Forrest, the founder of the Ku Klux Klan, was a training facility for eleven infantry divisions, two battalions of rangers, and a number of Army Air Corps personnel. It was one of the largest U.S. Army camps in the country.

Max was among eight hundred German American and Italian American prisoners interned at the seventy-eight-thousand-acre camp. A huge complex of buildings, the camp included a village used to give soldiers instructions in house-to-house combat. Not only were thousands of soldiers housed on the base, but also the army contracted with more than twelve thousand civilians to maintain the vehicles, operate the laundry, and run the post exchanges. Outside of Nashville and Memphis, the camp was one of the largest population centers in Tennessee.

Max wasn't impressed by the accommodations. The camp was filled with long trenches that contained stagnant water, and his cabin was inhabited by black widow spiders. But he was relatively happy there, since he was allowed to help physicians in the operating rooms as a result of his interest in first aid. Recalls daughter Karen: "When he talked about Camp Forrest, he wasn't as harsh as he was about Ellis Island." Even so, he reported disturbances at the camp and occasions when guns were pointed at the prisoners by persons he described as "sawed-off shrimps."

On May 28, 1943, Max was moved from Camp Forrest to make room for German and Italian prisoners of war. By the end of the war, the camp held twenty-four thousand members of the German army. Ironically, one of the POWs sent to the camp was Max's first cousin, a draftee who had served in the German army. Max's new destination was Fort Lincoln, located south of Bismarck, North Dakota, on the east side of the Missouri River.

Fort Lincoln was one of about two dozen detention camps set up by the Justice Department and the U.S. Army. The Justice Department camps were administered by the INS, and the military camps were administered by the army. These camps were different from the camps operated by the War Relocation Authority, a civilian agency, in that they were more rigid in their expectations of inmate behavior and less understanding of inmate family problems caused by the imprisonment. Most were located at existing military facilities, which typically meant that inmates were housed in tents or tar paper barracks. But there were exceptions, such as the army prison at Stringtown, Oklahoma, where inmates were assigned to prison cells formerly occupied by violent felons. The camps, which were separately administered by the army and the Justice Department, were never meant to be permanent facilities, and their status changed from year to year throughout the war, with many being shut down after only a year or two of operation to make room for rapidly escalating numbers of prisoners of war.

One of the difficulties faced by all the camps was what to do with the prisoners. Neither the prisoners nor the camp officials thought confining them to their barracks, tents, or prison cells day after day was a good idea. Work was the answer to better manage the prison population, but that was a problem, since the Justice Department had ordered that the facilities had to meet the standards set by the Geneva convention for prisoners of war. One of the provisions was that prisoners could not be forced to do labor that assisted their enemy's war effort.

American officials found a way around that in March 1942, when U.S. senator Robert Reynolds, who served on the Senate Committee on Military Affairs, noted that Germany and Italy used enslaved manpower to build their railroads. Why couldn't America use its prisoners to help build its railroads? he asked. It was a solution that appealed to both camp officials and prisoners.[12]

As a result, when the Justice Department held parole hearings in April 1943 for interned seamen at Fort Lincoln, sixty-two of these men were released into the custody of the Northern Pacific Railroad, which wanted the men to work as track gang workers.[13] The experimental program was so successful that the government made railroad work an option for more than five hundred prisoners.

Max Ebel was among the prisoners allowed to leave Fort Lincoln to work on the Northern Pacific Railroad. They were housed in boxcars that were heated by coal stoves. The only water source was the tank car. There were no bathroom facilities, so the men went outdoors. As harsh as those conditions were, they were preferable to living in a crowded camp where the most useful duties were peeling potatoes or washing dishes.

One of the best things for Max about working on the track gang was the opportunity it offered to interact with local Native Americans. The track gang once worked on a spur that veered onto the Standing Rock Indian Reservation, where there was a community of Lakota. Max was shocked to see that the Indians lived in huts with dirt floors, the original planking having been ripped up for firewood. Trees are a rarity on the plains, and to keep warm during the severe winter months, the Lakota burned anything they could find, including the floors of their dwellings. Karen tells the story of an experience Max had when the men attended a church on the reservation near Cannonball. Seeing the men in the congregation, the minister pleaded with them for money so that they could replace the church roof, not fully understanding the extent of the men's poverty. Even so, the prisoners pooled the hard-earned money they'd made on the railroad and donated what they could to help the church.

Max was among a group of one hundred prisoners who successfully pleaded with the government to give them new hearings, because from their perspective they were helping the American war effort by replacing the rails on the very tracks upon which wartime munitions were shipped. Their argument was that they should receive consideration because they were indirectly aiding the U.S. war effort. It was during that process that the board questioned why Max had been arrested.

Oddly, while the evaluation of his case was ongoing, Max was drafted and sent to a selective service center in Minnesota for his physical. He went with misgivings, not sure what to expect. His imprisonment seemed to be a direct result of the conflict at his previous hearing, at which he expressed unwillingness to fight in the European theater. He was fearful of being put in a position in which he would have to kill family members. There was also the matter of his being a pacifist, a position that never failed to elicit hostility from authorities.

To his surprise, he flunked the physical and was rejected for service. He couldn't help but wonder if the entire matter of his imprisonment might have been avoided if he had been given a physical in the beginning, which was normal procedure. If he had flunked the physical, they could not have prosecuted him. Knowing that, authorities prosecuted him without giving him a physical, which guaranteed that he would go to prison. Regardless of his draft status, he was aware of the irony of being confined to a camp because he was considered too dangerous to be on the streets yet being perfectly acceptable as a combatant in the service of the United States.

When Karen Ebel was growing up, the only thing she knew about World War II was that her father had worked on railroads in North Dakota during the war and had many pleasant experiences with Native Americans on a nearby Indian reservation. He told many stories about the Indians and made it sound like an adventure. She always thought it odd that he helped build railroads in such a faraway place during the war and made friends with Indians, but she was young and never asked why. She was in her midtwenties and in law school in Washington when she learned that her father had been declared an enemy alien and worked on the track gang at Fort Lincoln as a prisoner. His acknowledgment of his experiences came about in a roundabout way. Recalls Karen: "There was some publicity coming out about the Japanese redress efforts, and that came up and he said, 'You know, Karen, something like that happened to me.'"

Karen was shocked. She had no idea he'd ever been imprisoned. Due to the shock of learning that he had been a prisoner, she didn't ask him to go into detail. It was not until much later that she learned the entire story. That occurred when her husband, a serious Civil War buff who enjoyed researching military history, put "Fort Lincoln" and "internment" into his computer search engine and made the connection.

"He found pictures of Fort Lincoln and I was blown away," recalls Karen. "The whole thing had been shrouded in bits and pieces, but when I saw those pictures, I was living in New Hampshire, in the fall, and some of that early spring sun was streaming in the window, and it really hit me and I was so upset about the whole thing—to think that my country would do something like that! I knew that my father was never a threat to anyone."

From that time on, Karen committed herself to finding out more about his story. One result was the establishment of the German American Internee Coalition, a group that maintains a Web site onto which she has assembled an impressive collection of interviews and historical information about internment. She comments, "It was an astonishing time in history."

9

ITALIAN AMERICANS DODGE A BULLET

The first Italians interned in America during World War II were neither citizens nor aliens. They were sailors captured on Italian merchant ships that ventured into American waters or ports. The first detention facility opened by the Justice Department was at Fort Stanton, New Mexico. The fort had been established in 1855 to imprison the Apache rounded up by the army during the Indian wars. Years later, it was used to hold the outlaw Billy the Kid while he awaited a hanging that never took place. In January 1941, eleven months before the attack on Pearl Harbor, it was used to house 410 German seamen seized on the S.S. *Columbus*, a passenger liner. They remained in the prison for the duration of the war, their numbers inflated by the arrival of Italian seamen yanked from freighters and passenger liners.

Like Fort Stanton, Montana's Fort Missoula was built in response to the Indian wars. In 1941, it was converted to a detention facility for war-related internees, the first arrivals being 125 Italian sailors who were seized offshore. A couple of months later they were joined by an additional 400 Italian sailors who were transferred from Ellis Island.

Because of the Justice Department's use of detention facilities for Italian seamen, the army felt justified in requesting permission to lock up Italian American citizens and aliens. President Roosevelt shot down that request and made it clear to Attorney General Biddle that he wanted the government to go easy on the Italians. A few days after Pearl Harbor he told Biddle, "I don't care about the Italians. They are a lot of opera singers. But the Germans are different. They may be dangerous."[1]

That unfortunate "opera singers" phrase was his flippant way of discouraging further discourse about the matter. The truth is complex and not very flattering to the president. Italians, citizen and noncitizen, were a powerful political influence on the East Coast, where they had a large presence in a variety of industries related to the war effort, especially on the docks. Italian citizens, for the most part, voted Democratic, unlike German Americans, who tended to split their votes with the Republican Party.

Stephen Fox, who wrote a book about the problems experienced by Italian Americans during World War II (*UnCivil Liberties: Italian Americans Under Siege During World War II*), concluded that a major reason for the exclusion of Italian Americans from mass relocation was because they had a public profile that was much higher than that of the Japanese Americans. He points to a noncitizen Italian fisherman in San Francisco named Giuseppe DiMaggio, whose son Joe had set the 1941 major league record for hits in consecutive games. Would the public tolerate the Yankee Clipper's father being sent to a concentration camp? Then there were the political leaders of Italian or German ancestry, all Republicans—former presidential candidate Wendell Willkie, New York mayor Fiorello Henry La Guardia, and San Francisco mayor Angelo Rossi. And let's not forget one of the most popular singers of the era, Frank Sinatra, the son of Italian immigrants. Would their immigrant families be interned in camps with Japanese Americans?

Besides the social and political considerations that drove his decisions about internment, Roosevelt knew that he would need the help of the Italian American community to defeat Italian leader Benito Mussolini, a founder of the National Fascist Party. Mussolini was very popular with the so-called common man in Italy, but he was not so popular with the Mafia, a criminal organization that he felt sapped his political strength. For that reason, he cracked down on the Mafia, imprisoning its leaders, often humiliating them by arresting them and parading them in public. American war strategists saw his Mafia obsession as a weak spot in the belly of the Italian war machine. So did the American Mafia, which viewed the war as a vehicle through which it could obtain favors from the U.S. government. The mastermind of the Mafia's scheme was Charlie "Lucky" Luciano, the Sicilian-born New York don who was sometimes referred to as the "Chairman of the Board." It was his view that the American Mafia should be operated like a major American corporation and not like a feudal, vendetta-driven Sicilian gang.

To that end, Luciano and his cohorts played FBI director J. Edgar Hoover like a Stradivarius violin, to the point where Hoover once proclaimed to Attorney General Francis Biddle, "No single individual or coalition of racketeers dominates organized crime across the country."[2] Hoover knew better than that, but in order to get what he wanted from organized crime leaders—Hoover had a deal with Mafia don and Luciano associate Frank Costello that he would stay out of their business if they stayed out of his business—he had to pretend that the Mafia did not exist; otherwise the American people would demand that he get tough with the mobsters.[3] To those who ask why Hoover adopted such an attitude, journalist Sanford Ungar has an answer: "One [reason] was that [he] did not want to cause trouble for powerful friends on Capitol Hill or in city halls and statehouses who were themselves cozy with mobsters. Another was that some of the director's own wealthy friends were involved in dealings with the underworld."[4]

During the early years of World War II, while confined at Dannemora State Prison, from which he continued to rule his underworld empire, Luciano devised a plan that he hoped would win his release and help him obtain American citizenship. The newspapers were filled with stories of spies operating along East Coast waterfronts. Military intelligence officers were a frequent sight on the docks, where they encouraged dockworkers to be diligent to the possibility of sabotage. To put the plan into effect, he went to one of his toughest enforcers, Albert Anastasia, brother of Tony Anastasia, a boss in the International Longshoremen's Association. After a French ship, the *Normandie*, burned under mysterious circumstances while docked in New York harbor, Anastasia put out word that the underworld would be agreeable to preventing future disasters of that kind. American admirals took the bait. A naval officer was sent to the prison to negotiate with Luciano, after which the gangster was transferred to more comfortable quarters at a prison just outside Albany, from which Luciano was granted leave to visit local roadhouses to conduct his private business.[5]

While in the prison Luciano had more than twenty meetings with Moses Polakoff, a lawyer and navy veteran recruited by the Office of Naval Intelligence to be its go-between, and organized crime kingpin Meyer Lansky, who was the contact person for the gangsters on the docks. Luciano later described the agreement in conversation with an undercover FBI agent: "They want to know if I'll get the boys into a meeting and set up a kind of organization that will watch out for any screwy stuff going on around the docks. I called a meeting of longshore guys right up there in the warden's office and we set up just what they wanted."[6]

For his part, Lansky encouraged his associates who owned restaurants to hire undercover German-speaking naval intelligence agents as waiters so that they could listen in on conversations of their German-speaking patrons. The navy-mob working relationship went so smoothly that navy agents ended up servicing Mafia-owned vending machines in nightclubs. Explained Lansky: "They handed over the money they collected and were always honest in their dealings. I think this just might be the only time the U.S. Navy ever directly helped the Mafia."[7]

After the war, Luciano's lawyer asked for executive clemency, armed with a letter from the naval officer he had met with. Without asking questions, the parole board released Luciano from prison. However, there was a catch to Luciano's freedom: instead of being granted U.S. citizenship, he would be deported to Sicily.

On February 2, 1946, Luciano was moved from prison to a cell on Ellis Island. One week later he was escorted by INS agents to the freighter *Laura Keene*, where he was made comfortable for his journey to Italy. He spent the evening aboard the ship with a few of his closest friends—Frank Costello, Albert Anastasia, Meyer Lansky, Bugsy Siegel, and Joe Bonanno. They were served a splendid meal aboard the ship, where they enjoyed the company of three showgirls sent to them courtesy of the world-famous Copacabana Club. "There was no difficulty in getting them aboard," noted Lansky. "The authorities cooperated even on that. Nobody going into exile ever had a better send-off."[8]

At a time when Japanese, German, and Italian noncitizens were being rounded up, it is odd that the government would not use wartime proc-lamations as an opportunity to arrest and deport the rank and file of the American Mafia, whose underworld membership was notorious for not seeking U.S. citizenship. The government didn't lean on the mobsters because officials concocted a scenario in which America would pit its bad guys against Mussolini's bad guys for a bare-knuckle, winner-take-all brawl. The result of that high-stakes wager, along with Roosevelt's con-cerns about the political fallout of offending Italian Americans, meant that only an unfortunate few were picked up and sent to internment camps. J. Edgar Hoover's announcement in December 1942 that he had arrested practically all the enemy aliens that would need to be taken into custody is of interest not so much because of the bravado of his statement (he was obviously incorrect, as history would prove) but because of the breakdown of those arrested—1,291 Japanese, 857 Germans, and 147 Italians.[9] Clearly, some Italians were afforded special treatment by the FBI. To those who would argue that the low Italian numbers were because only a small num-ber of Italians were guilty of crimes, it should be pointed out that very few of those arrested of any nationality were ever found guilty of crimes.

Not so willing to go easy on the Italians was the army, which forced more than a hundred thousand Italian Americans on the West Coast to leave their homes and move inland. Of those, more than fifty thousand were subjected to curfews. During the day, they were required to be at their place of residence or employment, in transit to either of those two places, or within five miles from their home.[10] In 2000, Congress asked the U.S. attorney general to prepare a report that, among other things, answered the question as to why some Italian Americans were subjected to civil liber-ties infringements and other Italian Americans were not. The best that the attorney general's office could come up with was that the Italian Americans affected by relocation simply lived in the wrong place at the wrong time.[11]

═══════════════════

Confirmation that President Roosevelt was not the least bit concerned about the clout of Italian "opera singers," as he derisively referred to Italians, can be seen in the arrest of Ezio Pinza, a world-famous Italian basso opera singer who lived in New York in the 1940s with his wife and daughter. In the spring of 1942, he became concerned when he didn't hear from the Metropolitan Opera about an upcoming tour. As the days went by, his concern grew. Something was wrong. But what?

Finally, on March 12, 1942, his questions were answered. Pinza was at his desk in the living room when he was confronted by two men in dark suits who had entered the house through the back door without ringing the bell.

> "Are you Ezio Pinza?" one of them asked sharply.
>
> "Yes, I am. What can I do for you?"
>
> "In the name of the president of the United States, you are under arrest!"
>
> There was such iron in his voice that I rose involuntarily. For one fleeting moment, I had the illusion of myself behind bars, handcuffed, condemned, lost to the world for all eternity.[12]

As he stood there, stunned, his daughter's voice came from another part of the house, startling the FBI agents. Pinza explained that it was his daughter and his wife would return soon. Would the agents mind waiting for her, so that his daughter would not be left alone?

They didn't mind. They had a warrant to search his house.

While they were in the process of going through his closets and drawers, his wife, Doris, came home and, though ashen and stunned, gave him practical advice about how to respond to their questions. At the conclusion of the search, they showed him an assortment of items that they took with them—a bill of sale for his motorboat, assorted letters, and several autographed photos.

Pinza was taken to the Foley Square Courthouse, where he was fingerprinted and photographed. Then he was taken by boat to Ellis Island and imprisoned with one hundred twenty-five Italian, German, and Japanese Americans. The next morning the *New York Times* ran a page 1 story about his arrest, using the headline:

Ezio Pinza Seized as Enemy Alien
FBI Takes Singer to Ellis Island

Twelve days later his case was heard by a review board. In his autobiography, *Ezio Pinza: An Autobiography*, he wrote:

Shocked by the arrest, demoralized by the prison-like life in the barracks, and ignorant of the charges against me, I put on the worst show of my life at the hearing. My English, imperfect under the best circumstances, must have been positively murderous as I stuttered, mumbled, and repeatedly proclaimed my innocence.

The board ruled against him. He later learned that two of the three board members believed him, but for him to be set free, the board's vote had to be unanimous. He marveled that it took only one vote to convict and three votes to acquit. His only appeal was to Attorney General Biddle, who could order a second hearing. Pinza's lawyer was optimistic, but success depended on Pinza remembering everything that was said so that a legal defense could be prepared. Since internees were never advised of the charges against them, it was difficult to prepare a defense. The only clues that an internee had to go on were the questions that were asked. What follows are some of the accusations made by the government and Pinza's explanation to his lawyer:

Accusation: He owned a ring with the Nazi swastika on it.

Pinza's explanation: It was not a Nazi ring; it was a Samoan tortoiseshell ring that had a primitive marking that looked like a swastika.

Accusation: He had a boat equipped with a radio that received and sent secret messages.

Pinza's explanation: He no longer owned the boat; he sold it after Pearl Harbor because gas was no longer available for pleasure boats; the radio was not functioning.

Accusation: He was a personal friend of Benito Mussolini.

Pinza's explanation: He never met Mussolini.

Accusation: That he proudly bore the nickname Mussolini.

Pinza's explanation: No one called him Mussolini. It was the nickname of another Metropolitan basso that resembled the dictator.[13]

At last, Pinza's lawyer had something to work with. With the help of New York mayor Fiorello La Guardia, who telephoned Biddle to arrange a meeting with Doris and the lawyer, he was granted a second hearing. This time he didn't attend. Instead, speaking up for him was Doris, who spoke for more than an hour and a half, and several singers from the Met who served as character witnesses for Pinza. Later, Pinza wrote that Doris told him: "If I thought there was the smallest grain of truth in the charges against you, I would not have been able to do what I did."[14]

The second time was the charm for Pinza. After spending three months at Ellis Island, he was ordered released, though he was required to report to a parole officer and he was not allowed to travel without permission. His story offers proof of the flimsy evidence that could keep internees confined. (Pinza went to his grave convinced that his troubles were caused by a jealous competitor at the Met.) It also offers proof of the political ramifications feared by Roosevelt.

━━━━━━━━━━

Marino Sichi was two years old in 1922 when he came to America with his mother. His father had come two years earlier to get things ready for their arrival in California, where he had established a chicken farm on the west side of Highway 101, which at that time ran all the way from Mexico to Grants Pass, Oregon. As he grew up, Marino never thought much about citizenship. He went to American schools. His friends were American. He didn't feel any different from anyone else.[15]

But when he was seventeen, he was drafted by the Italian army to serve in the Ethiopian campaign. He told them to go to hell. He did not owe them anything. That brought a call from the Italian consul in San

Francisco, who reminded him that he was a citizen of Italy and had legal obligations to that country. He then realized the time had come for him to become a U.S. citizen.

Before that could happen, Pearl Harbor intervened. Everyone of Japanese, German, or Italian descent who lived west of Highway 101 was ordered to relocate. That meant that Marino's father was forced to sell off his stock of five thousand chickens because he lived on the wrong side of the highway. He couldn't take the chickens with him across the highway, so they had to be sold. The best price he could get was twenty-five cents per chicken, less than half the going rate.[16]

A family that lived on the other side of the highway took them in, and they lived with them for a few months until they found a three-room shack that they could move into. It was a reflection of bureaucratic absurdity that they could see their home from their cabin, but they were prohibited from crossing the highway to visit it. By the end of 1941, Marino was twenty-one and in love with a woman he would eventually marry. However, the logistics of wooing a prospective bride were hindered considerably by the army's demand that no one in his family could leave the house after 8:00 P.M.

Marino's response to the curfew was "Oh, to hell with it!" He went out anyway.

"The next thing I know, I had a real sharp looking young man knocking on my door," he says. "He was looking for my dad, then found out he had the wrong guy and wanted me. He says, 'I understand you were out after eight o'clock?' What could I say? I said 'yes,' so he arrested me for violation of the curfew."[17]

Marino figured a so-called friend had squealed on him.

The friend quickly learned that squealing was not acceptable. "He didn't wake up very good the next morning. Some friends went in and busted his head open, blacked his eyes, and busted his nose. He didn't recuperate very fast."[18]

Marino was taken to the county jail with a group of other prisoners and locked up for five days. Then they were taken to an INS detention facility in San Francisco, where officials complained that they had no place to house them. Until they could be moved, they were locked in a closet. They sat on the floor and waited. Soon the door opened, and they were loaded into a paddy wagon and transported to an assembly center.

The first thing he noticed was that the Japanese were on one side of the camp and the white prisoners—Germans and Italians—were segregated from them on the other side of the camp. The entire camp, which had guard towers stationed at regular intervals, was surrounded by high barbed-wire fences, but there was a strip of land between his fence and the Japanese fence, so it was impossible for him to speak to them from his camp.

Once, he was playing baseball and ran after a ball that had soared over his head. When he reached down to pick up the ball, he heard an unmistakable sound—the ominous *click-click* of a machine-gun arming bolt. He looked up and saw a soldier pointing the weapon at him. He was warned that he was too close to the fence, and if he knew what was good for him he would back away. He did.

When he was released from the assembly center—like most Italians, he was sent home after a brief confinement—he went to work at a bakery. The draft board classified him as "essential labor," a classification that enabled him to be exempt from the draft, just long enough for him to feel secure in his new job; but then he was drafted, rather suddenly, despite his supposedly protected classification, and his world came crashing down once again. He reported to the selective service office, where he was interviewed by representatives of the three branches of military.

The marines quickly rejected him and passed his file to the navy, where he was turned down and sent to the army representative. The desperate army recruiter, who had a quota to fill and did not mind signing an Italian recruit, took one look at him and said, "We ain't particular. We'll take you." Marino was sent to Camp Fannan, Texas, where he and other noncitizens were loaded into a truck and driven to the county courthouse so that they could be sworn in as American citizens. It was a solemn occasion, but his memory of it is marked by humor.

"We went up to the judge's chambers, and there was a character strictly out of Judge Roy Bean: boiled white shirt, string tie, white suit, planter's hat lying on the bench next to him, and a big mouth full of chewing tobacco, which he spit into a spittoon," recalls Marino. "I remember him saying,

'You all swear to uphold and defend these here—spttt—United States of America—sptttt—?' and he'd clang that old spittoon every time."[19]

As it turned out, he never had to defend his country. He was discharged for health reasons. He was bumped and pushed around by the government, and his father's business was devastated, but he was never sent to a concentration camp to stay for the remainder of the war, which almost certainly would have happened if he had been Japanese. There were three main ways in which Italians were treated differently from the Japanese. When Japanese males were rounded up for concentration camps, authorities typically took everyone in the family—women, children, and the aged. Not so with Italians. Their families were seldom taken into custody, primarily because there was no organized anti-Italian faction demanding that they be rounded up.[20] The second difference is that Italians were given an opportunity to enlist in the armed forces or go to prison. The Japanese were not given that option. They were taken to concentration camps first and then offered an opportunity to enlist in the army. The third difference is that Japanese schools were routinely targeted by the FBI, although as California governor Culbert Olson testified before the Commission on Wartime Relocation and Internment of Civilians, "there were many Italian language schools which frequently inculcated Fascist values."[21]

The irony of Marino's experience is that he ended up with full citizenship rights despite being persecuted because of his Italian heritage. Italians, Germans, Japanese, and Jews were all subject to arrest during the war, and if some fared better than others, the fact remained that no one who was a member of those targeted groups could go from day to day without experiencing a constant state of fear. In all, more than 600,000 Italian-born immigrants to the United States and their families were restricted by government measures that required carrying identification cards, travel restrictions, and seizure of personal property, with thousands of Italian Americans arrested and hundreds interned in concentration camps.[22]

Typical of those targeted for arrest was Louis Berizzi of New York City. In the middle of the night, FBI agents knocked on the door of his apartment and awakened the entire family. Berizzi went to the door in his pajamas and was immediately told by agents to get dressed, since they had orders to arrest him. According to his daughter, Lucetta, the agents stayed in his bedroom while he dressed and prevented him from talking to his family. Then they took him away without saying where he was going. Recalls his daughter: "Several days after his arrest, we learned that my father's office at Rockefeller Plaza had been locked and sealed . . . and all my father's assets were blocked. In time we learned that when my brother's tuition was due at Lehigh College, we had to petition the Enemy Alien Custodian for the money to pay for it."[23]

Berizzi was initially sent to Ellis Island and then transferred to an army POW camp at Fort Meade, Maryland, that held more than sixteen hundred Italian and German prisoners of war, including a famed German submarine captain. After his son, Albert, was accepted into U.S. Army intelligence, Berizzi was given a new hearing and then paroled, as his son awaited orders to report to the European front to fight for his country.[24]

At the time that these incidents occurred, Italian Americans were the largest foreign-born group in the United States. Most were patriotic and served their country in countless ways. Five hundred thousand served in the U.S. armed forces during World War II and brought honor to their country.[25] If some escaped government attention because of political or Mafia connections, it is of less consequence than the 600,000 who were stripped of their freedom because they had no influence with the government.

If it could happen to the Italians, it could happen to anyone.

10

JEWS TURNED AWAY FROM A NEW PROMISED LAND

On May 1, 1939, more than two and a half years before the U.S. entry into World War II, the German luxury line SS *St. Louis* left the docks of Hamburg, Germany, bound for Havana, Cuba. On board the ship were 936 passengers, almost all of them Jews fleeing the barbarous concentration camps built by Adolf Hitler's Third Reich. Construction of the camps had begun in 1933 with Dachau. By 1939, the Germans had built six large camps that were used primarily to imprison political prisoners, Communists, and journalists who wrote unflattering articles about Hitler. As the years went by, more and more Jews were classified as "undesirables" and sent to the camps.

The mass exterminations that would occur in the early 1940s had not begun yet, but German Jews were fearful of that possibility. Many on board the *St. Louis* had applied to the United States for visas and planned to wait for approval in Havana, where there was a sizable Jewish population. As it turned out, it was an overly optimistic plan based on unreasonable expectations that, first, the Cuban government would allow them to set foot on Cuban soil and, second, that the United States would waive immigration quotas because of the turmoil taking place in Germany.

Since the 1920s, the United States had imposed limitations on the number of immigrants who could enter the country, and a quota system set a yearly cap of 154,000 persons. Almost 84,000 spots were awarded to British and Irish immigrants, with the remaining 70,000 divided among people from other countries. The combined quota for Germany and Austria was 27,370. Such quotas did not exclude any potential immigrant based on their religion or ethnic origin; it was based entirely on nationality.

Jewish passengers aboard the *St. Louis* were granted landing certificates from the Cuban government in advance of boarding the ship, so they had no reason to anticipate problems upon their arrival in that country. However, eight days before the *St. Louis* sailed, Cuban president Federico Laredo Bru invalidated all recently issued landing certificates and required that visitors to the island obtain written authorization from the Cuban government and post a $500 bond. The Hamburg-America Line, which owned the ship, shared none of the above information with its passengers because it had purchased the landing certificates wholesale and sold them to passengers for $150 each.[1] The ship sailed under false pretenses, its unsuspecting passengers ill prepared for what awaited them.

Also unknown to the ship's passengers, its voyage had attracted considerable media attention. Even before the ship arrived, right-wing elements within the Cuban government demanded that the president put a stop to Jewish visitors to the island. There were massive rallies in Havana in which protesters took to the streets and railed against Jews. American newspapers picked up on the story and scolded Cuban authorities, but no one in a position of authority in the United States stepped forward and made a case for admitting the Jews to the United States. All of this was completely unknown to the passengers.

When the ship arrived in Havana on May 27, only twenty-two Jews were allowed onto Cuban soil. Passengers were shaken by Cuba's refusal to honor their landing certificates. One passenger who was not among those allowed off the ship was sent to a Havana hospital after a suicide attempt. Two other passengers succeeded at suicide. Negotiations with the Cuban government ended in failure.

On June 2, the ship was ordered out of Cuban waters. As the *St. Louis* passed within sight of the light of Miami, passengers cabled President Franklin D. Roosevelt and pleaded for safe refuge. The president turned the matter over to the State Department, which sent a telegram to the ship stating that those wishing entry to the United States would have to wait their turn. The German quota had been filled much earlier in the year. Turned away from America, the ship crossed the Atlantic again while Jewish organizations negotiated with governments of various European countries until Belgium, Holland, France, and the United Kingdom agreed to accept the refugees. Within twelve months, all the passengers, except those who found refuge in the United Kingdom, were once again in Nazi hands. Many of them ended up in concentration camps where they were killed by their captors.

The U.S. government refused to accept the passengers of the *St. Louis* based on immigration law that was purported to be blind to a person's religion or ethnic origin. But there was much more to the story than that. Anti-immigration and anti-Semitic sentiment in the United States was running high. In 1938, the year before the *St. Louis* was turned away from Miami, four opinion polls disclosed that 71 to 85 percent of Americans opposed increasing quotas to assist refugees.[2] Reflecting that viewpoint were senators and congressmen who consistently voted to restrict the immigration of refugees, knowing full well that the vast majority of Europeans requesting visas were Jews. Some, such as Senator Rufus Holman, a Republican from Oregon, complained that Jews controlled the money markets. Senator Robert Reynolds, a Democrat from North Carolina, maintained that Jews were too powerful in America, one reason that he labeled Jewish refugees as troublemakers. Then there was Mississippi congressman John Rankin, who supported racial segregation and once called the United Nations "the greatest fraud in all history." In later years, when the Immigration and Nationality Act of 1952, which established a quota system for immigration, was proposed, he characterized opposition to the bill as coming from American Jews: "[Jews] have been run out of practically every country in Europe in the years gone by, and if they keep stirring race trouble in this country and trying to force their communistic program on the Christian people of America, there is no telling what will happen to them here."[3]

Once the United States entered World War II, anti-Semitism increased, resulting in a marked decrease in immigration. During the three and a half years that the United States was at war with Germany, only twenty-one thousand refugees were allowed to enter the United States, a number that represented only 10 percent of the number who could have been allowed entry under existing quotas.[4] Someone applied the brakes when it became obvious that most of those asking for visas were Jews.

For the U.S. State Department, it was more of a strategic problem than one associated with racism. To the annoyance of many conservative congressmen and senators, especially those from the South, the Roosevelt administration was notably pro-Jewish. He appointed more Jews to high positions than any previous president, most prominently Treasury Secretary Henry Morgenthau Jr., U.S. Supreme Court justice Felix Frankfurter, economic adviser Bernard Baruch, and presidential adviser David Niles. However, the Jewish "problem" facing the State Department was not with American Jews; it was with European Jews, whose requests to enter the United States affected American politics.

The State Department made it clear that it had no intention of coming to the rescue of Jewish refugees, a position that was shared by the British Foreign Office. The British and the Americans feared that if they opened the gate, even slightly, Germany would release hundreds of thousands of Jews. Such a move would pressure the United States to accept them, creating political unrest, and put pressure on Great Britain to open Palestine to Jewish refugees. The British were reluctant to do so, since they had assured Arabs following a major rebellion in 1937 that no Jewish state would ever be permitted to arise there. Great Britain had been put in charge of Palestine in 1922 by the League of Nations. To prevent European Jews from going to Palestine, England limited Jewish immigration to seventy-five thousand over a five-year period.

For Secretary of the Interior Harold Ickes, who would later garner the disapproval of other cabinet members by expressing opposition to the internment of Japanese Americans, the solution was to bypass the quotas by sending Jewish refugees to a U.S. territory where quotas did not apply. His first choice was Alaska. The plan never got off the ground because some American Jewish leaders thought that it would send the wrong message (namely, that Jews would take over the territory) and because Roosevelt was never enthusiastic about it. In fact, the president was so unenthusiastic that he suggested a limit of only one thousand Jews a year over a five-year period. It soon became apparent to Ickes that there was no support for the plan, so he quietly shelved it.

Ickes also devised a plan in which Jewish refugees could be sent to the Virgin Islands, another U.S. territory. But Roosevelt refused his request. As an alternative, the State Department offered to approve a program to send individual food parcels to Jews in German-occupied countries. Under that plan, twelve thousand dollars' worth of food would be shipped each month. Secretary of State Dean Acheson opposed that plan on the grounds that it was a "feeble gesture."[5]

In June 1944, Ruth Gruber, a special assistant to Harold Ickes, opened the *Washington Post* and saw a story that made her heart race. President Roosevelt was quoted as saying, "I have decided that approximately 1,000 refugees should be immediately brought from Italy to this country." She could hardly believe what she read. Roosevelt's decision meant that refugees who had made their way to Italy from the concentration camps in Austria and Germany would be brought to the United States as guests of the president, bypassing immigration quotas. Judging by the number of refugees involved and the timing of the offer, a reasonable person would conclude that it was payback for the Jews who were turned away on the *St. Louis*.

For years, the United States had turned its back on Jewish refugees. Commenting on the sense of betrayal felt by Jews, Saul Friedman, who founded the Judaic and Holocaust Studies program at Youngstown State University, later wrote, "A passage from the Dead Sea Scrolls begins: 'Lo, I am stricken dumb, for naught comes out of men's mouths but swearing and lying.' That ancient sage thus might have lamented the dismal record of the United States toward Jewish refugees between 1938 and 1945. It was a record blemished by fear, hesitance, insincerity, and deceit."[6]

Seemingly overnight the President Roosevelt had changed his mind. Was it a one-time-only offer? Or were the floodgates about to be opened? The story went on to say that the refugees would be selected by the War Refugee Board and transported to America by the army. Once they arrived, the article explained, the refugees would be housed in a "temporary haven" at a former army camp called Fort Ontario, near Oswego, New York. The camp would be under the authority of the War Relocation Authority, which recently had been transferred to the Interior Department.

That was of special interest to Gruber because she was Ickes's special assistant, his field representative for Alaska—and because she was a Jewish American. Gruber was an unlikely person to be serving in that position. At age thirty-three, she had earned a Ph.D. in German philosophy and modern English literature and had worked as a foreign correspondent for the *New York Herald Tribune*, becoming the first person, male or female, to ever report from the Soviet Arctic.

When she reported to work that morning, she went directly to Ickes's office to hear his take on the announcement. He told her that the subject had arisen at a cabinet meeting. Roosevelt was still in favor of finding havens for the Jews in Europe. Ickes suggested the Virgin Islands again. Someone else suggested northern New York State, near Lake Ontario. Gruber wrote: "I thought of the millions of Jews waiting to be rescued. . . . Of all the Cabinet members, Ickes, who told me he had never met a Jew until he was sixteen, was the most passionate in denouncing Nazi atrocities against Jews and the angriest that the doors of America were sealed."[7]

Gruber expressed concern about the refugees coming to America without someone to guide them. Before she could volunteer for the job, Ickes got Dillon Myer, head of the War Relocation Authority, on the phone. He told Myer about Gruber and explained that she was perfect for the job because she spoke both German and Yiddish and because she would have empathy for the women and children refugees and understand their needs. Myer expressed reservations and said he needed to meet with her.

The next morning she met with Myer, who wasted no time wondering aloud why Ickes would risk sending a woman on such an important mission. Myer was old-school bureaucrat. "Change" and "innovation" were not words that anyone would ever associate with him. He grimaced and sputtered and scratched his head and told her that he would have to get back to her.

But Ickes was a member of the cabinet; he had clout, even if he was one of the most liberal members of the Roosevelt administration. Ickes wanted Gruber. So Myers saw that he got Gruber. If the mission somehow blew up, it would be a liberal failure, not a conservative one. It would serve Ickes right if the woman botched the entire operation. The next day Myer called Gruber and told her that she had the job.

Before she left the country, it dawned on Gruber that it was not, strictly speaking, a rescue mission. The refugees would be supervised by the same people who supervised the relocation of the other internees; they would be assigned to a concentration camp not unlike the ones used to imprison Japanese Americans, Germans, and Italians. They would be safe in America, but they would not be free. And there was no guarantee that they would be able to stay once the war ended. Myer's instructions to her were succinct and void of sentimentality: "Don't make any promises we can't fulfill. We don't want to raise their hopes too high. That happened in our other camps."[8]

Even so, Gruber began her mission with great enthusiasm.

On July 14, the day before she left the country, Ickes called her into his office to give her a pep talk. To her astonishment, he told her that she had been made a general for the mission. He explained that she would be flying in a military plane, which meant that if it were shot down, the Nazis could kill her as a civilian spy. However, if she were a general, under the terms of the Geneva convention, they would have to give her shelter and food and keep her alive. It was a conversation that made her heart race.

When she arrived in Naples, "General" Gruber learned that the refugees were already on board the ship that would take them to America. The *Henry Gibbins* was an army transport that, in addition to holding one thousand refugees, also held about a thousand wounded American soldiers, many in bad shape, from the battles at Anzio and Cassino. She asked to be taken immediately to the ship, but she was told she could not board for another day. She spent the free day paying courtesy calls on the people Ickes suggested she visit.

One of the people she met with was Max Perlman, a representative of the Joint Distribution Committee in Italy, the overseas arm of the American Jewish community. Selecting the refugees who would go to America was one of the toughest jobs he'd ever had, he explained. The pain he saw in their faces was still with him. It was a pain that Gruber saw for herself the following day when she boarded the ship. More than three thousand refugees were screened for the voyage, which meant that two thousand were turned down. Many of the passengers were still dressed in the tattered clothing that they had been assigned in concentration camps. Many were shoeless. Some wore shoes made of newspaper. One woman gave birth in an army truck on the way to the ship. The baby was named International Harry.

Pale, gaunt faces greeted Gruber everywhere she turned. Some smiled. Others looked fearful. Mostly the passengers had questions for her. They asked where they would be taken. She explained they would be going to a former army camp. Later, she wrote about her exchange with them:

"A camp in America!" Leo Mirkovic waved his arms in disbelief. A skeletal figure in once-white silk pajamas, he had been the premier baritone of the Zagreb National Opera.

"I haven't seen the camp," I said, "but I know it's being completely remodeled so that family groups can live together."

[One of the other men] put his hand on my arm. "Liebes Fraulein, don't tell me you're taking us to a concentration camp in America."

"Be realistic!" A young man in his twenties limped toward us. He was Fredi Baum, from Yugoslavia. "They'll put us in a camp when we arrive, and then we'll find out where we go from there."

"We are realistic," a middle-aged man with a sagging paunch, wearing black-and-white striped concentration-camp pajamas, shouted angrily. "We have a right to know. Are we or are we not going to a concentration camp?"

The passengers had reason to inquire about whether they would be confined to a concentration camp. Before any of the adult passengers could board the ship, they had to sign a document that said they agreed to reside at Fort Ontario and they understood that they would have to return to their homelands after the war. The wording of the document was such that there was a great deal of confusion about whether they could freely leave the camp.

The *Henry Gibbins* left Naples on July 21, part of a convoy of sixteen cargo and troop ships, escorted by more than a dozen warships. Because of the threat of enemy warships and submarines, the convoy was ordered to sail in complete darkness. Even cigarettes were forbidden, since the faint glimmer could attract the attention of German bombers. As it made its way through the Mediterranean Sea, the convoy experienced several close calls—including a fleeting encounter with a German submarine and a formation of Nazi planes—but once the Mediterranean was cleared safely, the two-week journey across the Atlantic was uneventful.

The ship sailed into the Port of New York on August 3. The passengers spent the night on the ship, and the next day they were taken to a building on the wharf, where they were told to remove all their clothing, after which American soldiers sprayed them with DDT to disinfect them with the harsh insecticide. They then sprayed their clothing. After their clothing also was disinfected, it was returned to them.

Two harbor ferries took the refugees across the Hudson River to New Jersey, where they were assembled at a railroad terminal. They were told that, for security reasons, they were not allowed to contact any friends or family members in the United States. Then they were placed in boxcars for their journey to Oswego. The sight of the boxcars terrified some of the refugees, for they had memories of family members herded into boxcars by the Nazis and transported to death camps. It was hardly an auspicious introduction to freedom American style.[9]

When they arrived at Camp Ontario, they saw that their worst fears had been realized. The eighty-acre camp was filled with wooden barracks that were surrounded by a chain-link fence topped with three rows of barbed wire. They were kept under quarantine for one month. During that time they were questioned by army intelligence officials. No one could leave the camp. No one but army personnel could enter the camp.

Once the quarantine was lifted, they were allowed to go into Oswego for up to six hours at a time on the condition that they returned by midnight. It was forbidden for anyone to travel past Oswego unless it was a medical emergency. Children were allowed to attend the Oswego public schools, and thirty adult refugees were allowed to attend Oswego State Teachers College free of charge.

For people who thought they were being rescued from concentration camps, it proved to be a difficult adjustment. They had committed no crimes, they argued, so why were they being kept behind barbed wire? Both physical and mental health issues arose. Ruth Gruber tells the story of a twenty-eight-year-old female prisoner, Karoline Bleir, who divorced her husband in order to be with the man she loved. However, that love came at a high price, for she lost custody of her two children. She married her lover and gave birth to two more children, but she grieved for the children she had left behind in Germany.

One night she went to see a movie in the camp theater, leaving her second husband in charge of the children. At the time, there was a raging blizzard, and the camp was covered with deep snow. When the movie ended and she had not returned, her husband called the camp police, and a search was begun amid fears that she had gotten lost in the blinding snow. They looked everywhere, sometimes digging through ten-foot snow drifts. Her footprints had been covered by the falling snow, and there was no trace of her. The next morning, soon after sunrise, she was found on the banks of a canal, where, according to an autopsy, she had committed suicide by swallowing one hundred aspirin tablets.

Karoline's sad death only heightened the despair in the camp. Did she take her life because she couldn't bear to live behind barbed wire? Or did she die because the children she had did not assuage the grief she felt for the children she did not have? Perhaps she would have died even if she were living comfortably in the city, her life not defined by barbed wire and guards. No one would ever know for certain.

Compounding the sadness at the camp over losing a woman who appeared to have so much to live for was the continuing confusion over their imprisonment. They lived day to day, expecting each new day to bring news of their release. A psychologist who visited the camp in 1945 wrote a report that noted the rising tensions in the camp.[10] He suggested that the camp should be closed. One problem he pointed out was the work situation. As in the other camps, prisoners were asked to do all the menial labor in the camp—washing dishes, cooking, cleaning, distributing coal, and handling garbage. Each prisoner received eight dollars and fifty cents a month for expenses, and those who worked were paid eighteen dollars a month, only nine dollars and fifty cents more than those who did not work. Many of the prisoners had high incomes before the Nazis took everything from them, and they bridled at doing work that servants had done for them in their prewar life. Some refused to work. Those who did work sometimes regretted it. One prisoner was accidentally killed while unloading coal, a job he had accepted to earn extra money. He left behind a wife and four children.

Outraged that friends and relatives were being held captive like common criminals, American Jews began a campaign to secure their release. Why would the United States go to all this trouble to rescue them from Nazi imprisonment only to strip them of their freedoms? Also asking that question was the camp director, who requested that his employer, the WRA, offer the Jews the same parole system offered to Japanese Americans, a means by which Jews could leave the camp and live independently in the community. It was a plan that Secretary Ickes supported with enthusiasm.

President Roosevelt and Attorney General Francis Biddle opposed any type of sponsored leave. They pointed out that they had promised Congress that the Jews would be allowed into the country on a temporary basis and would be kept in detention while they were in the United States and then sent back to their countries of origin once the war ended. Besides, Roosevelt argued, simply releasing them would violate immigration law.

There were ways around that, of course. In a report that Ruth Gruber sent to Secretary Ickes eight months after the Jews were interned, she noted the "new life" that Camp Ontario had offered the internees, but she said "a camp is a camp is a camp" and was taking its toll on the prisoners.

She offered a solution to the problem: "We should permit those who are eligible for entry to the United States to cross the border into Canada and re-enter the United States under regular quotas on an individual basis. It is time we showed that this administration has a policy of decency, humanity, and conscience and the guts to carry that policy through."[11]

When he read the report, Ickes called Gruber into his office and told her that he agreed with her. "I would like to see the camp closed as soon as possible," he said. "But my hands are tied. . . . It would be a crime to send them back. A crime if a country of one hundred thirty-seven million could not absorb one thousand refugees."[12]

Everyone blamed Roosevelt for not taking a firmer hand with Congress; but his influence with that body was limited. Congress reflected the anti-Jewish sentiment that was prevalent at that time. One of those in Congress who expressed that sentiment on a regular basis was Senator Kenneth McKellar of Tennessee, who in January 1945 became the president pro tempore of the Senate, a position that made him third in succession to the presidency in the event of the president's death. He was especially antagonistic toward David Lilienthal, one of three directors of the Tennessee Valley Authority. Most people called the Harvard-educated Jew "Mr. TVA," because of his strong leadership of that organization, but McKellar liked to refer to him as "King David II."

McKellar's anti-Semitism was so over the top that Memphis mayor E. H. "Boss" Crump sent him a remarkable letter in 1944 chastising him for his position on Jews. "The Jewish people down this way have been your friends and I am sure you won't gain anything by making a fight on the Jews. . . . I do suggest that you refrain from making it appear that you are attacking the Jewish people. After considering this fairly, I believe you will agree with me."[13]

The controversy over what to do with the prisoners at Camp Ontario was still raging on April 12, 1945, when President Roosevelt collapsed and died while vacationing in Warm Springs, Georgia. The nation was stunned. The prisoners at Camp Ontario went into mourning for the man who had brought them to America. They had their differences with him over his policies after they arrived in the United States, but they felt only appreciation for the courage he had showed in allowing them into the country.

Vice President Harry S. Truman was the new president, but Roosevelt had exerted his powers as president with such confident dominance that few people knew Truman's views on the major issues of the day.

Camp Ontario sank into a deep depression, like the rest of the country, not just over the death of a popular president who had never waivered in his wartime leadership, but also over the uncertainty that surrounded the new president. Was Truman a friend of the Jew? No one knew what position he would take on Camp Ontario.

11

FINDING REDEMPTION IN A TROUBLED LAND

In 1926, sixteen-year-old Johnny Aiso was an honor student at Holly-wood High School, where he won a district oratory contest with a speech titled "The American Constitution and What It Means to Me." That victory put him in line to compete for the California state championship and then the national finals in Washington, D.C. Aiso's talents set him apart from his peers, but there was something else: Although American born and raised, he was the son of a Japanese gardener.[1]

Elated over his victory at the oratory contest, he was called into the principal's office, where he expected praise and perhaps a pep talk for the upcoming competitions. Instead, he was told that his excellent grades entitled him to be class valedictorian, and that created a problem for the principal. It just wouldn't do for a person of Japanese ancestry to receive the school's top two academic awards. The principal told him he had to choose between delivering the valedictory or advancing in the oratory contest. Aiso chose the valedictory, and the principal chose the white runner-up in the oratory contest, Herbert Wenig, to advance to the national finals.

When the sponsor of the contest, the *Los Angeles Times*, learned of the ultimatum given to Aiso, *Times* publisher Harry Chandler sent his assistant to Hollywood High to speak to the principal.[2] In his report to Chandler, the assistant said that he felt the real issue was racial discrimination. Chandler urged Aiso to talk to the principal again and ask to be reinstated. Aiso also spoke to the chairman of the Japanese Merchants Association, who gave him the same advice. Encouraged by the support of the newspaper and the association, he met with the principal, only to be told the truth: if he accepted both honors, white parents and students would be outraged. Discrimination was nothing new to Aiso. When he began high school, he asked to join the ROTC program, which offered military training and allowed students to wear uniforms, but the instructor rejected his application, saying, "The American army doesn't need any Japs." With that incident still fresh in his memory, Aiso again withdrew from the debate rather than be labeled a troublemaker. Only this time he felt doubly discouraged for disappointing the newspaper and the association.

There were eight speakers at the district oratorical contest. Herbert Wenig won, taking home five hundred dollars in cash, an expense-paid trip to Europe, and the right to represent the Pacific Coast in the final contest in Washington, D.C. As a consolation prize, Aiso was allowed to go to the contest as Wenig's traveling companion and coach (unknown to Aiso, all his expenses were paid by the *Los Angeles Times*). Aiso took letters of introduction from Chandler to the National Board of the Constitutional Oratorical Contest and from the Japanese Consul in Los Angeles to Ambassador Tsuneo Matsudaira in Washington, D.C.

When Aiso called on the Japanese ambassador, he was asked what university he planned to attend. When he replied that his family was not wealthy enough to send him anyplace other than a public university, the consul told him that he knew the president of Brown University and would be happy to inquire about the possibility of him receiving a scholarship to attend Brown. After what he had been through, Aiso was not overly optimistic about his chances of attending Brown, so when he returned to Los Angeles and was graduated from Hollywood High at the age of sixteen, he went to Japan to study the Japanese language. He had studied for ten months when the Japanese consul in Los Angeles called his parents and told them that he had been granted a generous scholarship to attend Brown University.

Aiso returned to the United States and enrolled at Brown while still sixteen years of age. After graduating with honors and a degree in economics, he entered Harvard Law School, becoming the first Nisei from the continental United States to be admitted (three Nisei from the Territory of Hawaii preceded him). After graduating in 1934, he accepted a position as a law clerk at a prestigious Wall Street law firm. For the next six years, he was involved in several important legal cases, one of which made him realize that he needed to return to Japan to study the language required to understand the nuances of Japanese law. When he returned to the United States in December 1940, he received advance notice of his selective service draft notice. He reported for active duty in April 1941 and was assigned to Company D of the 69th Battalion at Camp Haan, near March Air Force Base in Riverside, California. Although a Harvard-educated lawyer, he was put in charge of automobile parts.

One day a captain, who was looking for soldiers who could read Japanese, passed through the base and recruited Aiso for a new unit named the Fourth Army Intelligence School. Meanwhile, the government announced that all draftees over twenty-eight years of age would be discharged. Since Aiso was in his early thirties, he made plans to resume law practice in Los Angeles and marry his fiancée. However, when he asked for his discharge papers, he was told that the army wanted him to stay in service. He was sent to the Presidio of San Francisco, where Lieutenant Colonel John Weckerling put his arm around Aiso and told him, "John, your country is in need of you!"

For Aiso, those were the magic words. It was the first time that anyone had ever referred to America as his country. After a lifetime of being berated as a "Jap," he was deeply moved by the sentiment. As a result, he made a commitment to stay in the army. At first, he was assigned to the Fourth Army Intelligence School as a student. Then he was told he would be an assistant instructor. A few days later, he was stunned to learn that he would be the school's head instructor. That created a problem, since he was only a private second class. Many of his students would be officers. It was unthinkable for officers to be instructed by a private second class. Under existing regulations, the highest grade to which Aiso could be commissioned was as a master sergeant, still not high enough to teach officers. The army solved that problem by transferring him to the Enlisted Reserve Corps and hiring him as a civilian, warning that if he tried to quit his job, he would be reinstated as a private second class.

After war was declared, the training school, newly named the Military Intelligence Service Language School, was moved to Camp Savage, Minnesota, where, it was felt, local residents would not discriminate against Japanese Americans. One day the chief of army intelligence, General Clayton Bissell, stopped by the school for a visit and witnessed Aiso, who by then was director of academic training, giving orders to the students. Outraged at his low rank, he returned to Washington determined to correct the situation. As a result, Aiso was promoted to major and then to lieutenant colonel, becoming the first Japanese American to become a commissioned officer.

Aiso served with great distinction. By the end of 1942, the school had trained more than one hundred Nisei and sent them to the Pacific. Enrollment grew each year, so that by the time the school closed in 1946, more than six thousand soldiers had been trained at the school, with nearly four thousand of those serving in combat areas, where they translated captured documents, interrogated enemy prisoners, and persuaded enemy soldiers to surrender. Of the six thousand, five thousand were Nisei and one thousand were Americans of other racial heritages. Among the students' most notable achievement was the translation of a document acquired on Guadalcanal that listed Japanese ships with their call signs and code names. They also acquired and translated the entire Japanese naval battle plan for the Philippines.

For most of the war, the work of the Nisei was kept top secret by the army, for fear of jeopardizing the men's efforts. In due course, President Harry S. Truman labeled them "our secret weapon." But before then, in October 1945, with the publication of a newspaper article in the *Minne-*

apolis Star-Journal, the contributions of the Nisei were publicly acknowledged. In the article, the reporter, John Nyberg, wrote:

> Joe Rosenthal, photographer of the famed Iwo Jima flag raising, said of the Nisei: "They work so close to the enemy that along with the danger of being killed by Japs they run the risk of being shot unintentionally by our own Marines. Of fourteen Nisei who volunteered for service with Merrill's Marauders in Burma, six were commissioned as officers for meritorious service, one was decorated with the Legion of Merit, and three with the Bronze Star.[3]

After the war, John Aiso served as a U.S. commissioner for one year before being appointed in 1953 to the Los Angeles Municipal Court. By 1968, he had become an associate justice of the California Court of Appeal, Second Appellate District. President Lyndon Johnson awarded him the Legion of Merit in 1965, and in 1991 he was inducted into the Military Intelligence Hall of Fame.

════════════════════

If the heroic efforts of the Japanese Americans involved in intelligence work were a well-kept secret during World War II, the exploits of those who served in the 442nd Regimental Combat Team and in 100th Battalion were not. The extraordinary bravery and combat successes of the soldiers in the 442nd were celebrated by the news media and the War Department; but it was a success story that got off to a rocky start, primarily because of the racism directed toward Japanese Americans.

Not long after the attack on Pearl Harbor, the War Department banned anyone of Japanese descent from entering military service. Those who wanted to serve their country were turned away. Most of those already in service were reclassified IV-C (enemy alien) and discharged. The turn-around occurred because of Hawaiian commander Lieutenant General Delos Emmons, who argued that instead of releasing the men from active duty, they should be folded into a special all-Nisei battalion and transferred to the mainland and trained for overseas service. His argument was that they made excellent soldiers and were highly motivated to prove their loyalty to the United States. Listening to that argument was General George C. Marshall, who authorized the creation of the 100th Battalion especially for the Nisei, after obtaining approval from Secretary of War Henry L. Stimson. Shortly afterward, on February 1, 1943, President Roosevelt issued a statement about that decision, indicating that it had his full approval:

> No loyal citizen of the United States should be denied the democratic right to exercise the responsibilities of his citizenship, regardless of his ancestry. The principle on which this country was founded and by which it has always been governed is that Americanism is a matter of the mind and heart; Americanism is not, and never was, a matter of race or ancestry.[4]

By early June 1942, more than fourteen hundred members of the battalion had sailed for training at Camp McCoy in Wisconsin and then later for additional training at Camp Shelby in southern Mississippi. Also at Camp Shelby, a military installation that was surrounded by pine forests and swamps and vulnerable to frequent tornadoes, was another newly formed all-Japanese unit, the 442nd Regimental Combat Team, composed of volunteers from Hawaii and prisoners recruited from the concentration camps. When the two groups came together, there was a great deal of strife among the members of the 442nd and the 100th, which pitted Hawaiian recruits against mainland recruits. Clashing cultural differences were the primary cause of the dissension. Mainlanders made fun of the Hawaiians' fractured English and unsophisticated ways, and the Hawaiians showed a lack of understanding of the hardships endured by mainland Nisei.

The War Department was about to pull the plug on both units when a clear-thinking higher-up, whose name has since been lost to history, suggested that the men should be taken to the concentration camps for a tour so that perhaps they would obtain a better understanding of each other—and get acquainted with their new homes if they were unable to work out their differences at Camp Shelby. The scheme worked. The soldiers returned to Camp Shelby with a better understanding of one another and no wish to live in a concentration camp. For her book *Boyhood to War*, Dorothy Matsuo interviewed a Japanese American soldier who recalled that "the regiment was not formed when we volunteered, nor when we arrived at Camp Shelby, but rather it was formed after this [concentration camp] visit."[5]

Nearly a year after they arrived in Camp Shelby, the 100th was ordered to North Africa, where it served until it was sent to Italy and entered combat at Salerno three weeks later. The following year, in March 1944, it joined the campaign to advance up the Italian peninsula, suffering heavy losses—78 killed and 239 wounded in the first six weeks alone. By the time the 100th was allowed to pull out, it was reduced to a little more than 500 men, earning nine hundred Purple Hearts and the nickname Purple Heart Battalion. From there it was sent to the Anzio beachhead, where it was joined by the 442nd Regimental Combat Team. Fighting together, the two units distinguished themselves by battling their way through Italy. In June, the 100th was formally combined with the 442nd.[6]

In September 1944, the 442nd fought its way across the Arno River, sustaining casualties of 1,272, more than a fourth of its total strength. Later that month, the 442nd experienced its bloodiest battle ever when it was ordered to rescue the Lost Battalion, a unit made up mostly of men from the Texas National Guard. The men were cut off from the rest of their regiment when the Germans counterattacked and isolated three companies and a platoon and then blasted the Americans with heavy artillery.

For a time it seemed hopeless for the Americans. They were slaughtered one by one. After two unsuccessful attempts to rescue the men, U.S. Army commanders ordered the 442nd into the battle. In a remarkable display of courage and military ability, the Nisei fought their way through the forests and up the mountain, dislodging the Germans by going from bunker to bunker, engaging in hand-to-hand combat, bayonets being the preferred weapon. For four days the 442nd battled enemy tanks, infantry, and artillery before crashing through to rescue about 230 Texans who were without food or water. To save the Lost Battalion, the 442nd suffered 2,000 casualties, including 140 dead. For their efforts, the 442nd became one of the most decorated units in U.S. military history, winning more than 9,500 Purple Hearts, 350 Silver Stars, 810 Bronze Stars, 7 Distinguished Unit Citations, 52 Distinguished Service Crosses, and 2 Congressional Medals, one of which was awarded to Private First Class Sadao Munemori, who died when he threw himself on an enemy grenade in an effort to save his comrades. When President Truman attached the Presidential Unit banner to the 442nd's regimental colors in appreciation of the unit's extraordinary heroism in saving the Lost Battalion, he read the citation, which said, in part, that the unit "fought without respite for four days against a fanatical enemy." The president then added that the Nisei fought "not only the enemy, but prejudice."[7]

One of the brave soldiers who fought with the 442nd was Second Lieutenant Daniel K. Inouye, who had enlisted in 1943, at the age of eighteen, while enrolled as a freshman in premedical studies at the University of Hawaii. After training at Camp Shelby, Inouye was promoted to the rank of sergeant. Shortly after the 442nd began the Italian campaign, he was named a combat platoon leader.

Just before the unit was ordered to shove off to rescue the Lost Battalion, Inouye was called into his commanding officer's tent, where he was given an order to report to the adjutant at regimental headquarters. When he arrived, he was handed a letter notifying him that he had been promoted to second lieutenant. By the time he returned to his unit, the bloody battle of the Lost Battalion was over.

Inouye attributed his luck in missing the battle—his twenty-man platoon was cut down to eleven in the fight—to two lucky silver dollars that he carried with him through every campaign. They were his lucky charms. For the next six months, the lucky charms continued to protect him through one engagement after another. Then on the night of April 20, 1945, he discovered that the coins had disappeared. He looked everywhere. They were nowhere to be found.

The next morning his platoon was ordered to attack Colle Musatello, a high and heavily defended ridge. His platoon was assigned the right flank of a three-platoon attack.

At one point during the fighting, Inouye crawled up a steep slope to within five yards of a German machine gun and tossed two grenades into the emplacement, destroying the fortification. Then, before the enemy could respond, he stood up and, using his Thompson machine gun, took out a second machine gun nest. As he pushed on, leading his men ever deeper in battle, he was wounded by a sniper's bullet. It seemingly had no effect on him and he continued to urge his men forward.

Suddenly, he heard someone, yell, "Come on, you guys, go for broke!"

Inouye was fiercely proud of his men, but he didn't think they had a chance of making it up the mountain. There was one machine gun nest left. He rose to his feet to lob a grenade at the enemy nest, but as he reached for the pin to arm the grenade, something happened, as he later recalled: "A German stood up waist-high in the bunker. He was aiming a rifle grenade at me from a range of ten yards. And then as I cocked my arm to throw, he fired, and the grenade smashed into my right elbow. It exploded and all but tore my arm off. I looked at my hand stunned. It dangled there by a few bloody shreds of tissue, my grenade still clenched in a fist that suddenly didn't belong to me anymore."[8]

Although in intense pain, he refused evacuation and stayed with his platoon, pushing them onward until the enemy resistance was broken. Inouye ended up losing his right arm and spending nearly two years in an army hospital in Battle Creek, Michigan, before being discharged with the rank of Captain. He was sent home with a Bronze Star, Purple Heart, and numerous other medals, including a Distinguished Service Cross, which was upgraded to a Medal of Honor in 2000 and presented to him by President Bill Clinton.

In 2003, Inouye, who by then had served many years first as a congressman and then as U.S. senator from Hawaii, wrote to a young girl who had visited his Washington office:

Please remember that the story of my experiences during World War II is by itself not important. Much more significant are values that the 442nd Regimental Combat Team and other segregated units represented: that patriotism and love of our great country are not limited to any ethnic group, and wartime hysteria must never again lead us to trample on our democratic principles.[9]

At the conclusion of the war, Japanese American soldiers returned home, not to parades and public adulation but rather to hatred and scorn. Nisei veterans encountered signs that read NO JAPS ALLOWED, and they were denied service in restaurants and stores. Sometimes their homes were attacked and set on fire. They were treated much as civil rights workers later were treated in Mississippi. After fighting courageously for their country, often against great odds, they came home to live in fear that they and their families would be murdered by flag-waving hooligans.

Among the 442nd veterans who returned was Tom Kawaguchi, who had been born in 1921 in Tacoma, Washington, two decades before the attack on Pearl Harbor, the sixth of seven children.[10] His parents were born in Kochi, Japan, and immigrated to Seattle in 1898 to work on the railroads. When Tom was three, his father purchased a shop in San Francisco and the family moved to that city, where Tom was raised in a Jewish neighborhood, not realizing that Japantown existed. He was working at Mitsubishi when the war broke out. One day the FBI visited him and asked a lot of questions and demanded to look through his personal papers. Not long after their visit, he was fired from his job at Mitsubishi and locked up in the assembly center at Tanforan Racetrack in San Bruno, twelve miles south of San Francisco.

Later, he was transferred to the concentration camp at Topaz, Utah, where he felt as if he had fallen off the end of the world. When he was told of the government's plans to create an all-Nisei military unit, he quickly volunteered. "I was a loyal American and I wanted to prove that the Japanese Americans were real Americans, just like anybody else," he later recounted. "And this is what a lot of my friends didn't understand."[11]

Once he became a member of the 442nd, he knew without a doubt that he had made the right decision. He knew many of the soldiers who came from San Francisco and the Bay area, and he felt a strong sense of kinship with those he met for the first time from Hawaii and other cities on the mainland. He later recalled: "It was teamwork, and we felt secure with each other. My war was only fifty feet in front of me and fifty feet to the right and fifty feet to the left. That was about it. So like any other GI, I really didn't know what the 442nd accomplished until after the war."[12]

Also amazed by the Nisei soldiers was *Delta Democrat-Times* editor Hodding Carter, whose work in army intelligence may have provided him with inside information about the contributions made by Japanese Americans in the war. When he returned to the newspaper after serving in the army, he had a long list of issues he wanted to address. One of the most pressing was the terrible treatment the Nisei solders received upon their return to civilian life. In August 1946, the *Houston Press* published a story about Sergeant George Otsuk, who had helped rescue the Lost Battalion. The story, which likely crossed Carter's desk, disclosed that Otsuk had been warned to keep away from a farm he wanted to purchase. Public response to the threats was so strong that Otsuk was able to purchase the farm without difficulty. On August 27, 1945, the *Delta Democrat-Times* published an editorial under the headline "Go for Broke."

Company D of the 168th Regiment, which is stationed in Leghorn, Italy, is composed altogether of white troops, some from the East, some from the South, some from the Midwest and West Coast.

Company D made an unusual promise earlier this month. The promise was in the form of a communication to their fellow Americans of the 442nd Infantry Regiment and the 100th Infantry Battalion, whose motto is "Go For Broke," and it was subscribed to unanimously by the officers and men of Company D.

In brief, the communication pledged the help of Company D in convincing "the folks back home that you are fully deserving of all the privileges with which we ourselves are bestowed."

The soldiers to whom that promise was made are Japanese-Americans. In all of the United States Army, no troops have chalked up a better combat record. Their record is so good that these Nisei were selected by General Francis M. Oxx, commander of the military area in which they are stationed, to lead the final victory parade. So they marched 3,000 strong, at the head of thousands of other Americans, their battle flag with three Presidential unit citationed streamers floating above them, their commander, a Wisconsin white colonel, leading them.

Some of those Nisei must have been thinking of the soul-shaking days of last October, when they spearheaded the attacks that opened the Vosges Mountain doorway to Strasbourg. Some of them were probably remembering how they, on another bloody day, had snatched the Thirty-Six Division's lost battalion of Texans from the encircling Germans. And many of them were bearing scars from those two engagements which alone had cost the Nisei boys from Hawaii and the West Coast 2,300 casualties.

Perhaps these yellow-skinned Americans, to whose Japanese kinsmen we have administered a terrific and long overdue defeat, were holding their heads a little higher because of the pledge of their white fellow-soldiers and fellow-Americans of Company D. Perhaps when they gazed at their combat flag, the motto "Go For Broke" emblazoned thereon took on a different meaning. "Go For Broke" is the Hawaiian-Japanese slang expression for shooting the works in a dice game.

The loyal Nisei have shot the works. From the beginning of the war, they have been on trial, in and out of uniform, in army camps and relocation centers, as combat troops in Europe and as front-line interrogators, propagandists and combat intelligence personnel in the Pacific where their capture meant prolonged and hideous torture. And even yet they have not satisfied their critics.

It is so easy for a dominant race to explain good or evil, patriotism or treachery, courage or cowardice in terms of skin color. So easy and so tragically wrong. Too many have committed that wrong against the loyal Nisei, who by the thousands have proved themselves good Americans, even while others of us, by our actions against them, have shown ourselves to be bad Americans. Nor is the end of this misconception in sight. Those Japanese-American soldiers, who paraded at Leghorn in commemoration of the defeat of the nation from which their fathers came, will meet other enemies, other obstacles as forbidding as those of war. A lot of people will begin saying, as soon as these boys take off their uniforms, that "a Jap is a Jap," and that the Nisei deserve no consideration. A majority won't say or believe this, but an active minority can have its way against an apathetic majority.

It seems to us that the Nisei slogan of "Go For Broke" could be adopted by all Americans of goodwill in the days ahead. We've got to shoot the works in a fight for tolerance. Those boys of Company D point the way.[13]

There was no groundswell of response for or against the editorial in Greenville, and Carter moved on to other pressing issues, of which there was no shortage. Meanwhile, the newspaper's general manager, John Gibson, put together a package of editorials for the Pulitzer committee in consideration for its annual competition. Gibson chose several editorials, including "Go for Broke," and an editorial that Carter had written about Theodore Bilbo, a racist politician with considerable populist appeal in Mississippi.[14] When Bilbo announced that he would run for a third term in the Senate, Carter wrote that Bilbo has sought office "with sickening regularity." One of the things that bothered Carter was Bilbo's treatment of minorities. When a woman of Italian descent wrote Bilbo a critical letter, the Senator responded with a letter of his own that began, "My Dear Dago." That infuriated Carter, who responded with an editorial: "It must take a great deal of courage to rampage against Italians and Catholics who in this state are such a small minority, or against Jews whose numbers here are infinitesimal, or against Negroes, who don't vote or talk back."[15]

When the Pulitzers for 1945 were announced in 1946, no one was more surprised than Carter to learn that he had won the award for editorial writing. The committee cited "Go for Broke" as its reason for selecting Carter. In a letter to a friend, Carter wrote: "The award provided me with the happiest and most astounded moment of my life. But my day of glory is going to be short lived. Bilbo is coming to Greenville on June 11 and has promised to tell everyone what kind of 'nigger loving communist' I am."[16]

═══════════════════════════

Reading Hodding Carter's editorials on a daily basis were the descendents of John Turner, who had made their way to the Mississippi Delta town of Greenville by way of the Great Depression. Audie, a lifelong newspaper reader whose father, Stephen, had coauthored the Mississippi constitution, and his wife, Rada, liked the idea of receiving a newspaper in the morning, the *Commercial Appeal* of Memphis, and another in the afternoon, Carter's *Delta Democrat-Times*. They adamantly refused to read the ultraconservative newspapers based in the capital city.

Audie and Rada had two sons who took to heart Carter's example of public service. Harold, at age twenty-eight, applied for admission to West Point. He was accepted based on his application but had to withdraw because the math education he'd received in the Delta was not up to West Point standards. Later, when war broke out, he joined the Seabees, a branch of the U.S. Navy that built roads and airstrips in the South Pacific. Following in his older brother's footsteps was Rex, who at age seventeen enlisted in the navy with the intent of avenging the attack on Pearl Harbor. After undergoing training, Rex also was sent to the Pacific, but his orders took him away from his older brother, all the way northward to China, where he experienced a mysterious motorcycle crash on the mainland that forever sealed his lips about his service in China. Both sons returned from the war, but Harold quickly became ill and died, the result of a tropical disease he contracted on some unnamed South Pacific island.

Growing up in and around Greenville, Rex and Harold's nephew, the author of this book and great-grandson of Stephen Turner, was aware not only of the war but also of the people across the Mississippi River who were kept in camps not unlike the wire pens Delta sportsmen built for their hunting dogs. Some of the author's earliest memories are of hearing adults of that era refer to Japanese Americans as "those people." Whispered voices gossiped about "those people" who had to be kept behind barbed wire in Arkansas because of heinous crimes they'd supposedly committed against freedom-loving Americans. That was all a lie, of course, and it was finally put to rest by Hodding Carter, who educated Deltans on the honorable role that Japanese Americans played in the war.

Redemption is one of those miracles of human discourse that sometimes arises in unexpected and unlikely places. Who ever would have thought that one of the lone voices of moral leadership of the war years would come from a small-town newspaper editor? Unlike the television news of today, when one set of talking heads gives one position and another set of talking heads offers the opposing position, leaving the viewer adrift, thoughtful newspaper editors of Carter's era digested the positions of all sides and came down squarely on a definable position that readers could embrace or reject.

That was not difficult for Carter. He had a passion not just for the written word but also for the redemptive power of moral persuasion. His wartime experience revealed to him the truth about Japanese American courage on the battlefield, and his own eyes revealed to him the savagery of the treatment of "those people" across the river. He had to speak out, even if no one listened. If you believe in God, you have to consider the possibility that Carter's solitary voice was the only thing that stood in the way of eternal damnation of an entire nation.

12

PRISONER, GO HOME!

What do you do after being released from a concentration camp? How do you make up for all the lost years, and how do you pick up where you left off, when your homes, jobs, and social standing in the community have been erased? How do you go from being a nonperson suspected of treason to resuming your life as a citizen in good standing?

Early on, the government had pondered the possible negative effects of releasing tens of thousands of concentration camp prisoners at one time. There could be riots all up and down the West Coast. Racist vigilantes could run amok. There could be retaliation against American POWs in Japan. The negative possibilities were endless.

As a means of reducing the camp population, male prisoners of military age were allowed to enlist for overseas service, and starting in early 1944 selected groups of inmates were offered certificates of exemption, or pardons, for the charges against them and released. Included in that group were family members of soldiers serving in the 442nd Regimental Combat Team, Japanese American women who were married to white citizens, and prisoners who could demonstrate unimpeachable loyalty to the United States, subject to government review and verification.

Of course, the 120,000-plus Japanese American prisoners interned by the army and supervised by the War Relocation Authority were only part of the problem. The Justice Department operated camps for tens of thousands of so-called enemy aliens—Germans, Italians, Jews—who would have to be released at some point in the near future.

As early as spring 1943, Secretary Stimson's War Department had concluded that its policy of exclusion was a mistake, but as long as the war continued, Stimson saw no politically acceptable way to rectify that mistake.[1] As a result, the imprisonment continued until December 1944, when mass exclusion was replaced by individual exclusion, a process that took nearly a year and a half to implement. Meanwhile, Harry Truman, who had ascended into the presidency on April 12, 1945, with the unexpected death of President Franklin D. Roosevelt, issued an executive order on July 14 that proclaimed that "all dangerous alien enemies" could be deported. The purpose of that order was to pave the way for the Justice Department to close its concentration camps by processing prisoners to determine whether they should be paroled or deported.

Granada, the camp at Amache, Colorado (the camp alternatively was called Amache and Granada), closed on October 15, 1945, making it the first to release prisoners. It was followed by the camp at Minidoka, Idaho (October 28), and the camp at Topaz, Utah (October 30). The camps at Gila River, Arizona, and Heart Mountain, Wyoming, followed on November 10.

When Manzanar closed on November 21, 1945, some of the elderly prisoners who had no family and nowhere else to go because they had lost everything they owned refused to leave, staying in the barracks until civic groups found homes for them. The camps at Poston, Arizona, and Rohwer, Arkansas, followed on November 28 and November 30 The last camp to close in 1945 was the one at Rohwer, Arkansas (November 30). As the closings continued into 1946, it was not until March 20 that the camp at Tule Lake, California, was shut down. The War Relocation Authority itself followed on June 30, 1946.

In Hawaii, Doris Berg's mother and father were released on parole in 1943, several months apart. As a condition of their release, they were required to report to a parole officer once a week. Despite their joy at being reunited with their children, putting their lives back together was difficult. They were lucky in the sense that they were able to hang on to their marriage, finding strength in adversity. Many interned couples were not lucky that way and ended up divorced because of the toll that the stress took on their marriage.

All family members of camp prisoners were altered by the experience, even those who had not been interned. Doris Berg went from outgoing tomboy—always exploring the outdoors—to a person always on alert, especially for anyone who asked questions about her past. Her demeanor of complete control was a mask; she went to a psychologist to help her cope. Her psychologist told her that she and her family had gone through the same post-traumatic stress that the children of the Holocaust went through. Recalls Doris: "My parents were very distrustful when they returned, so it was very difficult for us to become autonomous again. There was a tremendous amount of psychological separation. We had separation anxiety and guilt."[2]

Denial became the coping mechanism of choice. Early on, the family decided to simply stop discussing what had happened to them. Explains Doris: "My mom and dad didn't talk about it because my mom would get upset and my dad would get angry, so we just didn't go there."

Martial law in Hawaii did not end until October 1944: the beaches were covered with barbed wire, there was no free speech and no exchange of ideas, and the territory lacked a court system with which to address grievances. Hawaii was a closed society, and everyone treaded softly, ever fearful of being arrested again for some unknown offense.

Doris kept her thoughts to herself until she was sixteen, at which time she broke down and told her boyfriend about her family's internment: "I cried the whole time I told the story. Before that I hardly talked about it because no one believed me. As soon as I saw the person's eyes change, I stopped talking about that subject."

Doris went on to attend the University of Hawaii, where she was elected Pineapple Bowl Queen in 1949. She also was chosen by the governor to represent Hawaii at President Harry Truman's inauguration, but she had a difficult time appreciating honors like that because she was constantly preoccupied with hiding her past. The question that always made her freeze was, *What did your parents do during World War II?*

Perhaps the unkindest cut of all came from her mother-in-law, who said, "Doris, if the government didn't have anything on your folks, they wouldn't have taken them away." The sentiment was common at that time. There was widespread ignorance of the fact that not a single internee during the war was ever convicted of a crime.

Mitsuye Yamada was among those who received an early release. In fact, she recalls being encouraged by authorities to leave the camp. Not needing much encouragement, she and her family left Minidoka, Idaho, in August 1943 on a bus that took them to the train station, where they purchased tickets to Cincinnati, Ohio, so that they could join her brother, Mike, who had been accepted as a student at the University of Cincinnati.

Mitsuye applied to the university, but she was turned down because she was not an American citizen.[3] She was shocked that her brother was accepted, because he had answered "no-no" to the loyalty questions on the grounds that he was a pacifist. "They let him out of the camp, anyway, which is surprising," she recalls, noting that a year after he enrolled, the FBI visited the university and questioned him again. "We suspect they asked the school to expel him from the university because two weeks before his final exams, he was expelled." Mike didn't allow his expulsion to break his spirit. He went on to complete his education and become an Episcopal priest.

Not willing to give up on being admitted to the University of Cincinnati, Mitsuye found a job on the campus and worked until her application was approved. She stayed at the university for two years and then left to attend the University of Chicago, only to discover that the tuition, about nine thousand dollars a quarter, was more than she could pay. She had to discontinue her education at that point for a time, but she went on to receive degrees from New York University and the University of Chicago. She became an accomplished poet, board member of Amnesty International (where she once met Pulitzer Prize–winning Mississippi journalist Hodding Carter when he spoke at one of Amnesty's meetings), and an instructor in the Asian American studies program at the University of California at Irvine.

Mitsuye did not become eligible to become an American citizen until passage of the Immigration and Nationality Act of 1952, sometimes called the McCarran-Walter Act. As she was growing up in Seattle, she frequently complained to her father about perceived slights because she was not an American citizen, and his response to her was that if she ever hoped to become a citizen, she would have to be careful not to ever do anything that could be considered un-American. When she finally became a citizen in 1955, an event that should have been cause for celebration after living in the country for twenty-eight years without citizenship, she had an experience that made her feel more unwelcome than ever before.

In the interviewing room at Brooklyn College, where she had gone to be sworn in, she was asked by an immigration officer if she was willing to bear arms in defense of the United States. To someone who had never been unjustly imprisoned, it was at worst an innocuous question and at best one that made the heart soar, but to a concentration camp survivor it was an insult of the highest order. She later wrote:

> Suddenly I became aware that the officer was barking at me, "Whatsa matter? Why do you hesitate? You don't wanna defend your country?" I answered lamely, "Well, since I'm a woman, would I be asked to do that?" He mellowed a little, and said, "If you was a man, would you?" I felt like saying, "Not really," but I knew that this was not the time to argue about pacifism.[4]

Mitsuye was shaken when she left the interviewing room. She fell into another line, where she witnessed an officer shouting at an Asian woman, giving orders as to where she and the man she was with should stand. Mitsuye followed her line into a "processing" room and then into a large room, along with several hundred additional applicants, to listen to a judge deliver a short speech that stressed that citizenship was a privilege and not a right. The more that the judge celebrated American citizenship, the more he seemed to be diminishing the value of her Japanese citizenship. Couldn't he praise America without degrading other citizenships? Did America's greatness have to come at the expense of someone else? The proceedings left her with confused feelings about the entire citizenship process.

On the subway ride home with a friend, a naturalized European immigrant who had attended the ceremony as her witness, she came to terms with what she had done. The friend explained that her feelings were normal because she had been raised as an American and all Americans grow up thinking that citizenship is a right that belongs to them by virtue of their upbringing. Mitsuye realized then that she would never take her American citizenship for granted, nor would she feel that she "owned" this country in the same way that a white, native-born American did. She concluded: "I was no longer an alien at that moment, but I was acutely aware that in 1942, the evacuation orders posted on telephone poles referred to the American-born Nisei not as American-born citizens but as 'nonaliens.'"[5]

═══════════════

Before Aiko Yoshinaga and her family left the camp in Rohwer, Arkansas, in June 1945, they had to have references from people who knew them before they were incarcerated, people who would vouch for their loyalty. It seemed like such an indignity. They had never done anything remotely disloyal. The very idea of having a sponsor seemed like another contradiction to the American promise. Yet, to secure their freedom, they complied and found people who remembered them and stood up for them.

On their last day at the camp, they were driven to the train station and presented with twenty-five dollars each and one-way tickets to Denver, the city that they had specified as the place they wanted to start a new life. Aiko's husband, Jacob, had enlisted in the army and was in Germany when she made the long train ride to Colorado. "When he came back, we had a very, very hard time adjusting to each other again," she says. "I think we realized that we'd been very impulsive and had made a mistake."

Eventually, they divorced. She married another Japanese American, a Nisei soldier who was sent to Japan after the war as part of the occupation army, and she moved to New York to await his return. He was assigned to intelligence with orders to ferret out possible Communists. At that time, General Douglas MacArthur, who oversaw the occupation of Japan, used Japanese American Nisei to help keep Japan from going Communist. She recalls:

> I joined my husband a year later, and I was in Japan for five years. We were not permitted to fraternize, because of the nature of his work, so I didn't learn the language. I had very little contact with the Japanese people. What Japanese I know, I learned from my mother and father. When we returned, I had a couple of children that were born in an American hospital, so they were American citizens.[6]

Not long after they returned to the States, they separated and then later divorced. After two divorces, she didn't think about marriage again for almost two decades. Then she became reacquainted with a man named Jack Herzig, a soldier who had worked in intelligence with her ex-husband in Japan. Jack was German Irish, and he'd never met a Japanese American person growing up. When war broke out, he became a paratrooper assigned to the 503rd Parachute Infantry Regiment, which was sent to liberate Corregidor. Says Aiko: "He was part of the first unit to jump over enemy lines. It was a pretty difficult situation."

After the war, Jack was discharged from the army and went to New York, where he enrolled in New York University. However, his retirement from the army was short-lived. He was called back to active duty during the Korean War and made more than three dozen jumps the first year, before being assigned to the intelligence unit in Japan. That was where he was introduced to Aiko, not thinking much about it until they met again twenty years later and married in 1978.

"The third time was the charm for me," says Aiko. "I think I'm the black sheep of my family [for marrying three times]. I once asked my youngest sister why she never got married. She told me, 'You married enough for all of us.'"

George Aratani came under unexpected pressure while he was serv-ing with the intelligence unit in Minnesota and his Japanese-born step-mother, Masuko, was still imprisoned at Gila River. One day she returned to her barracks after having lunch at the mess hall and found an official letter from a government agency awaiting her. She opened the envelope and examined the signature before reading the letter. It was signed by Herman R. Landon, chief of the Exclusion and Expulsion Section and district director of the Immigration and Naturalization Service in El Paso. That alone made her knees shake. She read the letter and saw that she was being deported to Japan.

Masuko had entered the United States on a sightseeing visa. Her sta-tus changed after her marriage to Setsuo, George's father. Since Setsuo was a partner in a trading company that imported fish meal from Hiro-shima, he was eligible for special status as an immigration merchant. After Setsuo's death, Masuko was named president of the trading com-pany, an act that made her eligible for an exemption as an international trader. However, the outbreak of war with Japan nullified that protected status, since the United States and Japan no longer had a trade treaty because of the war. As a result, the government wanted Masuko to leave the country.

When George received a letter from Masuko and a copy of the let-ter she had received, he went to his boss, Major John Aiso, who told him that it was a very serious matter. He recommended that they talk to Col-onel Rasmussen, the white officer who headed up the intelligence train-ing school.

"Oh, bullshit," the colonel said after reading the letter. "What the hell. Don't worry about it. I'm gonna pick up the phone and call the War Department, all right? I'll squash this stuff."[7]

A week later, George was summoned to the colonel's office. George was told that his stepmother would be fine as long as George worked with military intelligence. It was a not-so-subtle form of blackmail, but George agreed to the terms in order to save his stepmother. The news was a great relief to Masuko, although she did long to see her aging mother, who lived with relatives in Hiroshima. It had been ten years since she left her family to forge a new family in America.

With the deportation order withdrawn, life went on as usual, with George in Minnesota and Masuko still at the concentration camp at Gila River. Then in early August 1945 their worlds were rocked again with news that the United States had dropped atomic bombs on Nagasaki and Hiroshima. No one knew exactly what an atomic bomb was, since it was developed in such secrecy, but news accounts made it clear that the cities had been destroyed. In Hiroshima, where both George and Masuko had family, more than 140,000 people were killed, most of them women and children. Another 80,000 were killed in Nagasaki. Six days later Japan announced its surrender.

Because of his military connections, George was able to find out which family members had survived the blasts. His grandmother Aratani had survived, as had his half sister, Sadako. It took longer to get word of Masuko's family. The bodies of her older sister, Yoshie, and her two daughters were never found, but her mother survived.

Now that the war was over, George and Masuko had to put their lives back together. The country that had imprisoned them and threatened to deport one of them had used a weapon of mass destruction against family and friends, erasing countless physical and emotional landmarks associated with loved ones. For Masuko there were no immediate decisions to be made. The end of the war did not mean that she would be released overnight from Gila River. On the contrary, she remained a prisoner until November 1945, at which time she moved into George's two-bedroom apartment, where he had made a home for his new wife, Sakaye, who was pregnant with their first child. George remained in the army, not sure what would happen to Masuko if he resigned and grateful for the income and status that his position provided as he sorted out his private business interests, which were in shambles. Making matters worse was the hostility expressed by whites in California. For example, in 1943 the Santa Maria Chamber of Commerce, of which George's father had once been a member, submitted a petition to the government asking that evacuees not be allowed to return to their farms.

In the summer of 1946, the intelligence school was moved from Minnesota to Monterey, California, a move that put George within a two-hour drive of his property. He was happy about the relocation, but he still had not made up his mind about how long he would continue in military service. Before turning in his resignation, he wanted to establish business connections with Japan that would allow him to reactivate the trading company founded by his father. Not only would that enable him to raise capital to get his farmland in operation again, but it would also reestablish Masuko's protected status and allow her to remain in the United States.

By the end of 1946, George was able to revive his father's trading company and establish offices in the Little Tokyo section of Los Angeles. That was his cue to resign from the protective environment of the army and try his hand at American capitalism. For much of the first year, he worked to establish connections with Japanese business firms, efforts that culminated in March 1948 with his first business trip to Japan. According to his biographer, Naomi Hirahara, "George, normally not given to displays of emotion, felt tears come to his eyes when he saw Tokyo."[8] The city had been leveled by American bombers that dropped nearly two thousand incendiary devices on the city, totally clearing it of its wooden buildings.

Establishing trade ties with Japan was difficult at first because much of Japan's economy was controlled by the U.S. military, but George persisted and eventually established a porcelain business that evolved into a multimillion-dollar chinaware company. He dropped the old name and renamed his business American Commercial, Inc. Within ten years, he introduced new chinaware that he named Mikasa, and by 1961 he was the owner of Kenwood, a multimillion-dollar electronics company.

━━━━━━━━━━

Like everyone else, Estelle Ishigo and her husband, Arthur, were given twenty-five dollars and one-way transportation from their concentration camp at Heart Mountain, Wyoming, back to Southern California. They left in the dead of night, carted on trucks to the train station, where they boarded the train, their possessions tucked beneath their seats, and pulled away from the magnificent mountain, hoping to emerge into their former lives.

Through the night they traveled, and then through more days and nights, until the familiar skyline of Los Angeles appeared. With their bundled lives tossed over their shoulders, they stepped off the train and were herded past startled whites who seemed shocked to see the shabbily dressed refugees. Estelle and Arthur had begun their journey by reporting to an assembly center. Now they were ending that journey by reporting to a center in Burbank from which they were expected to move forward into new lives. As before, armed guards patrolled the perimeter of the camp.

Estelle and Arthur had nowhere to go. Their $25 was not enough to rent an apartment, buy new clothing, and purchase food to sustain them until they could find work. At their new camp they slept on the floor and stared up at the sky through the holes in the ceiling of their barracks. But even that was temporary. Estelle and Arthur were told that they had to find work right away that included housing or they would have to report to a work camp, where they would live in a trailer, one of many moved there from the construction site at Boulder Dam. Since Estelle and Arthur were unable to quickly find work, they were taken to Lomita, California, and paid $15 a month to live in a trailer and $1.05 per person per day for meals. At that rate, their $25 would come up $0.50 short of lasting one week.

When the War Relocation Authority announced that it was shutting down on May 1, 1946, and would no longer bear any responsibility for former concentration camp prisoners, it left nearly two thousand ex-prisoners homeless in Los Angeles alone. Hostels were provided by charitable organizations, but there were not enough beds for everyone. Estelle and Arthur reluctantly accepted an offer from the Welfare Department, which had taken over from the WRA, to live in a trailer camp at a fish cannery with thirty-five other families that, for various reasons, had been unable to resume their former lives.

For two years, Estelle and Arthur lived in trailer camps and worked in fish canneries. In her memoir, Estelle wrote: "Trailers leaked in the winter rains, beds became moldy, the ground a muddy swamp, then water stood in deep pools with green slime. 'White people' avoided the camp—except social workers and religious friends. . . . We used a washtub of burning hot coals for our hearth. 'Relocation' was completed."[9]

Eventually, Arthur was able to find work at the Los Angeles International Airport. Fewer than ten years later, Arthur died at the age of fifty-five, worn out by the stresses and strains of "relocation." After his death, Estelle went into seclusion and worked on her paintings and her memoir, *Lone Heart Mountain*, which was published in 1972. Two years before her death in 1990 at the age of ninety-one, director Steven Okazaki released the film *Days of Waiting*, a poignant look at the lives of Estelle and Arthur during and after internment. The film won an Academy Award for Best Documentary Short Subject and the Peabody Award.

Estelle's feelings about internment were expressed in her memoir, viewed through the guileless eyes of young children:

> Two small boys sat on the log, coals glowed in the tub before them.
>
> "Are we Americans?" asked one.
>
> "No, we are not Americans," his friend answered.
>
> "But we were born here. If we are not Americans, what are we?"
>
> "We are human beings."
>
> "Who are the Americans?"
>
> "White people are Americans."[10]

The concentration camp at Crystal City, Texas, closed its doors on November 1, 1947, making it the last alien facility operated by the Justice Department to shut down. Among the last to leave were George and Emma Neupert. Their up-and-down experiences with internment left them bewildered and confused from the stress of never knowing what to expect next.

During the war, some prisoners in the camp, many of whom had lived in America for years, were shipped to Germany in exchange for American prisoners of war. Would the Neuperts be next? They simply didn't know what to expect. There was no twenty-four-hours-a-day news cycle. They lived in isolation of the events taking place in the rest of the country.

Emma, who had never been a citizen, was sent by authorities to live with family members who included her daughter Rose Marie, while

George, who had been a citizen only to have his citizenship revoked, was sent back to Ellis Island, where he was imprisoned with noncitizens earmarked for deportation.

Emma and Rose Marie visited George at Ellis Island on numerous occasions over the months that he was confined there, but one visit was especially disturbing in light of the notification he had received that he and other prisoners were about to be deported. Luckily, their lawyer was able to go to court and obtain a stay to delay his deportation. It was his closest call yet. His baggage already had been sent to the ship.[11]

George was eventually released, but it took years for his case to come to court. In the end, his citizenship was restored in 1956, just weeks after he died, giving meaning to the phrase "justice delayed, justice denied."

═══════════════

In June 1944, Max Ebel was paroled and allowed to return to Boston. There were restrictions, of course. Despite never being convicted of a crime, he had to report to a parole officer once a week for a year, and he was prohibited from going anywhere near a railroad or subway line. He went back to work for his father and met Doris Eckert, whom he married in 1948. An important part of resuming his old life was picking up where he left off with his citizenship application. Like everything else in his life for the past few years, his parole was a complicated process that required an intense evaluation of his application by the government. When he finally was granted a sit-down review, he was astonished at the size of the folders pertaining to his case. Finally, he was granted citizenship in 1953, more than twelve years after his first filing.

Max never protested his imprisonment. He never wrote letters home tinged with bitterness as did some of the prisoners. Although unfairly treated by his new country, he simply wrote it off as bad luck. The last thing he wanted to do was spend the rest of his life reliving the experience. Mostly, he wanted to forget. Recalls his daughter Karen: "He wasn't bitter. If anything, maybe I am bitter because of what happened to him."[12]

Max was grateful that he was not sent back to Germany. His seventeen-year-old brother, who had not left Germany, was drafted by the German army, shipped to the Russian front, and ended up going AWOL. "My father was aware of what a hellish existence he would have had in Germany," says Karen. "He might have had some guilt that he wasn't fighting for the United States. But as upset as he was about what happened to him, I don't think it affected his personality. Many of those families, where the people were established in their community and then got taken away, it just wrecked them mentally and economically."

Once Max had a family of his own, he observed a few German cultural traditions, but he did not encourage his children to speak German. Max and Doris spoke to each other in German when they wanted to keep a secret from the children, but otherwise the children grew up in a home that didn't differ greatly from that of their neighbors. Max wanted to embrace his adopted country, not promote the country of his birth.

By the time that Karen was aware of her surroundings, Max and Doris had moved the family to New Hampshire, where they put down roots in a small town that was mostly populated with old-time Yankee WASPs. If people whispered behind their backs, it was not because they knew about Max's imprisonment but rather because they were Catholics.

In 2000, Karen persuaded her eighty-year-old father to tell his story to the local newspaper, the *Concord Monitor*. In a story that was headlined "Germans, Too, Were Imprisoned in WWII," Max shrugged off his previous silence by saying, "There just wasn't that much to say." What really got to him was the way that whole chapter in American history has been forgotten. "Life brings along a lot of different things in eighty years," he told the reporter. "[But] I have absolutely no malice."

After Max's death in 2007, Karen made her father's cause her own. "You didn't have to be a different race for something like this to happen to you," she explains. "It is not a story that is as likely to get as much sympathy, but that doesn't mean it is not an important story. For the individuals who went through it, it was a hellacious experience. Witness the fact that so many of them do not want to talk about it even to this day."

In 1948 the Japanese American Evacuation Claims Act was passed by Congress. No mention was made of German or Italian Americans, but persons of Japanese ancestry were given the legal right to file claims with the government for "damage to or loss of real or personal property" that was not compensated by insurance.

Right away victims encountered problems. To receive compensation, Japanese American internees had to provide proof of their losses. That proved to be very difficult. Many of those sent to concentration camps returned to their homes to find that they had been ransacked, so it was difficult to find the receipts and contracts required by the law. The obvious source of information was the Internal Revenue Service, but by the time the claims procedure began, most of the income tax returns filed by internees already had been destroyed by the IRS. In testimony before Congress, the Japanese American Citizens League brought that to the lawmakers' attention by explaining that when someone was ordered to vacate their home to go to prison, the natural inclination was to pack food, medicine, and clothing and not books and financial records that may or may not be needed at a later date. No one knew if they even had a future.

Added to the difficulty of presenting proof of loss was the snail's pace of government review of the claims. For example, in 1949 and 1950 more than 26,000 claims totaling $148 million were filed under the act, but the government found time to adjudicate only 232 of those claims.[13] As the years went by, more and more claims were settled, especially when the government dropped the formal adjudication requirement and allowed claims to be settled for the lesser of $2,500 or 75 percent of their value, resulting in a rush of settlements. By the time the books were closed on the settlement process, the government had paid out about $37 million, a fraction of the losses sustained by the internees—and this process excluded Germans, Italians, and others detained in the camps.

With the end of the war came a reevaluation of the Jews at Camp Ontario. There were those in Congress who were impatient for them to live up to their part of the bargain—namely, to leave America and return to their various homelands, wherever that happened to be—Germany, Poland, or Austria. In the eyes of some, America already had enough Jews.

In the Camp Ontario newspaper, someone wrote: "Could it be really the intention to send a resident, who unfortunately was born in Germany or Austria, back to the countries of Buchenwald, Auschwitz and Dachau? . . . For many of us a return to 'their homelands in Europe' signifies no more or less than a death warrant."[14]

As word spread through the camp that everyone was about to be deported, it was announced that a subcommittee of the House Committee on Immigration and Naturalization would travel to Camp Ontario to conduct an investigation. That could not be a good sign, they concluded. Where was President Truman? Where did he stand on the issue?

After the subcommittee conducted its investigation, it approved a resolution that requested that the Departments of State and Justice ascertain the practicality of returning the prisoners to their homelands. In the event that was not practical, it was suggested that the attorney declare them illegal aliens and initiate deportation proceedings.

The matter lingered for another six months, and then on December 5, 1945, the Departments of Justice and State drafted a letter recommending that the refugees leave the United States. The letter was sent to Secretary Ickes for his signature, but he refused to sign it. The matter dragged on for several weeks, and then, to the surprise of everyone, President Truman, who was still a mystery to most Americans, took charge of the issue on December 22 with a radio address.

The speech began with an overview of the situation, his stern tone giving no encouragement to the refugees and those who had fought for their freedom, such as Ruth Gruber and Harold Ickes. He addressed the larger issue of the millions of Jewish refugees who were desperate for a place of safety, but he reiterated the reality of an immigration law that allowed only thirty-nine hundred refugees into the country each month. Listeners sympathetic to the cause of the refugees began to lose hope, when suddenly, without warning, Truman took a position on the Jews at Camp Ontario that stunned the nation:

In the circumstances, it would be inhumane and wasteful to require these people to go all the way back to Europe merely for the purpose of applying there for immigration visas and returning to the United States. Many of them have close relatives, including sons and daughters, who are citizens of the United States and who have served and are serving honorably in the armed forces of our country.

I am therefore directing the Secretary of State and the Attorney General to adjust the immigration status of those members of this group who may wish to stay here, in strict accordance with existing laws and regulations.[15]

Under President Truman's directive, the Camp Ontario refugees were allowed to be the first to qualify for immigrant status under the thirty-nine-hundred-per-month allocation. To qualify, they had to leave the country and then reenter. It was the plan that Ruth Gruber had suggested months before. On January 17, 1946, the first three busloads of refugees drove across western New York to Niagara Falls, where they crossed over into Canada on the Rainbow Bridge. Waiting for them was the American consul to Canada, who handed each refugee a ribbon-wrapped visa that allowed him or her to recross the bridge and enter the United States, free at last. And so it went, three busloads at a time, until Camp Ontario was emptied of all its prisoners. With the help of social workers employed by the War Relocation Authority, they chose cities across America as their new homes.

Fifty-nine years later, in July 2003, when the *New York Times* sent a reporter to a reunion of camp survivors at the home of Judy Goldsmith, daughter of a deceased camp member, there were only 134 survivors left, according to the newspaper tally. Several were interviewed by reporter Claudia Rowe. Most had adapted to their new lives. But few had forgotten the ordeal. Walter Greenberg said that it had taken him many years to be able even to talk about his experiences at the camp: "I'd known what prison was. I'd lived behind bars in Italy. But I'd never known freedom. In America, I looked out at the rest of the world [from behind a barbed wire fence] and I saw normal people with everyday lives, and I felt deceived."[16]

From Goldsmith's perspective, the refugees confined at Camp Ontario were just one aspect of a gigantic mystery regarding America's attitude toward Jewish refugees. "They came here thinking they would be welcomed. And these were the only people that America—this big, powerful country—even tried to save. It's pretty shameful."[17]

13

RIGHTING THE WRONGS

Twenty-five dollars and a one-way ticket home.

That's what the government provided to tens of thousands of Japanese Americans, most of them American citizens, who had been held for years in concentration camps, without criminal charges ever being leveled against them.

They could go home. But where was home?

Those who rented houses found strangers living in their former space, their possessions having been dumped onto the street. Homeowners often found that their homes had been sold by the government for nonpayment of taxes. Some had white friends who rescued their possessions and put them in storage until their release, but most did not have anyone. Most lost everything they owned before the roundup, a lifetime collection of possessions.

Those who had jobs found others working in their place. Those who owned businesses found them either shuttered or limping along in the hands of caretakers. When they returned to the workforce, most had to accept any job they could find, and typically those jobs were menial positions that whites did not want. Those who returned to civilian life with little or no capital faced beginning new businesses from scratch, which at that time usually meant start-up companies related to gardening or lawn care.

There were exceptions, of course. George Aratani was able to build a financial empire because he was able to nurture a network that protected his family's finances in his absence. John Aiso did well after the war because of his service to the country in military intelligence. Others emerged from concentration caps or from military service to build very successful lives. Those Americans who supported the use of concentration camps, which was most of the country at that time, have used those success stories to advance their agendas by suggesting that the negative effects of confinement in the camps were minimal.

To accept that argument is to ignore the fact that for every success story of Japanese American achievement there were countless economic hardships, psychological traumas, and cultural assaults (ethnic slurs of "Jap," "dago," "kike," or "Kraut" shouted in supermarket aisles or from street corners) that were experienced not only by the individuals imprisoned but also by their young children who, in many instances, grew up in households in which it was forbidden to discuss the injustices of the past out of embarrassment or a fear of violent reprisals, or because of event-induced depression or behavior disorders that left former internees emotionally unable to deal with day-to-day life without the suppression of the past.

Michael Yeshii, a third-generation Japanese American, first learned of his parents' internment as a youth and found that it was a difficult matter to discuss with them: "My perception of them was that they did not speak honestly about the camp experience. . . . My feeling was that there was much more to their experience than they wanted to reveal. Their words said one thing, while their hearts were holding something else deep inside."[1] Echoing that was Dr. Tetsuden Kachima, who was imprisoned as a child with his parents at Topaz, Utah, and went on to become a sociology professor of American ethnic studies at the University of Washington. It is his belief that imprisonment created a social amnesia in which there was an effort, conscious or otherwise, to suppress "less than pleasant memories."[2]

That feeling was prevalent. For the most part, the Japanese, German, and Italian Americans who were arrested and imprisoned during World War II mounted few legal challenges to the government's actions, a passive acceptance of the circumstances that amazed later generations of Americans, especially those who came of age during the protest years associated with the Vietnam War.

However, there were reasons for that passivity. Many of the Germans, Italians, and Jews imprisoned in concentration camps were not citizens and rightfully feared that if their goal was to remain in the United States, claiming rights available to citizens would not be in their best interests. The situation for Japanese Americans was different, because more than two-thirds of them were U.S. citizens who possessed constitutional rights. Their reluctance to confront authority seems to have been based on cultural differences, learned from their Japanese-born parents, about the proper relationship between the individual and his or her governmental authority. Like Michael Yeshii's parents, many wanted to suppress memories of the event, simply because the pain of remembering was never accompanied by a satisfying emotional resolution.

Some internees sought resolution in the courts. The most notable legal case to arise during that period was *Korematsu v. United States*. Fred Korematsu, one of three young men who in 1942 resisted the government order to leave their homes and report to an assembly center for transfer to a concentration camp, was born in the United States to a Japanese American family that owned a flower nursery. At the time that the evacuation order was issued, he was working as a welder and engaged to a white woman. To keep his freedom, he took several evasive actions. He doctored his draft card. He underwent plastic surgery so that he would no longer have strong Asian facial features. And he kept a low profile. He was arrested after a friend betrayed him and notified authorities of his whereabouts.

Coming to Korematsu's defense was a wily San Francisco attorney named Wayne M. Collins, who often took so-called controversial cases for the American Civil Liberties Union. He also represented more than six thousand Japanese Americans who renounced their citizenship under the pressure of the times but later wanted to reclaim their citizenship.

And he represented Peruvian Japanese who had been kidnapped and transferred to American concentration camps for the duration of the war.

Collins took Korematsu's case while he was still imprisoned in a concentration camp. After losing in federal district court and in the court of appeals, Collins took the case all the way to the U.S. Supreme Court, which in 1944 ruled, six to three, that the army was justified in establishing an internment policy directed against Japanese Americans. In the majority opinion, Justice Hugo Black wrote that Korematsu was not excluded from the military area because of hostility to him or his race, but because America was at war with Japan and because

> properly constituted military authorities feared an invasion of our West Coast and felt constrained to take proper security measures, because they decided that the military urgency of the situation demanded that all citizens of Japanese ancestry be segregated from the West Coast temporarily, and finally, because Congress, reposing its confidence in this time of war in our military leaders—as inevitably it must—determined that they should have the power to do just this.[3]

Offering a dissenting opinion was Associate Justice Robert Jackson, who later became chief U.S. prosecutor at the Nuremberg Trials. He concluded:

> Once a judicial opinion rationalizes such an order [internment based on race] to show that it conforms to the Constitution, or rather rationalizes the Constitution to show that the Constitution sanctions such an order, the Court for all time has validated the principle of racial discrimination in criminal procedure and of transplanting American citizens. The principle then lies about like a loaded weapon, ready for the hand of any authority that can bring forward a plausible claim of an urgent need.[4]

In 1944, the Supreme Court dashed hopes that justice ever would be extended to those confined in American concentration camps. However, once the war ended, there were a series of official actions that attempted to build a consensus, even if only one brick at a time. In 1948, Congress passed the Japanese American Evacuation Claims Act, which gave Japanese Americans the right to make claims for real and personal property losses during internment. The law provided no mechanism for economic loss or pain and suffering, and awards ended up being too low to address the problems caused by imprisonment. In 1972, the Social Security Act was amended to credit former prisoners with contributions during their confinement. In 1978, federal civil service retirement provisions were changed to give Japanese Americans eligible for civil service retirement credit for time spent in detention.

As time passed, more and more Americans began to wonder if piecemeal administrative solutions would ever absolve the national guilt over what was increasingly being viewed as one of the greatest institutional failures since the enslavement of African Americans and the decades of discrimination that followed.

━━━━━━━━━━

After serving in Germany, Lieutenant Colonel John "Jack" Herzig was assigned to the Pentagon. He and his wife, Aiko Yoshinaga-Herzig, moved to Washington, D.C., the perfect place for Aiko to live in view of her interest in her family's internment experiences. Each day that Jack drove to work at the Pentagon, he dropped Aiko off at the National Archives so that she could pore over documents related to her family and others who were sent to internment camps.

For Aiko the National Archives was a wonderland, with massive numbers of documents, letters, and government reports. One file would lead to another, then another, and she slowly entered a dark world that was more vast and informative than she'd ever imagined. At lunch, Jack joined her at the archives and helped with her research, then returned to the Pentagon, where current issues generated new documents, letters, and reports. At the end of the day he and Aiko drove back home, only to start all over again the next morning, mining government information.

Curiosity transformed into an intellectual passion for the pursuit of ideas. When Jack learned about the loyalty questionnaire, he became irate, telling Aiko, "I was German and I never had to answer questions like that. Why did you guys [Japanese Americans] have to do that?"[5]

Aiko did not have to search for an appropriate answer, for she had thought about it for a long time. She explained: "The government could not possibly incarcerate people of German and Italian descent the way they did Japanese Americans. Eisenhower's top general was a German. You would have had a civil war on your hands."

The more that Jack learned from Aiko's research, the more upset he became about the treatment of Japanese Americans. He felt betrayed by his government. He'd lost many good friends in Corregidor and New Guinea and the Philippines. Aiko recalls: "He thought they were fighting to preserve all the wonderful facets of democracy and our constitutional guarantees and at the same time this [internment] was happening to people like me. He felt betrayed and really got into the research."

One result of that research was that Jack and Aiko became involved with the National Council for Japanese American Redress (NCJAR), cofounded and chaired by William Hohri of Chicago, who had been imprisoned at the age of fifteen with his family at Manzanar. Hohri recruited Aiko to help the NCJAR lobby Congress for redress. At the same time, he asked Aiko to help research a class-action lawsuit against the government.

As a result of the lobbying efforts of NCJAR and other Japanese American groups, in 1980 Congress authorized the establishment of the Commission on Wartime Relocation and Internment of Civilians to review the facts and circumstances of World War II internment and to recommend appropriate remedies. To accomplish that mandate, the nine-member commission—with three members appointed by the president, three appointed by the Senate, and three appointed by the House of Representatives—held twenty days of hearings and heard from more than 750 witnesses between July and December 1981. During that time—and until the end of 1982—the commission gathered and reviewed relevant archival documents and historical writing on the subject of internment. By that time, Aiko's reputation for research was so well known that she was asked by the commission to provide assistance as a researcher.

In February 1983, the commission submitted its report to Congress. Titled *Personal Justice Denied*, the report included summaries of testimony, historical references, and an analysis of the decisions made by the government during internment. It concluded that Executive Order 9066 was not justified by military necessity, and it attributed the mistakes that were made to racial prejudice and widespread ignorance about Americans of Japanese descent. Furthermore, it concluded: "A grave personal injustice was done to the American citizens and resident aliens of Japanese ancestry. . . . [They] suffered enormous damages and losses, both material and intangible."[6]

The commission estimated that Japanese Americans collectively lost between $108 and $164 million in income and between $41 and $206 million in property as a result of being committed to concentration camps. Recommended by the commission as a remedial measure to address the wrongs not addressed by previous efforts was a joint resolution passed by Congress and signed by the president that acknowledges a "grave injustice" was done and offers the apologies of the nation, along with presidential pardons for those convicted of violating curfew laws. Other recommendations included the establishment of an educational foundation to conduct research on the causes of the injustices inflicted on Japanese Americans and a $1.5 billion fund set up by Congress to provide personal redress to those who were excluded or imprisoned. Specifically, the fund would provide compensatory payment of $20,000 to each of the survivors who suffered because of Executive Order 9066.

There were two dissenters from the final recommendation, Commissioner Dan Lungren, a right-wing Republican congressman from California, who stubbornly clung to the belief that the military might have had justification for the roundup, and Commissioner William M. Marutani, a concentration camp survivor who served in the army's military intelligence unit. Marutani, a respected judge and staunch critic of internment, was opposed to any monetary compensation to survivors, presumably in the belief that draft-age males had the same option that he had to join the armed forces.

In 1983, the year the commission's report was released, Fred Korematsu's attorneys went back to court, using Aiko Yoshinaga-Herzig's research to show that the government had suppressed, altered, and destroyed evidence that showed there was no military necessity for the evacuation and relocation of Japanese Americans in the months following the Japanese attack on Pearl Harbor. The evidence was so compelling that the following year the convictions of Korematsu and the other resisters were vacated by the courts.

The class-action lawsuit filed by Hohri and the NCJAR, which listed claims that totaled $27.5 billion, made its ways through the courts, encountering a series of ups and downs, before it reached the U.S. Supreme Court, only to be sent back to the U.S. Court of Appeals, where it lingered for five years before being dismissed on grounds that the statute of limitations had expired.

On August 10, 1988, President Ronald Reagan signed the Civil Liberties Act, which was the culmination of the struggle to approve the recommendations made by the commission. The law called for a national apology and twenty thousand dollars in reparations for each individual survivor of the concentration camps. However, before the terms of the act could be implemented, eligible survivors had to be identified and located. To accomplish this task, the Civil Liberties Act established the Office of Redress Administration (ORA) within the Justice Department. The redress agency was given ten years to find the individuals and authorize tax-free restitution payments of twenty thousand dollars to eligible individuals of Japanese ancestry. Not surprisingly, the ORA turned to the two people who had done more research on the subject than anyone else, Jack Herzig and Aiko Yoshinaga-Herzig.

"I was a big job to find out who was eligible," says Aiko. "The biggest part of the job was made easier because the War Relocation Authority that ran the camps had a wonderful collection of ten books that listed the inmates in each camp."

Aiko and Jack pored over the books and tracked each name until they could classify each person as living, deceased, or unknown. Even so, Aiko is certain that a lot of names "fell through the cracks." It took a full year for them to compile enough names and addresses for the apology and restitution process to begin. By then, Reagan was no longer president and the responsibility fell to President George H. W. Bush, who issued the apology in October 1990 by sending letters to the survivors.

The letter, in its entirety, read:

A monetary sum and words alone cannot restore lost years or erase painful memories; neither can they fully convey our Nation's resolve to rectify injustice and to uphold the rights of individuals. We can never fully right the wrongs of the past. But we can take a clear stand for justice and recognize that serious injustices were done to Japanese Americans during World War II.

In enacting a law calling for restitution and offering a sincere apology, your fellow Americans have, in a very real sense, renewed their traditional commitment to the ideals of freedom, equality, and justice. You and your family have our best wishes for the future.[7]

Not eligible for apologies or restitution were the prisoners of Japanese ancestry who were not born in the United States or who did not obtain legal permanent residency. Also excluded were ethnic Japanese who were taken from their homes in Latin America and brought to the United States and imprisoned in concentration camps. Notably absent from the apology and restitution list were the persons of German, Italian, or Jewish ancestry who were imprisoned in the United States during the war, without regard to their citizenship status.

By the time the ten-year payment provision of the act expired in 1998, 82,219 individuals were paid the full twenty-thousand-dollar amount, including 189 Japanese Latin American claimants who were eligible because they had proof of U.S. citizenship or permanent residency status.[8]

Because of a class-action lawsuit brought by Japanese Latin Americans who were deported to the United States at the request of this government, a settlement was reached during the final year of the Civil Liberties Act that provided for the payment of five thousand dollars to each of 145 survivors, along with a letter of apology. At the termination of the payment provision, President Bill Clinton settled a class-action lawsuit with an award of five thousand dollars to each of 1,200 surviving Japanese Latin Americans who were among those arrested in Latin American and transported to concentration camps in the United States. Two-thirds of this group were Japanese nationals, and over 80 percent were from Peru.[9]

Since Clinton was president at that time, he issued the letter of apology. In the letter, he noted the "unjust" internment, relocation, and evacuation of Japanese Americans during World War II and continued:

> Today, on behalf of your fellow Americans, I offer a sincere apology to you for the actions that unfairly denied Japanese Americans and their families fundamental liberties during World War II. In passing the Civil Liberties Act of 1988, we acknowledged the wrongs of the past and offered redress to those who endured such grave injustice. In retrospect, we understand that the nation's actions were rooted deeply in racial prejudice, wartime hysteria, and a lack of political leadership.[10]

There is no doubt in Aiko's mind that the Civil Liberties Act would never have occurred without the class-action lawsuit filed by William Hohri and the National Council for Japanese American Redress. Says Aiko: "When we spoke to Barney Frank [Democratic congressman from Massachusetts], who was subcommittee chairman, he said a class-action lawsuit would have cost our treasury twenty-seven billion dollars because it was computed on causes of action. Every survivor would have received around two hundred thousand dollars."

Faced with possible reparations of $27 billion imposed by the courts, Congress passed legislation that paid out more than $1.6 billion, a considerable savings for taxpayers. Aiko feels that justice could have been obtained much earlier if Japanese Americans had not been so reluctant to discuss their experiences in the camps. "It was a cause of shame that you were in prison, even though you were innocent," she explains, and she continues:

> Who wants to talk about that? Especially such a proud people. Many of the people of my generation didn't even tell their children what had happened. Asian people have a tendency to be very respectful of authority. It is passed down from the warlords, a long history of respecting authority. If the government said you had to go, you went. Little by little the story came out.

A story that has been slower to come out involves the World War II treatment of German and Italian American internees, along with Jewish refugees who were imprisoned. Congress has been slow to provide all three groups of individuals with considerations similar to those afforded Japanese Americans. There are sociological, political, and practical reasons for those groups being overlooked for an apology and reparations, but the main reason is that Japanese Americans were rounded up and interned in such large numbers that it was impossible to ignore them for long. In addition, they put together a very effective lobbying effort that Jack and Aiko supplied with unimpeachable documentation.

In November 2000, an effort was made to address the injustices committed against Italian Americans with a bill titled the Wartime Violation of Italian Americans Civil Liberties Act, sponsored by U.S. representative Rick Lazio (Republican of New York) and eighty-two cosponsors. The bill passed in the House of Representatives by voice vote, which prevented a record of each representative's position, and by unanimous consent in the Senate, a procedure that made unnecessary a record of each senator's position. The legislation was signed by President Bill Clinton.[11]

The act directed the attorney general to prepare a report detailing injustices suffered by Italian Americans during World War II, including those taken into custody, ordered to move to designated areas, arrested for curfew violations, or prevented from fishing in prohibited zones. The justification of the act was contained in the wording of the legislation, which stated:

> The story of the treatment of Italian Americans during World War II needs to be told in order to acknowledge that these events happened, to remember those whose lives were unjustly disrupted and whose freedoms were violated, to help repair the damage to the Italian American community, and to discourage the occurrence of similar injustices and violations of civil liberties in the future.[12]

The attorney general submitted the report to Congress on November 7, 2001. No mention was made of reparations. However, the act expressed the sense of the Congress that the story of the treatment of Italian Americans should be told by federal agencies in various ways, including traveling exhibits, seminars, lectures, and the production of a documentary film suited for public broadcast.[13]

The act was the result of a compromise between Democrats, many of whom also wanted reparations and recognition of the injustices suffered by German Americans and Jewish refugees, and Republicans, who did not. Democrats decided that recognition of the injustices against Italian Americans was sufficient for the moment, and Republicans agreed on the condition that the votes were cast so that they could not be personally linked to the legislation. As is the case for most legislative compromises, unfinished business related to the legislation was cast adrift to find its own way to acceptance.

The issue arose again in 2006, when President George W. Bush signed a law that authorized the National Park Service to spend up to $38 million to preserve historically significant Japanese American World War II concentration camps. The gesture is culturally important for the type of generational healing that is necessary for the matter to finally be put to rest. But can that healing ever happen as long as the injustices inflicted on the German, Italian, and Jewish injured parties are not addressed in a meaningful way? History has taught us that it is never over until it is over.

The most recent effort to redress the wrongs inflicted on Jewish refugees and Italian and German Americans was contained in an amendment to the 2007 Kennedy-Specter Comprehensive Immigration Bill, sponsored by the late Senator Edward Kennedy and Senator Arlen Specter. For the previous four Congresses, Democratic senators Russ Feingold and Chuck Grassley had attempted to pass a bill they cosponsored titled the Wartime Treatment Study Act. The goal was to establish a commission to study the injustices committed against Italian and German Americans and Jewish refugees. Even though the wartime problems faced by Italians were addressed in previous legislation, Feingold and Grassley felt that a commission review, similar to the review that was done on behalf of Japanese Americans, would be a beneficial supplement to the review undertaken by the Justice Department. Each time, the bill was blocked by Republican members of Congress. This time they attached the bill as an amendment to the immigration bill. The amendment required an independent review of the U.S. government's treatment of German Americans, Italian Americans, and Jewish refugees and the creation of commissions to preserve documents and record testimony of an aging population. The wording of the amendment was straightforward: "The wartime policies of the U.S. Government were devastating to the Italian and German American communities, individuals and their families. The detrimental effects are still being experienced."[14]

On the floor of the Senate, Feingold explained his amendment approach by saying that he would have preferred to have moved the bill on its own merits, but the political climate was such that he felt it would yet again be blocked by Republican members. "Let me again repeat that this amendment does not call for reparations," he said. "All it does is ensure that the public has a full accounting of what happened. We should be proud of our victory over Nazism, as I am. But we should not let that pride cause us to overlook what happened to some Americans and refugees during World War II."[15]

The Kennedy-Specter Comprehensive Immigration Bill and all its amendments were rejected by Congress in 2007. And so the story continues. Nearly seventy years after World War II–era concentration camps left a dark stain on America's legacy of "life, liberty and the pursuit of happiness," Americans are still debating government responsibility in the use of concentration camps and torture.

PART III

ASK NOT FOR WHOM THE BELL TOLLS

As a nation, we began by declaring that "all men are created equal." We now practically read it "all men are created equal, except Negroes." When the Know-Nothings get control, it will read "all men are created equal, except Negroes and foreigners and Catholics." When it comes to this, I shall prefer emigrating to some country where they make no pretense of loving liberty.

—ABRAHAM LINCOLN, LETTER TO JOSHUA F. SPEED

14

MODERN-DAY INTERNMENT

In the immediate aftermath of World War II, U.S. concentration camps disappeared from the political landscape, a casualty of the horror and deep shame felt by most Americans over the treatment of their fellow citizens in detention camps during the war. It was the dirty secret no one wanted to discuss, especially the part about innocent children being imprisoned because of their skin color and ethnic background.

Who can ever forget the photographs of frightened children being packed into cattle trucks for transport to the camps? No less innocent or frightened were the parents of the children, the vast majority of them American citizens, none ever convicted of crimes other than protesting their wrongful imprisonment.

When America's next crisis—the Korean War—sent American soldiers into combat in 1950, Congress passed the Detention Act of 1950, which gave the government the authority to arrest any individuals deemed to be subversive and to detain them in concentration camps built in Arizona, California, Florida, Oklahoma, and Pennsylvania. This time the stated purpose for the camps was to imprison communists. That idea never gained serious traction because the American public could not be convinced that there were enough communists in America to fill one concentration camp, much less six. It only served to stoke fears that the camps really were meant for Korean Americans. However, at that time it was unthinkable that Korean Americans, a substantial minority on the West Coast and a political force nationwide, would be rounded up with their children and sent to concentration camps.

A decade and a half later, with the arrival of the Vietnam War, U.S. officials rejected any consideration of concentration camps for either Vietnamese Americans or the Vietnamese nationals who had been relocated to American soil. Atrocities against civilians were committed by U.S. soldiers in Vietnam, but there was never any serious effort to herd Vietnamese families into concentration camps, either in Vietnam or on the U.S. mainland. That was because the stigma of the World War II camps still affected ordinary citizens throughout the 1950s, 1960s, and 1970s. In those decades, during which peace and civil rights movements gained prominence and political influence, there would have been a groundswell of opposition if the U.S. government had attempted to build new concentration camps for racial minorities.

Not until the 1980s, with the marginalization of the peace and civil rights movements—and the arrival of the conservative Reagan administration—did the memory of World War II concentration camps recede from public consciousness. By the 1980s, the "enemy" was no longer foreign soldiers but rather "invaders" from Mexico who illegally entered the United States to find work and build new lives. It mattered little that most of the illegal immigrants came from Mexico to build America, not destroy it. They were targeted for imprisonment as a matter of policy.

The Reagan administration encountered little opposition, mainly because it was difficult to argue that foreign nationals who broke the law in coming to America should not be held accountable for breaking the law, but also because the agency in charge of the camps was the Immigration and Naturalization Service (INS), an agency that had no authority over American-born ethnic minorities, who had acquired considerable political influence.

In 1986 Congress passed legislation that legalized some categories of illegal immigrants. Those who could prove that they had entered the country prior to January 1, 1982, would receive amnesty. Throughout the 1980s and 1990s, INS detention camps attracted little public scrutiny. They were not concentration camps in the traditional sense in that they did not target citizens of a particular race or ethnic background. Instead, they targeted lawbreakers. What could be wrong about that?

Shouldn't America put America first?

If only it were that simple.

The young woman had fled to America from Africa, where the military had kidnapped her older sister before looking for her. At the airport she was asked by an INS official if she was seeking asylum. She didn't understand the meaning of the word. She was looking for freedom. Were the two concepts—asylum and freedom—compatible?

The INS official broke that line of thinking when he muttered, "You African monkeys should go back to your country."[1] Was it his standard greeting?

Until her right to remain in the United States could be determined by government officials, the twenty-year-old woman was transported to an INS detention center, where all the prisoners were asylum seekers. Like all the other women, she was ordered to lift her skirt, part her feet, and bend over and cough three times while her orifices were inspected for contraband. She was menstruating at the time.

"They took me as an animal, not a human being," she later testified before a fact-finding hearing. "I promised myself whatever happens I will not cry."

Later that afternoon at the detention center, she was shackled to a Hispanic detainee and transported to another INS facility. The truck was filthy, filled with human excrement. None of the women in the van had been charged with a crime. All had come to America in search of freedom, lured by the promise of the Statue of Liberty.

Once again, the young woman was told to bend over and cough three times so that her vagina and rectum could be searched. Why three times?

she wondered. And why did they have such a fascination with her vagina and rectum? Were all Americans like that?

After she was taken to her holding cell, she broke the promise she'd made to herself. She cried, prompted perhaps by the screams of other women she could hear but not see. Identified as a problem prisoner, she was taken to the Behavioral Adjustment Unit, known to other prisoners as the Bad Attitude Unit. It was where troublemakers were processed. Ordered to remove her uniform, she balked at first, but then, consumed with fear, she did as they asked. Then they asked her to take off her bra and panties.

"No, even if you are female, I cannot do that."

For the correctional officers the young woman's words were nothing more than static. They held her down and undressed her, peeling away her bra and panties. As that happened, two male officers, wearing masks to conceal their identity, came into the room and watched. One man in particular frightened her. He was tall and well built, the kind of man who could hurt you if he wanted to. She tried not to look at him. She crawled under the bed to hide her private parts. Naked and terrified of what was going to happen next, she answered their questions from beneath the bed, her voice growing smaller and smaller with each answer.

"Do you feel like killing yourself?"

If she had wanted to die, she explained, she would have stayed in her native land.

"Do you ever hear voices?"

She heard their voices. Were those the voices they meant?

They dragged her from under the bed and gave her an injection, slapping the needle into her flesh. Terrified, she spoke in her native language, her words directed toward God: "Do you know what's going on?"

The only sound she heard in reply was the gritty sound of the men's feet on the concrete floor and their curses as they maneuvered to spread her legs and arms so that she could receive a second injection. Men and women watched as her legs were forcibly spread. She looked away from them, choosing not to see their staring eyes. The room was cold. She shivered, not just from the temperature but from the fear that surged through her. They tossed her a rag of some kind. She used it to cover herself.

Then she lost consciousness.

When she awoke, she was fully dressed. She had no idea what was done to her while she was unconscious or who had dressed her. Before she was taken back to the dorm, someone handed her a rosary. The other detainees voiced sympathy for her. One of the women asked her about the guard dog. She had not noticed a dog. The very thought of a dog being in the room with her caused her to collapse. She was afraid of dogs. The women picked her up and bathed her and braided her hair.

Sometime later she received a visit from a minister.

"Let me go and die in my own country," she pleaded. "I can't die in America."

The young woman's request was refused. Instead, she was held in detention for a year and a half and then abruptly granted political asylum, without apology or explanation. Later, she confessed that she sometimes missed the friends she had made in prison. They had stayed up with her through the night, comforting her as she wept. "I felt that that was my home for the rest of my life."

Obviously, while coming of age in Africa, where the nights on occasion can be cool and soothing, fragrant with the scent of exotic blooms, the young woman had never learned the American hard-knocks mantra: "Freedom is just another word for nothing left to lose."

As a concept, INS detention camps don't seem unreasonable. The law says that anyone who comes to America without following proper procedure is guilty of a crime. To accommodate all those "criminals," prisons must be built. The problem comes when you equate the crime with the time. Is the young African woman's sentence of a year and a half in a concentration camp, where she was subjected to what most people would reasonably consider torture, appropriate for the crime of not completing the proper paperwork before traveling to America? Many American-born criminals don't get prison sentences that severe for assault, child abuse, robbery, or drug trafficking. As it turns out, she committed no crime at all. She was granted political asylum and welcomed to America.

Historically, immigrants who have traveled to America without the proper paperwork have been deported and returned to their country of origin. That becomes problematic when immigrants cannot be returned without facing persecution or even death. In those cases, is imprisoning them in INS camps the right thing to do if no other crimes are at issue? In the young woman's case one cannot help but feel that her biggest crime was not being born white.

If one had to pick a time when the Reagan administration's 1980s policies regarding concentration camps for illegal immigrants kicked into manic overdrive, it would be 1996, the year that Republican Speaker of the House Newt Gingrich's Contract with America produced two landmark pieces of legislation, the Antiterrorism and Effective Death Penalty Act of 1996 (AEDPA) and the Illegal Immigration Reform and Immigrant Responsibility Act (IIRIRA). Both were signed into law by President Bill Clinton, who had no real choice, since both were passed by veto-proof majorities.

The AEDPA was rushed through Congress to commemorate the anniversary of the 1995 Oklahoma City bombing of the Murrah Federal Building. The attack was the work of U.S. Army veteran Timothy McVeigh, a right-wing militia movement sympathizer who planned the attack as a protest against the federal government. The purpose of the legislation was to deter terrorism by making it easier for prosecutors to obtain the death penalty, but in the process of doing that, it redefined habeas corpus law in the United States, which tangentially made it more difficult for immigrant detainees to be released from detention centers. It is ironic that a terrorist act by a white, right-wing radical could be used to justify closing the door on nonviolent immigrants of color.

The IIRIRA was more of a frontal assault on illegal immigrants, the vast majority of whom in the mid-1990s were Hispanic. The law expanded the number of crimes for which immigrants could be deported or subjected to mandatory detention. INS officials were required to detain large numbers of legal resident aliens without setting a bond, and the law also increased detention of asylum seekers. The harsh measures were a direct response to the government's inability to deport Mexican immigrants and its frustration at not being able to prevent them from reentering the United States within days of their deportation.

If illegal immigrants could not effectively be deported and could not be allowed to remain in the United States, the only workable solution, so the reasoning went, was to place the immigrants in concentration camps, state prisons, and local jails. The practical effect of IIRIRA and AEDPA was to put about two hundred thousand illegal immigrants a year into detention. Most were moved out of the system within a year, but the net effect by the end of the 1990s was about thirty thousand people in detention at any given time.

15

"WHY IS THIS THING HAPPENING IN THIS COUNTRY?"

The only event in American history that is even remotely similar to the surprise attack on Pearl Harbor is the airborne terrorist attack that took place on September 11, 2001, at the Pentagon and at the World Trade Center in New York City. In many ways, perhaps because it was broadcast on live television and the horror was there for all to see in real time, it struck an even deeper chord in the American psyche than did the Pearl Harbor attack. It was television's ultimate reality show.

Despite the similarities of the two events—3,000 killed in New York; 2,403 killed at Pearl Harbor—there are stark differences in the two attacks. The Pearl Harbor attack was a strategic gambit by an expansionist Japanese government intent on replacing the economic and military presence of United States and Great Britain in Southeast Asia. The September 11 attacks were carried out by a small group of Muslim immigrants in response to U.S. policy in the Middle East that they interpreted as being anti-Muslim, or at the very least excessively pro-Israel. However, unlike the Japanese attack, which was transparent in its origins and responsibility, all those responsible for the September 11 attacks have yet to be fully identified, much less held accountable. Indeed, some critics feel that funding and planning for the attack may have originated in American corporate offices, a suspicion that has been fueled by electronic government "snooping" that often seemed more concerned about protecting corporate secrets and stifling journalistic investigation of government wrongdoing than in bringing the guilty to justice. The result has been a high level of public hysteria that has been easily manipulated into public acceptance of irrational responses to potential threats.

Once al Qaeda's involvement in the September 11 attacks became known, President George W. Bush initiated a "war on terror" that sent the United States into military quagmires in Afghanistan, where al Qaeda operated training camps for terrorists, and into Iraq, which had no al Qaeda presence until the United States invaded with a substantial number of combat troops and mercenaries, thus drawing scores of al Qaeda operatives into that country.

A reaction to the hysteria of the times can be seen in the Bush administration's decision to establish a concentration camp in Guantánamo Bay, Cuba. The camp, which was opened in December 2001 and supervised by the U.S. military, was the destination for hundreds of orange-jumpsuit-clad prisoners from the war zone in Afghanistan (and later from Iraq). As with the initial camps set up in Hawaii during World War II, the camp was situated outside the legal jurisdiction of the United States so that prisoners could be held securely beyond reach of the U.S. Constitution.

Unlike the camps in Hawaii, which were built to contain persons of Japanese, German, or Italian ancestry, Guantánamo had the sole purpose of providing a government location where prisoners of Middle Eastern descent could be held without regard to American law. Here they could be subjected to torture and psychological manipulation by the military and the CIA as part of an interrogation program designed to obtain information at any cost. As with the World War II concentration camps, where innocent people were sometimes held based solely on anonymous tips made by unscrupulous business competitors, jealous suitors, or other predators, many of the prisoners at Guantánamo may be there because someone had a grievance against a neighbor or wanted someone's wife, daughter, or business. When legal proceedings are kept secret, it is easy for life-destroying abuses to occur and for the innocent to be swallowed up by a system that believes that everyone who is imprisoned at Guantánamo is guilty of terrorism simply by virtue of having been brought there.

Incredibly, the interrogation techniques used at Guantánamo were adapted from a 1957 air force study of Chinese Communist techniques used to obtain confessions from American prisoners during the Korean War.[1] Listed as approved techniques were forcing prisoners to stand for long periods of time in extreme weather conditions, housing prisoners in filthy, infested surroundings, the "exploitation of wounds," and sleep deprivation. However, when Guantánamo interrogators were provided with a list of approved torture techniques, they were not advised that the air force study had determined that the Chinese Communist techniques mostly resulted in false confessions. The military demanded confessions, whether they were true or not, just as the North Vietnamese military demanded confessions from captured Americans, whether true or not, during the Vietnam War. Propaganda is the goal of torture, not truth.

Perhaps the most inhumane torture technique used at Guantánamo was waterboarding. It calls for the prisoner to be strapped down on his back, usually with his feet elevated. Typically the prisoner's face is covered with a towel (to collect moisture) or cellophane (to increase breathing difficulty) and water is poured over his face. The result is simulated drowning. The prisoner feels he is about to die. As he chokes on the water, he undergoes a terrifying fear of drowning. Sometimes the technique results in death by heart attack or stroke. Other times it causes long-lasting psychological damage to the prisoner. Tests show that the average length of time that someone can survive waterboarding before saying whatever his torturers want to hear is about twelve seconds.

In late 2008, Vice President Dick Cheney told ABC News and the *Washington Times* that he personally had signed off on waterboarding prisoners at Guantánamo. "Was it torture? I don't believe it was torture," he told ABC News. "The CIA handled itself, I think, very appropriately. They came to us in the administration, talked to me, talked to others in the administration about what they felt they needed to do in order to obtain the intelligence that we believe these people were in possession of."[2]

Apparently the Bush administration was unaware that the Mississippi Supreme Court had outlawed waterboarding in the 1920s, describing it as torture.[3] At that time, it was used routinely to extract information from African Americans accused of crimes. The record shows that it never failed to garner a confession. Whether the accused were innocent or guilty, they always confessed, usually in quick order after the torture began. Typically, the hanging took place within a matter of days. It strains comprehension to think that the Bush administration would adopt the same barbaric torture techniques that a court in the most racially troubled state in the union has defined as torture.

One of the most harshly treated prisoners at Guantánamo was Mohammed al-Qahtani, an al Qaeda suspect from Saudi Arabia who was thought to have been involved in the September 11 attacks. His treatment was straight out of the Chinese handbook. In one session, he was brought to an interrogation booth in shackles and bolted to the floor. His hood was removed, and for forty-eight of the next fifty-four days he was allowed only four hours of sleep a night. At one point he was forced to strip naked and to perform dog tricks while attached to a leash. He was made to wear a bra and thong underwear on his head. He was forced to undergo enemas and ordered to dance with a male interrogator. He was also subjected to a procedure called "invasion of space by female," in which a female interrogator straddled him in a humiliating manner.

Susan Crawford, the retired judge who oversaw the military tribunals at Guantánamo, told the *Washington Post* that Qahtani was tortured to the point where his life was endangered. "For 160 days his only contact was with the interrogators," said Crawford. "Forty-eight of fifty-four consecutive days of 18-to-20-hour interrogations. Standing naked in front of a female agent. Subject to strip searches. And insults to his mother and sister."[4]

The rationale for those techniques, according to Jane Mayer, author of *The Dark Side*, was based on the belief that devote Muslims cannot pray if they feel unclean. One way to make them feel unclean was for them to be touched by non-Muslim women. The thinking was that if they could stop Muslim men from praying, they would come between them and Allah and thus be in a position to break them psychologically to the point where they would tell everything that they knew.

Faced with daily torture, Qahtani eventually confessed. However, eighteen months later the value of his confession was nullified by the confession of a higher-up, Khalid Sheikh Mohammed, who was condescending in his comments about Qahtani. While admitting that Qahtani was selected to help carry out the September 11 attacks, he dismissively described him as someone who was not intelligent enough to be a participant. In *The Dark Side*, Mayer writes that Mohammed had no further use for Qahtani after he failed to talk his way past customs officials. Qahtani knew he was on a suicide mission, but he was given no details. Writes Mayer: "He was brought in near the end as muscle, to round out the numbers on the hijack teams. . . . In other words, the gap-ridden story that Qahtani had told his interrogators, which caused them to disbelieve him and push him to the point of medical emergency and, in the view of some colleagues, criminal excess, had been true from the start."[5]

In May 2008, the Pentagon dismissed charges against Qahtani after officials became concerned that the inhumane treatment he had received in Guantánamo would make it difficult to obtain a conviction. Mohammed's statements about Qahtani's lack of involvement in the attack also raised serious questions about the credibility of the confession. However, in November 2008, the Pentagon announced that it had decided to file new war-crime charges against Qahtani. Explained Colonel Lawrence Morris, chief prosecutor for the army: "His conduct is significant enough that he falls into the category of people who ought to be held accountable by being brought to trial."[6]

Meanwhile, Qahtani was confined to a mattress-size cell from which he was allowed to leave only two or three times a week, usually in the dead of night so that he will not see sunlight. It is a subtle way to induce clinical depression, a mental state that enhances the effectiveness of torture techniques. It is also a way in which to induce a variety of life-threatening diseases, including cancer. Other torture techniques were aimed at Muslim aversion to homosexuality (in some Middle Eastern countries homosexuality is a crime, sometimes punishable by death). To capitalize on that "weakness," the military used homosexual interrogators to insert their fingers in the anuses of prisoners. One prisoner, according to lawyer Zachary Katznelson, had a stick shoved into his rectum.[7]

Tom Wilner, a lawyer with the Washington, D.C., firm of Shearman and Sterling, told author Mahvish Rukhsana Khan that when he first went to Guantánano to represent prisoners in the concentration camp, it was to support basic principles of American jurisprudence, specifically the belief that everyone is entitled to legal representation. However, once he spent time talking to the prisoners, his motivation became more personal as he concluded that most of his clients were innocent.

"It's naïve for us to think that evil is committed only by people who appear like monsters or ogres," he says. "Guantánamo is evil. It's a place where men have been imprisoned for more than five years without charge and without any sort of fair hearing on the basis of only the flimsiest of allegations. . . . The way they've been treated and what they've had to suffer makes me ashamed. It brings shame on our country."[8]

One of the anomalies that Wilner noted in his legal arguments is that while the iguanas in Guantánamo are protected by U.S. law—anyone who inflicts abuse on an iguana can be prosecuted—the prisoners at the camp are considered foreigners outside of U.S. jurisdiction and therefore not protected by U.S. law, a throwback to military philosophy toward Japanese Americans during World War II. It is a philosophy that runs counter to the American belief that it is better to free a guilty suspect than to punish an innocent person. When pondering the effectiveness of Guantánamo, it is helpful to remember that the imprisonment of tens of thousands of Japanese, German, and Italian Americans in concentration camps produced not a single conviction related to sabotage.

"It is a matter of international law that you can intern aliens from hostile nations, and so people say the U.S. is just doing what other countries do," says Karen Ebel, whose father of German heritage lived a nightmare in internment camps. "I guess that's true, but I hold my country to a higher standard. . . . If you were a man, thirty-five, married, with children, and you were taken out of commission for seven years or so, it is very difficult. You go back and there is a stigma. Family lives were destroyed."[9]

For survivors of the World War II concentration camps, Guantánamo is a disturbing reminder of the country's inability to learn from
the past. Notes World War II concentration camp survivor Mitsuye
Yamada: "I don't think we learned anything [from World War II intern-
ments]. There is so little sense of history, a lack of any historical memory. We seem to keep forgetting what happened in the past. I would like
a greater educational component in our schools so that children can
learn what happened before. Our textbooks are still simplified. I think
people need to know the truth of what has gone on so that they will be
more aware."[10]

U.S. representative Bennie Thompson, chairman of the House Committee on Homeland Security, was not impressed by his visit to Guantánamo. He questioned the lack of legal representation that was made available to the prisoners, and he questioned the tactics used to interrogate
them. "It's come out now that those tactics have been outlawed by various
agreements," he says. "For us to do them and then criticize another country that does it is the height of hypocrisy. If those individuals are this bad,
we need to have a trial. We put on our evidence. They should be provided
an adequate defense to say, 'I'm not who you say I am.'" Thompson trusts
the American jury system to make the right decisions when they listen to
cases involving alleged terrorists. "You can't wave the flag of democracy
when it's convenient," he maintains. "You have to wave it all the time."[11]

In many ways Guantánamo was less a destination for suspected foreign terrorists, very few of whom were ever proved to be guilty of any
wrongdoing, than it was a launching pad for an unprecedented assault on
American civil liberties that began forty-five days after the September 11
attacks with passage of the USA Patriot Act by Congress. This controversial legislation increased the power of the federal government to monitor ordinary Americans' e-mail and telephone communications, medical records, library and bookstore records, and bank accounts. It also
provided government agencies with the power to surreptitiously enter a
citizen's home for the purpose of conducting searches of a type that has
traditionally been prohibited on constitutional grounds. The law was set

to expire on December 31, 2005, but instead it was given new life when Congress approved an extension on March 2, 2006.

==

Shortly after the September 11 attack in New York, the INS required nationals from various counties, including Iraq, Iran, Libya, Sudan, Syria, Afghanistan, Algeria, Bahrain, Pakistan, Eritrea, Lebanon, Morocco, North Korea, Oman, Qatar, Somalia, Tunisia, Yemen, and the United Arab Emirates to register with the agency so that they could be interviewed by INS and FBI agents. Failure to register was a serious offense that could result in deportation. Today more than 150 countries are on the registration list.[12]

Pakistani Sadru Noorani escaped registration by virtue of having arrived in the United States prior to 1982, which meant that he had earned amnesty for his illegal entry into the country. A crewman on a Greek merchant ship, Noorani never meant to become an illegal immigrant. It happened when his ship docked in San Diego to unload its cargo and he was granted permission to leave the ship with a few crewmates to eat dinner in a local restaurant and purchase souvenirs to take back home. When he returned, he found that his ship had sailed, stranding him in California. Noorani called a cousin who lived in Chicago and was advised to take a bus there. Once in Chicago, he found work busing tables in a restaurant. Over the next few years, he purchased a downtown gift shop and gained a reputation as a professional interpreter. He became so well known that the *Chicago Tribune* heralded him as an example of a local immigrant who had found success in the city.

As a result of his high profile in the Pakistani community, Noorani was visited often by INS and FBI agents who inquired about certain people. Noorani cooperated by answering their questions. "I welcomed them because I'm clean," he explained to author Tram Nguyen. When FBI agents visited him in the wake of the September 11 attacks, he answered questions about whether he thought anyone in Chicago was involved. Soon he began to have misgivings, primarily because of the lack of feedback he received from the agents. "They don't even send you a thank-you note acknowledging that they ate with you, they drank your water. No response, nothing, and they just disappeared."

Because the United States had been good to him, even if federal agents had not reciprocated his friendship, in 2003 he returned the favor by urging fellow Pakistanis to register with the INS. He really saw no option. If undocumented immigrants failed to register, they could be arrested and then deported. What he didn't understand at the time was that undocumented Pakistani immigrants who did register often were detained and sent to INS concentration camps for processing and then deported. To his dismay, the people he sent in good faith to register with the INS soon were arriving on his doorstep to ask for his help in finding lawyers to fight their deportation.

"Now people are coming back to me and saying, 'You're the one who encouraged us. You're the one who put us in this situation'" Noorani said. "In some cases people even thought I am an agent of the government. . . . As I'm talking my heart is crying. They used to trust me so much. . . . I have love for this country because I have made myself in this country. What I have achieved here would not have been possible in other countries." He paused, perplexed by his dilemma, avoiding eye contact with his interviewer. "Why is this thing happening in this country?"[13]

16

WHICH CAMP WILL YOU SOMEDAY CALL HOME?

One of the most ominous developments since the September 11 attack was a plan that allows the U.S. government to outsource the construction of new concentration camps of the type built during World War II. The camps, which are earmarked to be built on American soil, were not debated in Congress prior to the awarding of a $385 million contract by the Bush administration to Kellogg, Brown and Root (KBR), a subsidiary of Halliburton Company, which Vice President Dick Cheney had headed up before his election. KBR is perhaps the most knowledgeable construction company in the world when it comes to concentration camps, having built the facilities at Guantánamo and high-security prisons throughout Iraq. Under the terms of the contract, construction of the American camps would not begin until such time as there is an immigration "emergency." Meanwhile, KBR was granted nearly a half million dollars a year for "administrative" costs.

Not until news of the contract was published by newspapers did Homeland Security Committee chairman Bennie Thompson learn of the administration's plans, a surprise that inspired him to write a letter to Department of Homeland Security secretary Michael Chertoff asking for information about the contract. Specifically, he asked for a definition of an "immigration emergency." Chertoff's response was provided in a letter that limited an emergency to "humanitarian interventions, mass migrations, populations rapidly arriving in the United States, and other unforeseen situations." It's the latter phrase that gives chills to those who monitor constitutional abuses by government. Chertoff went on to explain that Homeland Security was the only agency that had the power to declare an immigration emergency.

Congressman Thompson was not satisfied with Chertoff's response, since he felt it offered an interpretation that was too broad to prevent abuses of the type witnessed during World War II. Says Thompson: "Obviously that kind of internment doesn't really work and is clearly undemocratic and clearly has no judicial benefit, and from a long-term standpoint does more to harm relationships not just with the people interred but with the people around the world in terms of how we are looked at as a country."[1]

Homeland Security named its secret plan, ENDGAME, a remarkably bad choice of words. The dictionary defines "endgame" as the "final stage of some action or process," wording that is awkwardly similar to Adolf Hitler's "final solution" for the Jews imprisoned in concentration camps during World War II. No one believes that ENDGAME has as its goal the extermination of Muslim Americans, but it is a word choice that demonstrates an incredible lack of knowledge of world history.

"Our people fought vociferously to undo the laws that established the authority to create camps for dissidents," says Aiko Yoshinaga-Herzig. "I thought that we had been successful in doing that, but they have let it happen again. What have we learned from the World War II experiences? We've established new laws allowing things like Guantánamo. I know the Arab Americans are fearful because they are being racially profiled the way we were. If I had changed my name to Johnson, it would not have helped me, because I don't look like a Johnson. I'm sure they are not living comfortably right now and that is a shame."[2]

The problem with secret plans to suspend the Constitution is that there is no way to anticipate who will be on the list. Who did the Bush administration target for its secret plan? Aliens of a half dozen different nationalities? Arab Americans? African Americans? Hispanic Americans? Democrats? Republicans? American journalists? Americans who did not contribute to the election campaigns of those in power? Judges who render decisions that run counter to the master plan? The list is secret, and the possibilities are endless.

Congressman Thompson understands why people are unnerved by the camps, since they could be for anyone. "That's the scary thing," he says, and continues:

> So much of what has happened is being done under the claim of getting ready for the terrorists. A bogeyman scenario. You're almost afraid to ask questions because then you'll be viewed as unpatriotic and put on the list. For someone like myself, to now chair the committee [Homeland Security], it's been a challenge to get information before these occur. A lot of members of Congress read about things like this after the ink is dried on the contract.

For Thompson, an African American Democrat who represents Mississippi's Second District, someone who literally put his life on the line during the rough days of the civil rights movement, the secrecy that was inherent in the Bush administration's "war on terror" was of great concern. During the 1960s, while he was attending Tougaloo College in Jackson, Mississippi, Thompson came under scrutiny from both the Mississippi State Sovereignty Commission, the state's super-secret spy agency during the 1950s and 1960s, and the FBI, because of his strong advocacy of civil rights. One incident that put Thompson under Sovereignty Commission scrutiny occurred in 1971, when he filed a report with the FBI that Mississippi Highway Patrolmen had set up a roadblock and beat several blacks with fists and shotgun butts in an effort to prevent voter registration.[3] He identified twenty-five blacks who had been beaten in that manner, some of whom had their teeth knocked out, with others sustaining serious abdominal injuries. The FBI investigated his complaint but took no action other than to open a file on Thompson.

Once Thompson was elected to Congress, he asked for his FBI files. "They wasted money," he says, shaking his head. "I didn't warrant an FBI file. Let's don't get back in the business of spying on citizens. It has created a climate that we shouldn't have in America." Perhaps as a result of Thompson's personal experiences with abuses of power, the Homeland Security Committee pays close attention to complaints regarding civil liberties as they arise from actions taken by the Department of Homeland Security. Explains Thompson: "We also look at how the Department of Homeland Security does business in general."

Since 2003, the year the Immigration and Customs Enforcement (ICE) division of the Department of Homeland Security was created to investigate illegal immigration, there have been 107 deaths in detention centers, according to information obtained and published by the *New York Times* under the Freedom of Information Act.

In February 2007, an ICE spokesman stonewalled a *New York Times* reporter's queries regarding a dying African man, a fifty-two-year-old Guinean tailor named Boubacar Bah, held in the privately run Elizabeth Detention Center in New Jersey, by saying that he could not check into the case without the man's alien registration number. Once the reporter obtained information under the Freedom of Information Act, she discovered that the spokesman not only knew about the man but also had alerted ICE management officials that the newspaper was conducting an investigation. Instead of providing the information to the public, officials secretly conferred about sending the man back to Africa so that the agency could avoid embarrassing publicity.[4]

Bah's story is chilling in its implications for thousands of other detainees. He was held in an isolation cell without treatment for more than thirteen hours before an ambulance was called for him. Once he arrived at the hospital, he underwent emergency brain surgery that left him in a coma. According to the reporter's story, "Ten agency managers in Washington and Newark conferred by telephone and email about how to avoid the cost of his care and the likelihood of 'increased scrutiny and/or media exposure.'" ICE officials explored the option of sending the unconscious man to Guinea, despite an e-mail message from the supervising deportation officer that warned, "I don't condone removal in his present state as he has a catheter."[5] Instead, ICE officials decided to release the man to cousins in New York despite their protests that they had no way to care for him. Days before the planned release, Bah died.

By 2007 the largest INS concentration camp in the United States was in Raymondville, Texas, a town of fewer than ten thousand people situated in the Rio Grande Valley in the southern tip of the state. Texas was no stranger to concentration camps, having had its share during World War II, but the idea of putting thousands of illegal Hispanic immigrants in a town that already was more than 80 percent Hispanic impressed many observers as unusual, to say the least. "Unusual" does not begin to describe the appearance of the camp. The $65 million city is composed of ten oversized circus tents that are surrounded by a fourteen-foot-high chain-link fence topped by skin-shredding barbed wire. The windowless tents, made of a Kevlar-like material blown into shape with giant fans, are divided into individual pods that each hold about fifty people. The sandy, endlessly flat landscape gives the puffy tents a surreal moon-mission appearance. There are no doors or partitions to separate the five toilets, five sinks, and five showers in each tent. Since there is usually a lack of eating utensils, prisoners often eat with their hands.[6]

The entire spectrum of detention camps, from Guantánamo to immigration detention camps, came under close scrutiny during the 2008 presidential campaign, with both the Democratic candidate, Barack Obama, and the Republican candidate, John McCain, taking similar positions that Guantánamo should be closed. The candidates also took similar positions on outlawing the use of interrogation techniques that cause physical or emotional suffering. Likewise, both candidates backed away from the issue of concentration camps for illegal immigrants, focusing instead on comprehensive immigration reform that would better control illegal immigration and provide means by which illegal immigrants could obtain citizenship or work permits.

Following the 2008 presidential election, in which Obama was elected by a convincing margin, the *New York Times* published the results of a yearlong investigation of a concentration camp located in Central Falls, Rhode Island.[7] The Donald W. Wyatt Detention Facility, the first privately owned detention center in the country, was built to house about six hundred federal prisoners designated by the U.S. Marshals Service as meeting one of three criteria: detainees awaiting trial on immigration charges, detainees awaiting deportation, or detainees awaiting transportation into the Federal Bureau of Prisons. For the most part, the facility's prisoners were individuals who had never been charged with a crime. Rather, they were caught up in the nation's crackdown on illegal immigration, unlucky Hispanic workers without documents. The facility attracted national attention when Hiu Lui Ng, a thirty-four-year-old Chinese computer engineer from New York who had been arrested after he overstayed a visa, died in Wyatt's custody after spending a year in various detention camps.

Despite months of complaints about pain, Ng's cancer went undiagnosed until shortly before his death. Never charged with a crime, he died in a hospital not far from a facility filled with people who were denied basic human rights. After Ng's death became public, there was a demonstration outside the prison, where local pastors and Hispanic advocacy groups demanded an investigation. Watching from a distance, a guard spoke to a reporter of "good, hard-working people" detained in the prison and inexperienced guards "who talk to people with no respect, like they're dogs."[8]

As a result of the publicity, the Wyatt Detention Facility conducted an internal investigation of Ng's death and concluded that while disciplinary action against seven prison employees was justified, there was no evidence that Ng was provided inadequate medical attention.[9] U.S. immigration officials conducted a separate investigation and found that facility supervisors had denied Ng appropriate medical treatment on numerous occasions and once dragged him from his cell to a van as he screamed in pain.

Surveillance videotapes, according to the *New York Times*, told investigators all they needed to know: "At one point, [investigators] wrote, the captain cursed Ng, calling him an idiot, and ordered him to 'stop whining.'" Ng begged for a wheelchair but was told he could not have one. As he screamed, he was pulled from his bed and taken to another part of the prison, where he was shackled. John McConnell Jr, the lawyer representing Ng's family, told reporters that Ng never should have been detained: "The people involved in that torturous treatment should be ashamed of themselves."[10]

The Ng case was only one of many immigration nightmares to greet the new administration. Looming even larger were the detainees at Guantánamo, which Obama had pledged to close by the end of January 2010. To head up the Department of Homeland Security, which has responsibility for the nation's concentration camps, President Obama chose Janet Napolitano, a second-term governor of Arizona who had served as a U.S. attorney during the Clinton administration.

U.S. representative Bennie Thompson met with Napolitano before her Senate confirmation hearings. "Given her ancestry [she is of Italian descent, a group targeted during World War II], I would like to think that the sensitivity of this discussion would be greater with her," he says. "The fact is that the rule of law ought to apply to whatever we do, simply because we are a nation of laws. That should not be a foreign concept for [the Obama administration] to follow. But we will see."

════════════

On January 22, 2009, President Obama made history when he signed an executive order that ended the Central Intelligence Agency's secret overseas prisons, banned coercive interrogation methods, and served notice that the Guantánamo detention camp would be closed within a year. At the ceremony sixteen retired generals and admirals who had fought for a ban on torture stood behind the president and applauded. Noticeably absent were any career CIA officers or retirees. Said the president in a television address: "We believe we can abide by a rule that says, we don't torture, but we can effectively obtain the intelligence we need."

Massachusetts senator John Kerry, chairman of the Senate Foreign Relations Committee, applauded the president's decision, saying, "Today is a great day for the rule of law in the United States of America. . . . America is ready to lead again—not just with our words, but by our example."

Reactions by Republicans were predictable. Michigan congressman Peter Hoekstra, reflecting his party's long-standing support of torture and detention, attitudes developed during World War II and the Vietnam War, complained, "What are we to do with these people, bring them to the very place they hoped to attack: The United States? What do we do with confessed 9/11 mastermind Khalid Sheikh Mohammed and his fellow terrorist conspirators, offer them jail cells in American communities?"[11] It was a disingenuous argument. Homegrown American terrorists, such as Ku Klux Klan members convicted of murdering African Americans, have been held in mainland prisons without difficulty for decades. Did the Dutch-born Hoekstra mean to suggest that American citizens charged or convicted of hate crimes should be shipped to overseas detention centers and tortured to learn more about their activities? One suspects that Hoekstra's comments about the safety of American communities speaks more to his own political ambitions than it does to the reality of the American penal system's ability to serve and protect. Regardless of Hoekstra's reasons for advocating selective torture and detention, it is a position that resonates with a significant percentage of right-wing Americans and should be taken seriously as a harbinger of things to come if the balance of power in America again shifts to the right.

Not affected by President Obama's decision to shut down overseas detention camps such as Guantánamo Bay are twenty-two mainland detention centers acknowledged by the U.S. Immigration and Customs Enforcement division of the Department of Homeland Security.[12] Another eight hundred secret detention centers, many of which were authorized during the George W. Bush administration, are thought to be in place. Many are part of a loose network of federal centers, county jails, and privately run prisons. Some were built with illegal immigrants in mind, but the purpose of the remaining camps has never been made clear. Nor is it clear why new camps still are under contract to be built. That uncertainty has proved to be fertile ground for Internet and talk radio rumor, which in late 2009 had it that the camps would be used for opponents of Obama's foreign and domestic policies.

One of the most vociferous exponents of that theory is former FBI agent Ted Gunderson, who maintains that the federal government has stored thirty thousand guillotines and a half-million caskets for use when it rounds up dissenters.[13] In other words, those who disagree with the president will be sent to concentration camps, where they will be detained until they can be beheaded and their body parts harvested for government use. As absurd as that sounds, it is believed by millions of Americans whose fears are stoked by hate radio and right-wing television commentators.

Such beliefs are the foundation of a new militia movement in America, one dedicated to defending the country from what they call a socialist New World Order. Notes the Southern Poverty Law Center, an Alabama-based civil rights organization that has monitored hate crimes in the United States since 1971: "One big difference from the militia movement of the 1990s is that the face of the federal government—the enemy that almost all parts of the extreme right see as the primary threat to freedom—is now black. And the fact that the president is an African American has injected a strong racial element into even those parts of the radical right, like the militias, that in the past were not primarily motivated by race hate. Contributing to the racial animus have been fears on the far right about the consequences of Latino immigration."[14]

As hate rhetoric escalated throughout 2009, fed mainly by talk radio, Congress felt impotent to deal with the detention camp issue. As it now stands, Congress is convinced it does not have the power to cancel the contracts signed for new concentration camps, since they were issued by the executive branch. Lamented Representative Bennie Thompson, chairman of the Homeland Security Committee: "In my fifteen years in Congress, I have never seen a contract cancelled by Congress. It would take a new president to do that."

President Obama remained oddly silent about the issue in 2009, despite U.S. attorney general Eric Holder's admission that the United States' past policies on internment had left the nation with "some rebuilding to do." Explained Holder: "I think we are strongest when we adhere to what has always made this country great, adhering to the rule of law, following our moral precepts, and we are weakest when we have failed to do that. Great presidents have sometimes deviated from that path. Roosevelt did with regard to the internment of the Japanese."[15]

Not far into 2010, Obama backpedaled on the internment issue, making it clear that the concentration camp at Guantánamo would not be closed within the time frame he had promised. Critics wondered if it ever would be closed. One of the things that sets Guantánamo apart from the camps that imprisoned Native Americans, Japanese Americans, Italian Americans, German Americans, and Jewish immigrants is that Guantánamo was created because of failed government policies in the Middle East and government support of unrestrained corporate adventurism in Arab countries, not because of racism or misplaced fears about certain ethnic groups, or even economic issues based on land acquisition. Concentration camp supporters will argue for Guantánamo's existence for as long as America is under attack from terrorists—and, until such time as U.S. Middle East policy is modified to fit the times and international corporate expansionism is reined in, the attacks will continue, perhaps for several generations.

America's most dangerous threat to individual liberties is failed leadership. Two centuries of concentration camps and torture are not the fault of the innocent victims. It is the fault of leadership that allows bad things to happen to good people during times of crisis.

In Tennessee Williams's *A Streetcar Named Desire*, Blanche DuBois confesses that she has "always depended on the kindness of strangers" to get through life. It makes one wonder if it was the intent of the Founding Fathers to allow our individual liberties to be dependent on the "kindness" of the next president or the president after that. Our core freedoms should have a firmer foundation than presidential whim.

America's tormented past with concentration camps seems destined to repeat itself, again and again, until citizens intervene and demand safeguards to prevent the future establishment of detention centers whose sole purpose is to house people based on skin color or political beliefs or ethnic background or failed government policies overseas. Otherwise, we may awaken one morning in desperate straits, like Blanche DuBois, and discover that our cherished freedoms have been quietly stripped away in the dark of night because we entrusted them to the wrong stranger.

ACKNOWLEDGMENTS

I would like to thank Aiko Yoshinaga-Herzig; Mitsuye Yamada; Ted Eckardt, Doris Berg Nye, Karen Ebel, and the German American Internee Coalition; U.S. representative Bennie Thompson; Hodding Carter III, for permission to reprint his father's prize-winning editorial; Charlie Blanks at the William Alexander Percy Library; Jimmy Bryant and Heidi Reutter at the University of Central Arkansas; Brian Niiya, Resource Center Director, Japanese Cultural Center of Hawaii; the staff at the Memphis/Shelby County Public Library; the Jean and Alexander Heard Library at Vanderbilt University; staff at the Mississippi Department of Archives and History; the staff at the Nashville and Davidson County Public Library; Christina Brianik, Rutgers University Press; Julie Gardham, Special Collections librarian, University of Glasgow Library; Mary Kravenas and Devon Freeny at Chicago Review Press; and my assistants, Allie and Mattie.

NOTES

Introduction

1. Ashley F. Jespersen, Martin L. Lalumiere, and Michael Seto, "Sexual Abuse History Among Adult Sex Offenders and Non-sex Offenders: A Meta-analysis," *Child Abuse and Neglect* 33 (2009). The study concluded that "there is support for the sexually abused–sexual abuser hypothesis, in that sex offenders are more likely to have been sexually abused than non-sex offenders."

Prologue

1. James Turner, *Memoirs of His Own Life and Times* (repr. Edinburgh: Bannatyne Club, 1829). Regarding the degree, Turner wrote in his memoir: "It is both a disgrace to learning, and a hindrance to trades and other callings, that such as are grossly ignorant and unfit for any profession in letters be honoured with any degree or public testimony of learning; it is therefore earnestly recommended to the Faculty of Arts that such trial be taken of students especially of magistrands [sic], before the time of laureation [sic], so that those who are found altogether unworthy be not admitted to the degree and honor of Masters."
2. William McDowall, *History of the Burgh of Domfries* (Edinburgh: Adam and Charles Black, 1867).
3. Ibid.

4. Sir James Turner, *Pallas Armata: Military Essayes of the Ancient Grecian, Roman, and Modern Art of War* (London, 1683).

5. P. Hume Brown, *History of Scotland: From the Accession of Mary Stewart to the Revolution of 1689* (New York: Octagon Books, 1971).

6. Ibid; Rev. Archibald Stewart, *History Vindicated in the Case of the Wigtown Martyrs*, 2nd ed. (Edinburgh: Edmonston and Douglas, 1869).

7. Stephen Turner journal and other family records.

1. The Economics of Torture and Internment

1. Wilcomb D. Washburn, "Indians and the American Revolution," AmericanRevolution.org, www.americanrevolution.org/ind1.html.

2. James H. O'Donnell III, *Southern Indians in the American Revolution* (Knoxville: University of Tennessee Press, 1973).

3. Theda Perdue and Michael D. Green, eds., *The Cherokee Removal: A Brief History with Documents* (Boston: Bedford Books of St. Martin's Press, 1995).

4. Ibid.

5. Journals of Governors Winthrop Sargent and William Charles Cole Claiborne, Mississippi Territorial Archives.

6. H. B. Cushman, *History of the Choctaw, Chickasaw and Natchez Indians* (Norman: University of Oklahoma Press, 1999).

7. Perdue and Green, *The Cherokee Removal*.

8. Ibid.

9. Mississippi Band of Choctaw Indians, "Treaty of Dancing Rabbit Creek," www.choctaw.org/History/Treaties/treaty9.html.

2. Walking the Trail of Tears

1. John S. D. Eisenhower, *Agents of Destiny: The Life and Times of General Winfield Scott* (Norman, OK: University of Oklahoma Press, 1997).

2. Ibid.

3. Ibid.

4. As the 1830s began, America's five "Civilized Tribes"—the Choctaw, Chickasaw, Seminole, Creek, and Cherokee—so-called because they

adopted European traditions such as a written language and European styles of dress, and because they converted to European sects of Christianity, were targeted by the government under the terms of the Indian Removal Act. The Choctaw and Chickasaw were the first to be driven off their land, followed by the Creek and the Seminole of Florida. The Cherokee were saved for last.

5. Lieutenant General Winfield Scott, *Memoirs* (New York: Sheldon, 1864).

6. Vicki Rozmea, ed., *Voices from the Trail of Tears* (Winston-Salem, NC: John F. Blair, 2003).

7. Fort Smith National Historic Site, "Cherokee Round Up," National Park Service, www.nps.gov/fosm/historyculture/cherokee-round-up.htm.

8. Theda Perdue and Michael D. Green, eds., *The Cherokee Removal: A Brief History with Documents* (Boston: Bedford Books of St. Martin's Press, 1995).

9. Ibid.

10. Randy Golden, "Cherokee Removal Forts," About North Georgia, www.ngeorgia.com/history/nghisttt.html.

11. Cherokee Heritage Trails, "Sites in RedClay: Fort Cass and the Cherokee Internment Camps," www.cherokeeheritagetrails.org.

12. Perdue and Green, *The Cherokee Removal*.

13. John Ehle, *Trail of Tears: The Rise and Fall of the Cherokee Nation* (1988; New York: Anchor Books, 1989).

14. Stephen Turner journal and other family records.

15. Stephen Turner journal.

3. Pearl Harbor Under Attack

1. Doris Berg Nye, interview by the author, 2008. Subsequent unattributed quotations from Berg Nye are from this interview.

2. Gordon W. Prange, *At Dawn We Slept: The Untold Story of Pearl Harbor* (New York: Penguin Books, 1981).

3. Ibid.

4. Ibid.

5. Originally published in two volumes by the U.S. Government Printing Office in 1982 and 1983, the report of the Commission on

Wartime Relocation and Internment of Civilians was republished in 1997 by the Civil Liberties Public Education Fund and the University of Washington Press, using the title *Personal Justice Denied*. Commission on Wartime Relocation and Internment of Civilians, *Personal Justice Denied* (Seattle: University of Washington Press, 1997).

6. Ibid.

7. Ibid.

8. Tetsuden Kashima, *Judgment Without Trial* (Seattle: University of Washington Press, 2004).

9. Emmy E. Werner, *Through the Eyes of Innocents: Children Witness World War II* (Boulder, CO: Westview, 2000).

10. Doris Berg, *The Written Recollections of Doris Berg* (July 15, 2008), used with permission.

11. Ibid.

4. Executive Order 9066

1. Greg Robinson, *By Order of the President: FDR and the Internment of Japanese Americans* (Cambridge, MA: Harvard University Press, 2001).

2. Ibid.

3. Commission on Wartime Relocation and Internment of Civilians, *Personal Justice Denied* (Seattle: University of Washington Press, 1997).

4. Lt. General J. L. DeWitt, *Final Report: Japanese Evacuation from the West Coast, 1942* (Washington, DC: GPO, 1943), available online at Virtual Museum of the City of San Francisco, www.sfmuseum.org/war/dewitt1.html.

5. Attorney General Francis Biddle, memorandum to President Franklin D. Roosevelt, January 30, 1942, JERS, reel 7, Bancroft Library, University of California, Berkeley.

6. James A. Michener, introduction to *Years of Infamy: The Untold Story of America's Concentration Camps* by Michi Nishiura Weglyn (1976; Seattle: University of Washington Press, 1996).

7. Smithsonian Center for Education and Museum Studies, "Letters from the Japanese American Internment," Smithsonian Institution,

www.smithsonianeducation.org/educators/lesson_plans/
japanese_internment/index.html.

8. Attorney General Francis Biddle, "Luncheon Conference with the President," memorandum, February 7, 1942, CWRIC 5750, Biddle Papers, Franklin Delano Roosevelt Library, Hyde Park, NY; Commission on Wartime Relocation and Internment of Civilians, *Personal Justice Denied*.

9. Francis Biddle, *In Brief Authority* (New York: Doubleday, 1962).

10. Commission on Wartime Relocation and Internment of Civilians, *Personal Justice Denied*.

11. *San Francisco News*. "New Order on Aliens Awaited." March 2, 1942.

12. *San Francisco News*, "First Japanese Ready to Leave Coast," March 19, 1942.

13. *San Francisco News*, "FBI Rounds Up More Japanese," March 18, 1942.

14. *San Francisco News*, "Japanese on West Coast Face Wholesale Uprooting," March 4, 1942.

15. *San Francisco News*, "Jap Farm Land Is Transferred," April 3, 1942, from an interview with FSA regional director L. T. Hewes.

16. Testimony in *Personal Justice Denied* by Commission on Wartime Relocation and Internment of Civilians.

17. Ibid.

18. Ibid.

19. Ibid.

20. Ibid.

21. Ibid.

22. Carey McWilliams, *Prejudice: Japanese Americans; Symbols of Racial Intolerance* (Boston: Little, Brown, 1944).

23. Michi Nishiura Weglyn, *Years of Infamy: The Untold Story of America's Concentration Camps* (1976; Seattle: University of Washington Press, 1996).

24. Commission on Wartime Relocation and Internment of Civilians, *Personal Justice Denied*.

25. Ibid.

26. Red Cross Survey of Assembly Centers, in *Personal Justice Denied* by Commission on Wartime Relocation and Internment of Civilians.

27. War Relocation Authority, *Relocation of Japanese Americans* (Washington, DC: War Relocation Authority, 1943), available online at Virtual Museum of the City of San Francisco, www.sfmuseum.org/hist10/relocbook.html.
28. Smithsonian Center for Education and Museum Studies, "Letters from the Japanese American Internment."
29. Ibid.
30. Clara E. Breed, "All but Blind," *Library Journal*, February 1, 1943.
31. Claire Sprague, "Letter of the Week," *Saturday Evening Post*, August 15, 1942, Claire D. Sprague Collection, University of the Pacific.
32. Mitsuye Yamada, interview by the author, 2008. Subsequent unattributed quotations from Yamada are from this interview.

5. Manzanar's Gateway to Hell

1. Aiko Yoshinaga-Herzig, interview by the author, 2008. Subsequent unattributed quotations from Yoshinaga-Herzig are from this interview.
2. Commission on Wartime Relocation and Internment of Civilians, *Personal Justice Denied* (Seattle: University of Washington Press, 1997).
3. Thomas D. Campbell, memorandum to Assistant Secretary of War John McCloy, February 25, 1942, Franklin Delano Roosevelt Library, Hyde Park, NY.
4. Commission on Wartime Relocation and Internment of Civilians, *Personal Justice Denied*.
5. Jeanne Wakatsuki Houston and James Houston, *Farewell to Manzanar* (Boston: Houghton Mifflin, 2002).
6. Ibid.
7. John Tateishi, *And Justice for All: An Oral History of the Japanese American Detention Camps* (Seattle: University of Washington Press, 1984).
8. Ibid
9. William Minoru Hohri, *Repairing America: An Account of the Movement for Japanese-American Redress*, (Pullman: Washington State University Press, 1988).

10. Commission on Wartime Relocation and Internment of Civilians, *Personal Justice Denied*.

11. Renee Tawa, "Childhood Lost: The Orphans of Manzanar," *Los Angeles Times*, March 11, 1997.

12. Ibid.

13. Testimony in *Personal Justice Denied* by Commission on Wartime Relocation and Internment of Civilians.

14. Emmy E. Werner, *Through the Eyes of Innocents: Children Witness World War II* (Boulder, CO: Westview, 2000).

15. Ibid.

16. Tawa, "Childhood Lost."

17. *Manzanar Free Press*, April 11, 1942, www.nps.gov/archive/manz/ MFP/mfp-v1-n1.htm.

18. *Manzanar Free Press*, August 3, 1942, in *Remembering Manzanar: Life in a Japanese Relocation Camp* by Michael L. Cooper (New York: Clarion Books, 2002).

19. Commission on Wartime Relocation and Internment of Civilians, *Personal Justice Denied*.

20. John Tateishi, "Memories from Behind Barbed Wire," in *Last Witnesses: Reflections on the Wartime Internment of Japanese Americans*, ed. Erica Harth (New York: Palgrave Macmillan, 2001).

21. Ibid.

22. Ibid.

23. Commission on Wartime Relocation and Internment of Civilians, *Personal Justice Denied*.

24. Testimony, August 6, 1981, in *Personal Justice Denied* by Commission on Wartime Relocation and Internment of Civilians.

25. *Manzanar Free Press*, March 20, 1943, www.nps.gov/archive/manz/ mfp/mfp-v3-n23b.htm.

6. Life in an Arkansas Swamp

1. Aiko Yoshinaga-Herzig, interview by the author, 2008. Subsequent unattributed quotations from Yoshinaga-Herzig are from this interview.

2. The Arkansas Delta is almost as famous as the Mississippi when it comes to the blues—Sonny Boy Williamson II, Robert Junior Lockwood, *King Biscuit Time* radio show in Helena, to name a few.

3. John Tateishi, *And Justice for All: An Oral History of the Japanese American Detention Camps* (Seattle: University of Washington Press, 1984).

4. Marielle Tsukamoto, interview by fifth-grade students at Barbara Comstock Morse Elementary School, n.d., American Memory, Library of Congress, http://memory.loc.gov/learn/lessons/99/fear/interview.html.

5. Tateishi, *And Justice for All.*

6. Jeffery F. Burton et al., "Confinement and Ethnicity: An Overview of World War II Japanese American Relocation Sites," *Publications in Anthropology* 74 (1999, rev. July 2000): www.nps.gov/history/history/online_books/anthropology74/ce7.htm.

7. War Relocation Authority, "Riots, Strikes, and Disturbances in Japanese Relocation Centers," memorandum, 1943, Internment Archives, www.internmentarchives.com/showdoc.php?docid=00073.

8. Ibid.

9. Ibid.

10. Commission on Wartime Relocation and Internment of Civilians, *Personal Justice Denied* (Seattle: University of Washington Press, 1997).

11. George Takei, *To the Stars: The Autobiography of George Takei* (New York: Pocket Books, 1994).

12. Ibid.

13. Ibid.

14. Ibid.

15. Ibid.

16. Ruth Asawa's official Web site, "Internment," www.ruthasawa.com/internment.html.

17. Ibid.

18. Ibid.

19. Merill R. Pritchell and William L. Shea, "The Enemy in Mississippi (1943–1946)," *Journal of Mississippi History* 41 (November 1979).

20. Paul V. Canonici, *The Delta Italians* ([Madison, MS]: P. V. Canonici, 2003).

21. *Delta Democrat-Times*, "German Prisoners Arrive in City for Cotton Picking Job," October 4, 1943.

22. Associated Press, "Delta Planter's Wife Held After Flight with German POW," published in *Delta Democrat-Times*, January 6, 1946.

23. Ann Waldron, *Hodding Carter: The Reconstruction of a Racist* (Chapel Hill, NC: Algonquin Books, 1993).

7. Eastward Ho to the Wild, Wild West

1. Mitsuye Yamada, interview by the author, 2008. Subsequent unattributed quotations from Yamada are from this interview.

2. Testimony in *Personal Justice Denied* by Commission on Wartime Relocation and Internment of Civilians (Seattle: University of Washington Press, 1997); William Minoru Hohri, *Repairing America: An Account of the Movement for Japanese-American Redress* (Pullman: Washington State University Press, 1988).

3. Ibid.

4. Ibid.

5. *All Things Considered*, "Internment Camp Survivor Gets Honorary Degree," National Public Radio, May 16, 2008.

6. Governor Ralph Carr, letter to Dr. Rufus C. Baker, April 21, 1942, available online at "Documents from Colorado Governor Ralph Carr's Administration," Colorado Department of Personnel and Administration, www.colorado.gov/dpa/doit/archives/wwcod/granada4.htm.

7. Governor Ralph Carr, letter to U.S. Attorney Thomas J. Morrissey, June or July 1942, available online at "Documents from Colorado Governor Ralph Carr's Administration."

8. Ibid.

9. Governor Ralph Carr, address before joint session of the Colorado legislature, January 8, 1943, available online at "Documents from Colorado Governor Ralph Carr's Administration."

10. Santa Fe Trail Scenic and Historic Byway Mountain Branch Web site, "Camp Amache," www.santafetrailscenicandhistoricbyway.org/amache.html.

11. Estelle Ishigo, *Lone Heart Mountain* (Los Angeles: Anderson, Ritchie and Simon, 1972). Manuscript at Department of Special Collections, University of California at Los Angeles Library.

12. Ibid.

13. Tom Brokaw, *The Greatest Generation* (New York: Random House, 1998).

14. Naomi Hirahara, *An American Son: The Story of George Aratani* (Los Angeles: Japanese American National Museum, 2001).

15. Ibid.

16. Ibid.

17. Eleanor Roosevelt, "A Challenge to American Sportsmanship, *Collier's*, October 16, 1943.

18. Ibid.

19. Commission on Wartime Relocation and Internment of Civilians, *Personal Justice Denied*.

20. Robert Maeda, "Isamu Noguchi: 5-7-A, Poston, Arizona," in *Last Witness: Reflections on the Wartime Internment of Japanese Americans*, ed. Erica Harth (New York: Palgrave Macmillan, 2001).

21. Ibid.

22. Michael Brenson, obituary of Isamu Noguchi, *New York Times*, December 31, 1988.

23. Commission on Wartime Relocation and Internment of Civilians, *Personal Justice Denied*.

24. Elmer Davis, memorandum to President Franklin D. Roosevelt, October 2, 1942, CWRIC 13755, record group 407, National Archives, Washington, DC.

25. Secretary of War Henry L. Stimson, memorandum to Chief of Staff George C. Marshall, CWRIC 13753, record group 407, National Archives.

26. Commission on Wartime Relocation and Internment of Civilians, *Personal Justice Denied*.

27. Ibid.

28. Ibid.

29. Testimony in *Personal Justice Denied* by Commission on Wartime Relocation and Internment of Civilians.

30. John Tateishi, *And Justice for All: An Oral History of the Japanese American Detention Camps* (Seattle: University of Washington Press, 1984).

31. George Takei, *To the Stars: The Autobiography of George Takei* (New York: Pocket Books, 1994).

32. Ibid.

33. Testimony in *Personal Justice Denied* by Commission on Wartime Relocation and Internment of Civilians.

34. Ibid.

35. Ibid.

36. Attorney General Francis Biddle, memorandum to President Franklin D. Roosevelt, November 10, 1943, box 76, President's Secretary File (Justice Department) 194101944, Franklin Delano Roosevelt Library, Hyde Park, NY.

37. Michi Nishiura Weglyn, *Years of Infamy: The Untold Story of America's Concentration Camps* (1976; Seattle: University of Washington Press, 1996).

38. Tule Lake Committee official Web site, "History of Tule Lake Concentration Camp and the Pilgrimages," www.tulelake.org/history.html.

8. The Konzentrationslager Blues

1. Karen Ebel, "Max Ebel: A German Immigrant's Story," German American Internee Coalition, March 2006, www.gaic.info/real_ebel .html.

2. Testimony in *Personal Justice Denied* by Commission on Wartime Relocation and Internment of Civilians (Seattle: University of Washington Press, 1997).

3. John Christgau. *Enemies: World War II Alien Internment* (1985; New York: Authors Choice Press, 2001).

4. Ibid.

5. Ibid.

6. FBI official Web site, "History of the FBI: World War II Period," www.fbi.gov/libref/historic/history/worldwar.htm.

7. Commission on Wartime Relocation and Internment of Civilians, *Personal Justice Denied*.

8. Karen Ebel, interview by the author, 2008. Subsequent unattributed quotations from Ebel are from this interview.

9. Rose Marie Neupert, "The Neupert Family Story," German American Internee Coalition, March 2006, www.gaic.info/real_neupert.html.

10. Ted Eckardt, interview by the author, 2008. Subsequent unattributed quotations from Eckardt are from this interview.

11. Arthur D. Jacobs, *The Prison Called Hohenasperg: An American Boy Betrayed by his Government During World War II* (n.p.: Universal Publishers, 1999).

12. Christgau, *Enemies*.

13. Ibid.

9. Italian Americans Dodge a Bullet

1. Francis Biddle, *In Brief Authority* (New York: Doubleday, 1962).

2. Ibid.

3. Curt Gentry, *J. Edgar Hoover: The Man and the Secrets* (New York: Plume, 1991).

4. Sanford J. Ungar, *FBI* (Boston: Atlantic Monthly Press, 1976); Gentry, *J. Edgar Hoover*.

5. Thomas H. Flaherty, ed., *Mafia* (New York: Time-Life Books, 1993).

6. Tim Newark, *Mafia Allies: The True Story of America's Secret Alliance with the Mob in World War II* (St. Paul, MN: Zenith Press, 2007).

7. Dennis Eisenberg, Uri Dan, and E. Landau, *Meyer Lanksy: Mogul of the Mob* (New York: Paddinton Press, 1979).

8. Ibid.

9. Commission on Wartime Relocation and Internment of Civilians, *Personal Justice Denied* (Seattle: University of Washington Press, 1997).

10. U.S. Department of Justice, *A Review of the Restrictions on Persons of Italian Ancestry During World War II*, report to Congress, November 2001, www.justice.gov/crt/Italian_Report.pdf.

11. Ibid.

12. Ezio Pinza and Robert Magidoff, *Ezio Pinza: An Autobiography* (New York: Rinehart, 1958).

13. Ibid.

14. Ibid.

15. Stephen Fox, *UnCivil Liberties: Italian Americans Under Siege During World War II* (Boca Raton, FL: Universal Publishers, 2000).

16. According to the U.S. Department of Agriculture, the selling price of chicken in 1939–1940 was 53 cents per chicken. Agricultural Marketing Service, *Farm Productivity, Farm Disposition and Income: Chickens and Eggs, 1939–1940* (Washington, DC: U.S. Department of Agriculture, 1941).

17. Fox, *UnCivil Liberties*.

18. Ibid.

19. Ibid.

20. Commission on Wartime Relocation and Internment of Civilians, *Personal Justice Denied*.

21. Ibid.

22. Department of Justice, *Review of the Restrictions on Persons of Italian Ancestry*.

23. Lucetta Berizzi Drypolcher, "Orders to Take Him Away," in *Una Storia Segreta: The Secret History of Italian American Evacuation and Internment During World War II*, ed. Lawrence DiStasi (Berkeley, CA: Heyday Books, 2001).

24. Ibid.

25. House of Representatives of the State of New Hampshire, *A Resolution on Treatment of Italian American Citizens During World War II*, petition laid before the U.S. Senate, *Congressional Record* 149, no. 128, daily ed. (September 17, 2003).

10. Jews Turned Away from a New Promised Land

1. Henry L. Feingold, *The Politics of Rescue: The Roosevelt Administration and the Holocaust, 1938–1945* (New York: Holocaust Library, 1970).

2. David S. Wyman, *The Abandonment of the Jews: America and the Holocaust* (New York: New Press, 1984).

3. John Rankin, *Congressional Record*, April 23, 1952.

4. Wyman, *The Abandonment of the Jews*.

5. Harold Ickes Diaries, 7053-4, Library of Congress.

6. Saul S. Friedman, *No Haven for the Oppressed: United States Policy Toward Jewish Refugees, 1938–1945* (Detroit: Wayne State University Press, 1973).

7. Ruth Gruber, *Haven: The Dramatic Story of 1,000 World War II Refugees and How They Came to America* (1983; 1984; New York: Three Rivers Press, 2000).

8. Ibid.

9. Carole Garbuny Vogel, "Oswego, New York: Wartime Haven for Jewish Refuges," *Avotaynu*, winter 1998.

10. Wyman, *Abandonment of the Jews.*

11. Gruber, *Haven.*

12. Ibid.

13. E. H. Crump, letter to Kenneth McKellar, May 22, 1944, Kenneth McKellar Collection, Memphis and Shelby County Public Library.

11. Finding Redemption in a Troubled Land

1. *Time*, "One of the Rest," March 13, 1950.

2. Tad Ichinokuchi and Daniel Aiso, *John Aiso and the M.I.S.: Japanese-American Soldiers in the Military Intelligence Service, World War II* (Los Angeles: Military Intelligence Service Club of Southern California, 1988).

3. John Nyberg, "3,500 Minnesota-Trained Nisei Act as 'Eyes, Ears,'" *Minneapolis Star-Journal*, October 22, 1945.

4. Commission on Wartime Relocation and Internment of Civilians, *Personal Justice Denied* (Seattle: University of Washington Press, 1997).

5. Dorothy Matsuo, *Boyhood to War* (n.p.: Mutual Publishing Co., 1992).

6. Tanaka, Chester, *Go for Broke: A Pictorial History of the Japanese American 100th Infantry Battalion and 442nd Regimental Combat Team* (Richmond, CA: Go for Broke, 1982).

7. Selective Service System, *Special Groups*, Special Monograph no. 10, vol 1.

8. Daniel Inouye, *Journey to Washington* (New York: Prentice-Hall, 1967).

9. MedalofHonor.com, biography of Daniel Inouye, www.medalofhonor.com/DanielInouye.htm. This Web site is no longer available but is archived at Internet Archive, http://web.archive .org/web/20071027082945/http://www.medalofhonor.com/ DanielInouye.htm.

10. John Tateishi, *And Justice for All: An Oral History of the Japanese American Detention Camps* (Seattle: University of Washington Press, 1984).

11. Ibid.

12. Ibid.

13. *Delta Democrat-Times*, "Go for Broke," August 27, 1945. Reprinted with permission.

14. How the Pulitzer committee learned of Hodding Carter's award-winning editorial became a subject of controversy when a member of the committee said that the editorial had not been formally submitted and he had discovered the editorial on his own. In a conversation with John Gibson in the mid-1970s, the author of this book heard a credible account from Gibson of the process he went through in submitting the editorials.

15. Hodding Carter, editorial, *Delta Democrat-Times*, July 26, 1945.

16. Ann Waldron, *Hodding Carter: The Reconstruction of a Racist* (Chapel Hill, NC: Algonquin Books, 1993).

12. Prisoner, Go Home!

1. Commission on Wartime Relocation and Internment of Civilians, *Personal Justice Denied* (Seattle: University of Washington Press, 1997).

2. Doris Berg Nye, interview by the author, 2008. Subsequent unattributed quotations from Berg Nye are from this interview.

3. Mitsuye Yamada, interview by the author, 2008. Subsequent unattributed quotations from Mitsuye Yamada are from this interview.

4. Mitsuye Yamada, "Legacy of Silence," in *Last Witnesses: Reflections on the Wartime Internment of Japanese Americans*, ed. Erica Harth (New York: Palgrave Macmillan, 2001).

5. Ibid.

6. Aiko Yoshinaga-Herzig, interview by the author, 2008. Subsequent unattributed quotations from Yoshinaga-Herzig are from this interview.

7. Naomi Hirahara, *An American Son: The Story of George Aratani* (Los Angeles: Japanese American National Museum, 2001).

8. Ibid.

9. Estelle Ishigo, *Lone Heart Mountain* (Los Angeles: Anderson, Ritchie and Simon, 1972).

10. Ibid.

11. Rose Marie Neupert, "The Neupert Family Story," German American Internee Coalition, March 2006, www.gaic.info/real_neupert.html.

12. Karen Ebel, interview by the author, 2008. Subsequent unattributed quotations from Ebel are from this interview.

13. Commission on Wartime Relocation and Internment of Civilians, *Personal Justice Denied.*

14. Ruth Gruber, *Haven: The Dramatic Story of 1,000 World War II Refugees and How They Came to America* (1983; 1984; New York: Three Rivers Press, 2000).

15. Ibid.

16. Claudia Rowe, "59 Years Ago, They Fled to an Internment Camp," *New York Times*, July 21, 2003.

17. Ibid.

13. Righting the Wrongs

1. Commission on Wartime Relocation and Internment of Civilians, *Personal Justice Denied* (Seattle: University of Washington Press, 1997).

2. Testimony in *Personal Justice Denied* by Commission on Wartime Relocation and Internment of Civilians.

3. *Korematsu v. United States*, 323 U.S. 214 (1944).

4. Ibid.

5. Aiko Yoshinaga-Herzig, interview by the author, 2008. Subsequent unattributed quotations from Yoshinaga-Herzig are from this interview.

6. Commission on Wartime Relocation and Internment of Civilians, *Personal Justice Denied*.

7. Lawson Fuscao Inada, *Only What We Could Carry: The Japanese American Internment Experience* (Berkeley, CA: Heyday Books, 2000).

8. U.S. National Archives and Records Administration, "About the Redress Program," www.archives.gov/research/japanese-americans/redress.html.

9. Erica Harth, ed., *Last Witnesses: Reflections on the Wartime Internment of Japanese Americans* (New York: Palgrave Macmillan, 2001).

10. Bill Clinton, letter to victims of internment, October 1, 1993, available online at "Internment History," Children of the Camps Project, PBS, www.pbs.org/childofcamp/history/clinton.html.

11. U.S. Department of Justice, *A Review of the Restrictions on Persons of Italian Ancestry During World War II*, report to Congress, November 2001, www.justice.gov/crt/Italian_Report.pdf.

12. Ibid.

13. Ibid.

14. Russ Feingold, "Remarks of U.S. Senator Russ Feingold on the Wartime Treatment Study Act Amendment to the Comprehensive Immigration Reform Act," press release, May 24, 2007, http://feingold.senate.gov/record.cfm?id=309706.

15. Ibid.

14. Modern-Day Internment

1. The quotes and story line of the young African woman's experiences were gleaned from Mark Dow's excellent book *American Gulag: Inside U.S. Immigration Prisons* (Berkeley, CA: University of California Press, 2004).

15. "Why Is This Thing Happening in This Country?"

1. Scott Shane, "China Inspired Interrogations at Guantánamo," *New York Times*, July 2, 2008.

2. Jason Leopold, "Cheney Admits He 'Signed Off' on Waterboarding of Three Guantánamo Prisoners," *Online Journal*, December 29, 2008, www.onlinejournal.com/artman/publish/article_4170.shtml.

3. Alex A. Alston and James L. Dickerson, *Devil's Sanctuary: An Eye-Witness History of Mississippi Hate Crimes* (Chicago: Lawrence Hill Books, 2009); *Fisher v. State*, 145 Miss. 116, 127, 110 So. 361 (1926) and *White v. State*, 129 Miss. 182, 187, 91 So. 903 (1922).

4. Bob Woodward, "Detainee Tortured, Says U.S. Official," *Washington Post*, January 14, 2009.

5. Jane Mayer, *The Dark Side: The Inside Story of How the War on Terror Turned into a War on American Ideals* (New York: Doubleday, 2008).

6. William Glaberson, "Detainee Will Face New War-Crimes Charges," *New York Times*, November 19, 2008.

7. Mahvish Rukhsana Khan, *My Guantánamo Diary: The Detainees and the Stories They Told Me* (New York: Public Affairs, 2008).

8. Ibid.

9. Karen Ebel, interview by the author, 2008.

10. Mitsuye Yamada, interview by the author, 2008.

11. U.S. representative Bennie Thompson, interview by the author, 2008.

12. Migration Policy Institute, "'Special Registration' Program," Migration Information Source, April 2003, www.migrationinformation.org/USFocus/display.cfm?ID=116.

13. The quotes from Sadru Noorani and the background information can be found in Tram Nguyen's *We Are All Suspects Now* (Boston: Beacon Press, 2005).

16. Which Camp Will You Someday Call Home?

1. U.S. representative Bennie Thompson, interview by the author, 2008. Subsequent unattributed quotations from Thompson are from this interview.

2. Aiko Yoshinaga-Herzig, interview by the author, 2008.

3. Davis Smith, "Bolton Black Says Beatings Occurred," *Jackson Daily News*, June 11, 1971.

4. Nina Bernstein, "Officials Hid Truth About Immigrant Deaths in Jail," *New York Times*, January 10, 2010.

5. Ibid.

6. Spencer S. Hsu and Sylvia Morena, "Border Policy's Success Strains Resources," *Washington Post*, February 2, 2007.

7. Nina Bernstein, "City of Immigrants Fills Jail Cells with Its Own," *New York Times*, December 27, 2008.

8. Ibid.

9. Wyatt Detention Facility, "Wyatt Detention Facility Statement Re Internal Investigation of Detainee Death," Reuters, January 8, 2009.

10. Nina Bernstein, "U.S. Agency Issues Scathing Report on Death of Immigrant in Its Custody," *New York Times*, January 16, 2009.

11. Scott Shane, "Obama Orders Secret Prison and Detention Camps Closed," *New York Times*, January 23, 2009.

12. U.S. Immigration and Customs Enforcement, "Immigration Detention Facilities," www.ice.gov/pi/dro/facilities.htm.

13. Steven Thomma, "Secret Camps and Guillotines? Groups Make Birthers Look Sane," McClatchy Newspapers, August 28, 2009, www.mcclatchydc.com/2009/08/28/74549/secret-camps-and-guillotines-groups.html.

14. Larry Keller, "The Second Wave: Evidence Grows of Far-Right Militia Resurgence," *Intelligence Report* 135 (Fall 2009): www.splcenter.org/get-informed/intelligence-report/browse-all-issues/2009/fall/the-second-wave.

15. Daniel Klaidman, "Eric Holder, Jr.," *Newsweek*, December 28, 2009.

BIBLIOGRAPHY

Books

Alston, Alex A., and James L. Dickerson. *Devil's Sanctuary: An Eyewitness History of Mississippi Hate Crimes*. Chicago: Lawrence Hill Books, 2009.

Biddle, Francis. *In Brief Authority*. New York: Doubleday, 1962.

Brokaw, Tom. *The Greatest Generation*. New York: Random House, 1998.

Brown, P. Hume. *History of Scotland: From the Accession of Mary Stewart to the Revolution of 1689*. New York: Octagon Books, 1971.

Canonici, Paul V. *The Delta Italians*. [Madison, MS]: P. V. Canonici, 2003.

Christgau, John. *Enemies: World War II Alien Internment*. New York: Authors Choice Press, 2001. Previously published 1985.

Commission on Wartime Relocation and Internment of Civilians. *Personal Justice Denied*. Seattle: University of Washington Press, 1997.

Cooper, Michael L. *Remembering Manzanar: Life in a Japanese Relocation Camp*. New York: Clarion Books, 2002.

Cushman, H. B. *History of the Choctaw, Chickasaw and Natchez Indians*. Norman: University of Oklahoma Press, 1999.

Dow, Mark. *American Gulag: Inside U.S. Immigration Prisons*. Berkeley, CA: University of California Press, 2004.

Drypolcher, Lucetta Berizzi. "Orders to Take Him Away." In *Una Storia Segreta: The Secret History of Italian American Evacuation and Internment During World War II*, edited by Lawrence DiStasi. Berkeley, CA: Heyday Books, 2001.

Ehle, John. *Trail of Tears: The Rise and Fall of the Cherokee Nation.* New York: Anchor Books, 1989. First published 1988.

Eisenberg, Dennis, Uri Dan, and E. Landau. *Meyer Lanksy: Mogul of the Mob.* New York: Paddington Press, 1979.

Eisenhower, John S. D. *Agent of Destiny: The Life and Times of General Winfield Scott.* Norman: University of Oklahoma Press, 1997.

Feingold, Henry L. *The Politics of Rescue: The Roosevelt Administration and the Holocaust, 1938–1945.* New York: Holocaust Library, 1970.

Flaherty, Thomas H., ed. *Mafia.* New York: Time-Life Books, 1993.

Fox, Stephen. *UnCivil Liberties: Italian Americans Under Siege During World War II.* Boca Raton, FL: Universal Publishers, 2000.

Friedman, Saul S. *No Haven for the Oppressed: United States Policy Toward Jewish Refugees, 1938–1945.* Detroit: Wayne State University Press, 1973.

Gentry, Curt. *J. Edgar Hoover: The Man and the Secrets.* New York: Plume, 1991.

Gruber, Ruth. *Haven: The Dramatic Story of 1,000 World War II Refugees and How They Came to America.* New York: Three Rivers Press, 2000. Previously published 1983, 1984.

Harth, Erica, ed. *Last Witnesses: Reflections on the Wartime Internment of Japanese Americans.* New York: Palgrave Macmillan, 2001.

Hirahara, Naomi. *An American Son: The Story of George Aratani.* Los Angeles: Japanese American National Museum, 2001.

Hohri, William Minoru. *Repairing America: An Account of the Movement for Japanese-American Redress.* Pullman: Washington State University Press, 1988.

Houston, Jeanne Wakatsuki, and James Houston. *Farewell to Manzanar.* Boston: Houghton Mifflin, 2002.

Huxley, Aldous. *Brave New World.* New York: Bantam Books, 1942. Previously published 1932.

Ichinokuchi, Tad, and Daniel Aiso. *John Aiso and the M.I.S.: Japanese-American Soldiers in the Military Intelligence Service, World War II.* Los Angeles: Military Intelligence Service Club of Southern California, 1988.

Inada, Lawson Fuscao. *Only What We Could Carry: The Japanese American Internment Experience.* Berkeley, CA: Heyday Books, 2000.

Inouye, Daniel. *Journey to Washington*. New York: Prentice-Hall, 1967.

Ishigo, Estelle. *Lone Heart Mountain*. Los Angeles: Anderson, Ritchie and Simon, 1972.

Jacobs, Arthur D. *The Prison Called Hohenasperg: An American Boy Betrayed by His Government During World War II*. N.p.: Universal Publishers, 1999.

Kashima, Tetsuden. *Judgment Without Trial*. Seattle: University of Washington Press, 2004.

Khan, Mahvish Rukhsana. *My Guantánamo Diary: The Detainees and the Stories They Told Me*. New York: Public Affairs, 2008.

Matsuo, Dorothy. *Boyhood to War*. N.p.: Mutual Publishing Co., 1992.

Mayer, Jane. *The Dark Side: The Inside Story of How the War on Terror Turned Into a War on American Ideals*. New York: Doubleday, 2008.

McDowall, William. *History of the Burgh of Domfries*. Edinburgh: Adam and Charles Black, 1867.

McWilliams, Carey. *Prejudice: Japanese Americans; Symbols of Racial Intolerance*. Boston: Little, Brown, 1944.

Newark, Tim. *Mafia Allies: The True Story of America's Secret Alliance with the Mob in World War II*. St. Paul, MN: Zenith Press, 2007.

Nguyen, Tram. *We Are All Suspects Now: Untold Stories from Immigrant Communities after 9/11*. Boston: Beacon Press, 2005.

Orwell, George. *1984*. New York: New American Library, 1949.

Perdue, Theda, and Michael D. Green, eds. *The Cherokee Removal: A Brief History with Documents*. Boston: Bedford Books of St. Martin's Press, 1995.

Pinza, Ezio, and Robert Magidoff. *Ezio Pinza: An Autobiography*. New York: Rinehart, 1958.

Prange, Gordon W. *At Dawn We Slept: The Untold Story of Pearl Harbor*. New York: Penguin Books, 1981.

Robinson, Greg. *By Order of the President: FDR and the Internment of Japanese Americans*. Cambridge, MA: Harvard University Press, 2001.

Rozema, Vicki, ed. *Voices from the Trail of Tears*. Winston-Salem, NC: John F. Blair, 2003.

Scott, Lieutenant General Winfield. *Memoirs*. New York: Sheldon, 1864.

Stewart, Rev. Archibald. *History Vindicated in the Case of the Wigtown Martyrs*. 2nd ed. Edinburgh: Edmonston and Douglas, 1869.

Takei, George. *To the Stars: The Autobiography of George Takei.* New York: Pocket Books, 1994.

Tanaka, Chester. *Go for Broke: A Pictorial History of the Japanese American 100th Infantry Battalion and 442nd Regimental Combat Team.* Richmond, CA: Go for Broke, 1982.

Tateishi, John. *And Justice for All: An Oral History of the Japanese American Detention Camps.* Seattle: University of Washington Press, 1984.

Turner, Sir James. *Memoirs of His Own Life and Times.* Reprint, Edinburgh: Bannatyne Club, 1829.

———. *Pallas Armata, Military Essayes on the Ancient Grecian, Roman, and Modern Art of War.* London, 1683.

Ungar, Sanford J. *FBI.* Boston: Atlantic Monthly Press, 1976.

Waldron, Ann. *Hodding Carter: The Reconstruction of a Racist.* Chapel Hill, NC: Algonquin Books, 1993.

Weglyn, Michi Nishiura. *Years of Infamy: The Untold Story of America's Concentration Camps.* Seattle: University of Washington Press, 1996. Previously published 1976.

Werner, Emmy E. *Through the Eyes of Innocents: Children Witness World War II.* Boulder, CO: Westview, 2000.

Wyman, David S. *The Abandonment of the Jews: America and the Holocaust.* New York: New Press, 1984.

Yamada, Mitsuye. *Camp Notes and Other Writings.* New Brunswick, NJ: Rutgers University Press, 1992. Previously published 1976.

Periodicals

Agence France Presse. "Guantánamo Should Stay Open, Waterboarding OK; Cheney." December 15, 2008.

All Things Considered. "Internment Camp Survivor Gets Honorary Degree." National Public Radio, May 16, 2008.

Associated Press. "Delta Planter's Wife Held After Flight with German POW." Published in *Delta Democrat-Times,* January 6, 1946.

Bernstein, Nina. "City of Immigrants Fills Jail Cells with Its Own." *New York Times,* December 27, 2008.

———. "Officials Hid Truth About Immigrant Deaths in Jail." *New York Times*, January 10, 2010.

———. "U.S. Agency Issues Scathing Report on Death of Immigrant in Its Custody." *New York Times*, January 16, 2009.

Breed, Clara E. "All but Blind." *Library Journal*, February 1, 1943.

Brenson, Michael. Obituary of Isamu Noguchi. *New York Times*, December 31, 1988.

Burton, Jeffery F., et al. "Confinement and Ethnicity: An Overview of World War II Japanese American Relocation Sites." *Publications in Anthropology* 74 (1999, rev. July 2000): www.nps.gov/history/history/online_books/anthropology74/ce7.htm.

Carter, Hodding. Editorial. *Delta Democrat-Times*, July 26, 1945.

Caylor, Arthur. "Behind the News with Arthur Caylor." *San Francisco News*, March 2, 1942.

Delta Democrat-Times. "German Prisoners Arrive in City for Cotton Picking Job." October 4, 1943.

Delta Democrat-Times. "Go for Broke," August 27, 1945.

Glaberson, William. "Detainee Will Face New War-Crimes Charges." *New York Times*, November 19, 2008.

———. "Evidence Faulted in Detainee Case." *New York Times*, July 1, 2008.

———. "Post-Guantánamo: A New Detention Law?" *New York Times*, November 15, 2008.

Hsu, Spencer S., and Sylvia Moreno. "Border Policy's Success Strains Resources." *Washington Post*, February 2, 2007.

Jespersen, Ashley F., Martin L. Lalumiere, and Michael Seto. "Sexual Abuse History Among Adult Sex Offenders and Non-sex Offenders: A Meta-analysis." *Child Abuse and Neglect* 33 (2009).

Keller, Larry. "The Second Wave: Evidence Grows of Far-Right Militia Resurgence." *Intelligence Report* 135 (Fall 2009): www.splcenter.org/get-informed/intelligence-report/browse-all-issues/2009/fall/the-second-wave.

Ketcham, Christopher. "The Last Roundup." *Radar Magazine*, May/June 2008.

Klaidman, Daniel. "Eric Holder, Jr." *Newsweek*, December 28, 2009.

Leopold, Jason. "Cheney Admits He 'Signed Off' on Waterboarding of Three Guantánamo Prisoners." *Online Journal*, December 29, 2008, www.onlinejournal.com/artman/publish/article_4170.shtml.

Manzanar Free Press. April 11, 1942, www.nps.gov/archive/manz/MFP/mfp-v1-n1.htm.

Manzanar Free Press. March 20, 1943, www.nps.gov/archive/manz/mfp/mfp-v3-n23b.htm.

Nyberg, John. "3,500 Minnesota-Trained Nisei Act as 'Eyes, Ears.'" *Minneapolis Star-Journal*, October 22, 1945.

Oakland Tribune. "800 Japs to Go to Arkansas, Utah." September 30, 1942.

Phoenix Republic. "Evacuees Operate Factory Vegetable Farm at Rivers." N.d.

Pritchett, Merrill R., and William L. Shea. "The Enemy in Mississippi (1943–1946)." *Journal of Mississippi History* 41 (November 1979).

Roosevelt, Eleanor. "A Challenge to American Sportsmanship. *Collier's*, October 16, 1943.

Rowe, Claudia. "59 Years Ago, They Fled to an Internment Camp." *New York Times*, July 21, 2003.

Sacramento Bee. Editorial. February 23, 1942.

San Francisco Chronicle. Editorial. February 21, 1942.

San Francisco News. "Bay Area Japs Leaving Coast in Final Rush." March 27, 1942.

———. "FBI Rounds Up More Japanese." March 18, 1942.

———. "First Japanese Ready to Leave Coast." March 19, 1942.

———. "Jap Farm Land Is Transferred." April 3, 1942.

———. "Japanese on West Coast Face Wholesale Uprooting." March 4, 1942.

———. "New Order on Aliens Awaited." March 2, 1942.

———. "Olson Wants All Japs Removed." March 6, 1942.

———. "1000 Japs Arrive at Manzanar Colony." March 24, 1942.

———. "State Suspends All Japanese Employees." April 3, 1942.

Schor, Elana. "US Drops Charges Against 9/11 Suspect Detained at Guantánamo." Guardian.co.uk, May 14, 2008, www.guardian.co.uk/world/2008/may/14/usa.Guantánamo.

Shane, Scott. "China Inspired Interrogations at Guantánamo." *New York Times*, July 2, 2008.

———. "Documents Laid Out Interrogation Procedures." *New York Times*, July 25, 2008.

———. "Obama Orders Secret Prisons and Detention Camps Closed." *New York Times,* January 23, 2009.

Smith, Davis. "Bolton Black Says Beatings Occurred." *Jackson Daily News,* June 11, 1971.

Sprague, Claire. "Letter of the Week." *Saturday Evening Post,* August 15, 1942. Claire D. Sprague Collection, University of the Pacific.

Tawa, Renee. "Childhood Lost: The Orphans of Manzanar." *Los Angeles Times,* March 11, 1997.

Thomma, Steven. "Secret Camps and Guillotines? Groups Make Birthers Look Sane." McClatchy Newspapers, August 28, 2009, www.mcclatchydc .com/2009/08/28/74549/secret-camps-and-guillotines-groups.html.

Time. "One of the Rest." March 13, 1950.

Vlahos, Kelley Beaucar. "Critics Fear Emergency Centers Could Be Used for Immigration Round-Ups." Foxnews.com, June 7, 2006.

Vogel, Carole Garbuny. "Oswego, New York: Wartime Haven for Jewish Refugees." *Avotaynu,* winter 1998.

Woodward, Bob. "Detainee Tortured, Says U.S. Official." *Washington Post,* January 14, 2009.

Other Documents

Asawa, Ruth, and Albert Lanier. Oral history interview by Paul Karlstrom, June 21–July 5, 2002. *Archives of American Art, Smithsonian Institution, www.aaa.si.edu/collections/oralhistories/ transcripts/asawa02.htm.*

Carr, Governor Ralph. Letter to U.S. Attorney Thomas J. Morrissey, June or July 1942. Available online at "Documents from Colorado Governor Ralph Carr's Administration," Colorado Department of Personnel and Administration, www.colorado.gov/dpa/doit/archives/ wwcod/granada4.htm.

———. Letters and other documents. Available online at "Documents from Colorado Governor Ralph Carr's Administration," Colorado Department of Personnel and Administration, www.colorado.gov/dpa/doit/archives/wwcod/granada4.htm.

Cherokee Heritage Trails. "Sites in Red Clay: Fort Cass and the Cherokee Internment Camps." www.cherokeeheritagetrails.org.

Children of the Camps Project. "Internment History." PBS, www.pbs
.org/childofcamp/history/clinton.html.

DeWitt, Lt. Gen. J. L. *Final Report: Japanese Evacuation from the West
Coast, 1942.* Washington, DC: GPO, 1943. Available online at Virtual
Museum of the City of San Francisco, www.sfmuseum.org/war/
dewitt1.html.

———. "Instructions to All Persons of Japanese Ancestry." April 1, 1942.
Virtual Museum of the City of San Francisco, www.sfmuseum.org/
hist9/evacorder.html.

Ebel, Karen. "Max Ebel, A German Immigrant's Story." German American
Internee Coalition, March 2006, www.gaic.info/real_ebel.html.

Elsea, Jennifer K. *Detention of American Citizens as Enemy Combatants.*
Report prepared for Congress by the Congressional Research
Service, February 24, 2005.

FBI official Web site. "History of the FBI: World War II Period."
www.fbi.gov/libref/historic/history/worldwar.htm.

Feingold, Russ. "Remarks of U.S. Senator Russ Feingold on the
Wartime Treatment Study Act Amendment to the Comprehensive
Immigration Reform Act." Press release, May 24, 2007,
http://feingold.senate.gov/record.cfm?id=309706.

Fort Smith National Historic Site. "Cherokee Round Up." National Park
Service, www.nps.gov/fosm/historyculture/cherokee-round-up.htm.

Golden, Randy. "Cherokee Removal Forts." About North Georgia,
www.ngeorgia.com/history/nghisttt.html.

Migration Policy Institute. "'Special Registration' Program." Migration
Information Source, April 2003, www.migrationinformation.org/
USFocus/display.cfm?ID=116.

Mississippi Band of Choctaw Indians. "Treaty of Dancing Rabbit Creek."
www.choctaw.org/History/Treaties/treaty9.html.

Neupert, Rose Marie. "The Neupert Family Story." German American
Internee Coalition, March 2006, www.gaic.info/real_neupert.html.

Roosevelt, Franklin D. Executive Order no. 9066. Available online at
"Executive Order 9066: Resulting in the Relocation of Japanese
(1942)," Our Documents, www.ourdocuments.gov/doc.php?doc=74#.

Ruth Asawa's official Web site. "Internment." www.ruthasawa.com/
internment.html.

Smithsonian Center for Education and Museum Studies. "Letters
from the Japanese American Internment." Smithsonian Institution,
www.smithsonianeducation.org/educators/lesson_plans/japanese_
internment/index.html.

Tsukamoto, Marielle. Interview by fifth-grade students at Barbara
Comstock Morse Elementary School, n.d. American Memory,
Library of Congress, http://memory.loc.gov/learn/lessons/99/fear/
interview.html.

Tule Lake Committee official Web site. "History of Tule Lake Concentration
Camp and the Pilgrimages." www.tulelake.org/history.html.

United States Holocaust Memorial Museum. "Voyage of the St. Louis."
www.ushmm.org/museum/exhibit/online/stlouis/.

U.S. Department of Justice. *A Review of the Restrictions on Persons of
Italian Ancestry During World War II.* Report to Congress, November
2001, www.justice.gov/crt/Italian_Report.pdf.

U.S. Immigration and Customs Enforcement. "Immigration Detention
Facilities." www.ice.gov/pi/dro/facilities.htm.

U.S. National Archives and Records Administration. "About the Redress
Program." www.archives.gov/research/japanese-americans/redress
.html.

War Relocation Authority. *Relocation of Japanese Americans.*
Washington, D.C.: War Relocation Authority, 1943. Available online
at Virtual Museum of the City of San Francisco, www.sfmuseum.org/
hist10/relocbook.html.

———. "Riots, Strikes, and Disturbances in Japanese Relocation
Centers." Memorandum, 1943. Internment Archives, www
.internmentarchives.com/showdoc.php?docid=00073.

Washburn, Wilcomb D. "Indians and the American Revolution."
AmericanRevolution.org, www.americanrevolution.org/ind1.html.

Wyatt Detention Facility. "Wyatt Detention Facility Statement Re
Internal Investigation of Detainee Death." Reuters, January 8, 2009.

INDEX

Abbey, Roy, 75
Acheson, Dean, 177
African Americans, 67, 106, 248
Africans, 239–241
Aiso, Johnny, 187–191, 222
Akutsu, Jim, 122–124
al Qaeda, 246
al-Qahtani, Mohammed, 248–249
Alaska, 177
alien, term defined, 65
Alien Enemies Act, 146–147
Alien Registration Act, 147
Amache camp, 124–125, 126–127, 204
"Amazing Grace," 33
American Revolution, 16–17
amnesia, social, 222–223, 230
Anastasia, Albert, 164
Angel Island, 53
anti-Semitism, 175–176, 184
Antiterrorism and Effective Death Penalty Act (AEDPA), 242–243
apprehension warrants, 64
Aratani, George, 130–133, 210–212, 222
Aratani, Masuko, 210–211

Arkansas, 89, 104–109, 110–115, 204
Army, U.S., 149, 157, 165
Aue, Helmut von der, 118
Asawa, Ruth, 114–115
Asawa, Umakichi, 114
assembly centers, 77–81, 87, 89, 90, 114, 128, 131, 170. *See also* Manzanar

Bah, Boubacar, 258–259
Bambauer, Dennis, 95
Baruch, Bernard, 176
Behavioral Adjustment Unit, 240
Belenchia, Josephine Pandolfi, 117
Bendetsen, Karl R., 95
Berg, Anita, 39, 43–44, 50
Berg, Bertha, 39, 42–43, 44, 50, 52–58, 205–206
Berg, Doris, 39–45, 50–53, 55, 56, 57–60, 205
Berg, Frederick, 39–40, 44, 53–54, 56, 58, 205
Berizzi, Albert, 172
Berizzi, Louis, 171–172
Berizzi, Lucetta, 172

Biddle, Francis, 64, 65, 68, 149, 162, 183
Bilbo, Theodore, 199
Bissell, Clayton, 190
Black, Hugo, 224
Black Dragons, 100–101
Bleir, Karoline, 182
Boyhood to War (Matsuo), 193
Brave New World (Huxley), 74
Breed, Clara, 81–82
Britain, 176
Bru, Federico Laredo, 174
Burnett, John G., 30
Bush, George H. W., 228
Bush, George W., 232, 246, 248, 255, 257, 262

California
    assembly centers in, 77–78
    concentration camps in, 89
        (*see also* Manzanar)
    discrimination in, 67, 76, 92, 96
    forced-evacuation experiences, 70–75, 76–77, 79–80, 131
    Japanese in, statistics, 63
    university arrests, 70–71
Camp Clinton, 116–117
Camp Como, 116–117
Camp Crystal, 152–153, 155, 214
Camp Forrest, 156–157
Camp Honouliuli, 59–60, 62
Camp McCain, 116–117
Camp McCoy, 53–54, 56
Camp Ontario, 181–185, 217–219
Camp Rohwer, 104, 107–108, 110–115, 204
Camp Savage, 190
Camp Shelby, 116, 192
Campbell, Thomas D., 90

Canonici, Paul V., 117
Carr, Ralph L., 69, 125–127
Carter, Betty, 116, 120
Carter, Hodding, 116, 119–120, 197, 200–201, 207
Cavelier, Rene-Robert, Sieur de La Salle, 13
Central Falls detention facility, 260
Central Intelligence Agency (CIA), 261
certificates of exemption, 203
Chandler, Harry, 188
Charles II, King of England, 1, 2–3, 6
Cheney, Dick, 247–248, 255
Cherokees, 17, 18–20, 23, 29–33
Chertoff, Michael, 256
Chickasaws, 21, 25, 34
children
    deportation of, 155
    as detainees, 49, 94–96, 110–115, 139, 152
    imprisonment of parents, 43–45, 46–47, 50–53, 55, 57–61
Children's Village, 94–96
Choctaws, 21–22, 24–25
Chuman, Frank, 98
citizenship, 140, 152, 207–208, 215, 223–224
Civil Liberties Act, 228–230
Civil War, 18, 33–34
Claiborne, William C. C., 21
Clark, Thomas C., 74
Clinton, Bill, 229–231, 242
Collier, John, 135
Collier's (magazine), 133–134
Collins, Wayne M., 223–224
Columbus (passenger liner), 161
Commercial Appeal (newspaper), 108

Commission on Wartime Relocation and Internment of Civilians, 48–49, 79, 100, 110, 226–227
communists, 209, 238
Conoy tribe, 14, 18
Constitution of 1890, 35
construction contracts, camp, 255–257, 262
contraband, 64–65
Contract with America, 242
Costello, Frank, 163
Covenanters, Scottish, 1–9
Crawford, Susan, 248
Crockett, Davy, 23–24
Crump, E. H., 184
Cuba, 173–175, 246–251, 259, 261–264
curfews, 78, 129, 165, 169

Dade, Francis L., 28
Dalziel, Sir Thomas, 4–5
Dancing Rabbit Creek, Treaty of, 24
Dark Side, The (Mayer), 248–249
Davis, Elmer, 137
Days of Waiting (film), 214
Delawares, 17
Delta Democrat-Times (newspaper), 197–199
Delta Star (newspaper), 116
Democrat-Times (newspaper), 116
deportation
    choice between enlistment or, 132–133
    German Americans, 155
    as internment release strategy, 204
    of Jewish refugees, 217–219
    legislation assisting, 242–243

loyalty questionnaire answers resulting in, 143
    military blackmail to avoid, 210–212
    registration resulting in, 253
    as retaliation for complaints, 122–123
Detention Act, 237–238
Deutschamerikanische Volksbund, 147
DeWitt, John L., 64–65, 66, 69, 70, 71–74, 78
DiMaggio, Giuseppe, 162
DiMaggio, Joe, 162
District of Columbia, 18
divorce, 205, 208
Donald W. Wyatt Detention Facility, 260
Drum, Hugh A., 148

Ebel, Doris (nee Eckert), 215–216
Ebel, Karen, 150, 151, 156, 159–160, 215–216, 250
Ebel, Max, 145–146, 148, 150–151, 156–157, 158–160, 215–216
Eckardt, Albert, 152–153
Eckardt, Ruth (nee Jankwitz), 152–153
Eckardt, Ted, 152–153
Eisenhower, Milton, 69, 137
Eleanor (Berg's sister), 44–45, 49–50, 55, 57
Elizabeth Detention Center, 258–259
Ellis Island, 147, 151–152, 154–155, 156, 168, 215
Embrey, Sue Kunitomi, 91–92
Emmons, Delos, 191–192
ENDGAME (camp construction plans), 255–257, 262–263

enemy aliens, 49, 64–65, 70, 146–151, 252
equality, 235
espionage, 66–67, 149
"Evacuation" (Yamada), 37, 83
Executive Order 9066, 66, 68, 130, 227
Ezio Pinza (Pinza), 167

Farewell to Manzanar (Houston), 91
Farm Security Administration, 74
Federal Bureau of Investigation (FBI), 45–49, 68, 70–71, 84, 146, 149, 151, 206, 252, 257–258
Feingold, Russ, 232–233
Foote, Shelby, 116
Forrest, Nathan Bedford, 156
Fort Armstrong Immigration Station, 49–50
Fort Lincoln, 157, 158, 159–160
Fort Meade, 156, 172
Fort Missoula, 161–162
Fort Sixes, 31–32
Fort Stanton, 161
Fort Wayne, Indiana, 17
442nd Regimental Combat Team, 130, 191, 192–196, 203
Fourth Army Intelligence School, 189–190
Fox, Stephen, 162
Frankfurter, Felix, 176
Freedom of Information Act, 258
Friedman, Saul, 177–178
Fujimoto, Jack, 75

Geneva convention, 117, 157, 179
Georgia Guard, 30, 31, 32
German American Internee Coalition, 160

German Americans
arrests and internment, 70, 78, 147–155, 157–161
civil liberty violations investigations, 232–233
deportation to Germany, 155, 215
German prisoners of war compared to, 156
in Hawaii, 42–62
Japanese Americans compared to, 70, 148, 226
population statistics (1940), 148
postwar public perception of internment, 206
release and aftermath, 214–215, 215–216
war preparation and surveillance of, 146–147
German concentration camps, 173
German prisoners of war, 116–117, 117–119, 118–119
German spy rings, 149
Gila River camp, 89, 129, 132–134, 204
Gingrich, Newt, 242
"Go for Broke" (Carter), 197–199
Goya, Kuantoku, 48–49
Granada camp, 124–125, 126–127, 204
Grant (ship), 53
Grassley, Chuck, 232
Greenberg, Walter, 219
Greenville WWII POW camp, 115–118
Grier, Will, 3–4
Gruber, Ruth, 177–180, 183–184, 219

Guantánamo Bay detention center, 246–251, 259, 261–264
Gunderson, Ted, 262–263

habeas corpus, 56, 65
Harvard Law School, 189
Hawaii
    camp location and legal jurisdiction issues, 246
    camps on, 59–60, 62
    detention centers on, 48, 49, 57–58
    German Americans detainees, 42–62
    Japanese American detainees, 48–49, 59, 63, 110
    Japanese American military units from, 63, 130, 191, 192–196, 203
    Japanese populations in (1940), 63
    martial law on, 47, 205
Hawaii Defense Act, 47
Hawaiian Provisional Infantry Battalion, 63
hearings, 48–49, 150
Heart Mountain Relocation Center, 89, 127–129, 204
Henry Gibbins (ship), 179–181
Herzig, John "Jack," 209, 225–226, 228
Hiroshima bombing, 211
historical preservation of camps, 232
Hitler, Adolf, 146, 147, 173, 256
Hoekstra, Peter, 261–262
Hohenasperg prison, Germany, 155
Hohri, William Minoru, 93, 226, 228
Holder, Eric, 263

Holman, Rufus, 175
Holston, Treaty of, 19–20
Homeland Security, Department of, 255–257, 258, 261, 262–263
homosexuality, and torture, 249–250
Honda, Francis L., 95
Hoover, J. Edgar, 62, 149, 163, 165
Hopewell, Treaty of, 19
Huxley, Aldous, 74

Ickes, Harold, 176–177, 178–179, 183, 184, 218
Illegal Immigration Reform and Immigrant Responsibility Act (IIRIRA), 242–243
immigration
    American opposition to, 175
    citizenship interviews, 207–208
    illegal, 238–243, 252, 258–260
    Japanese restrictions, 84
    Jewish restrictions, 175–178, 184
    quota systems for, 174, 175
    registration of illegal immigrants, 252–253
Immigration Act, 84
Immigration and Customs Enforcement (ICE), 258–259
Immigration and Nationality Act, 175, 207
Immigration and Naturalization Service (INS), 140, 147, 154, 238–242, 252–253, 259
immigration detention camps, 239–243, 258–260
"immigration emergency," 256–257
In Brief Authority (Biddle), 68
Indian Removal (Neugin), 31

Indian Removal Act, 23–24
Indian Trade and Intercourse Act, 19
Inouye, Daniel K., 194–195
Inouye, Ruby, 124
International Harry, 180
Ishigo, Arthur, 128, 212–214
Ishigo, Estelle, 128, 212–214
Ishizuka, Mary, 74–75
Issei, 63, 76, 81, 100–101, 138–139, 210
Italian Americans
    arrests and internment, 70, 78, 147, 148, 149, 161–162, 165–170, 172
    civil liberty violations investigations, 171, 231–233
    internment exclusion of, 162–166
    Japanese Americans compared to, 70, 171, 226
    population statistics (1940), 148
    U.S. military drafting of, 170–171
    wartime restrictions on, 117, 171
Italian prisoners of war, 116–117
Ito, Jimmy, 100
Ito, Yasuko, 75–76

Jackson, Andrew, 11, 23–24, 25
Jackson, Mary Elizabeth, 25
Jackson, Robert, 224
Jacobs, Arthur, 154–155
James II, King of England, 1, 7
Japanese American Citizens League (JACL), 70, 98, 100, 101, 109, 217
Japanese American Evacuation Claims Act, 216–217, 225

Japanese American internment
    children in, 95–96, 106–107, 139
    complaints and retaliation, 122–124
    conflicts between Nisei and Issei, 100–101
    creative writings on experiences, 37, 81–82, 83
    for dissidents, 133, 139–143
    facility descriptions, 91–92, 103–104, 108, 121–122, 124–125, 126–127
    leaves outside camp, 105–106, 126–127
    living conditions, 85–86, 88–89, 91–92, 96–98, 110–115, 128–129, 134
    locations and population capacity, 89
    location selection, 69–70, 90, 104
    loyalty assessments during, 109–110, 132–133, 136, 138–141
    medical care, 79, 92–93
    newspapers published at, 96–97, 100
    orphanages in, 94–96
    psychological impact of, 205–206, 207, 222–223
    riots, protests and demonstrations, 98–100, 109, 134, 142–143
    statistics of, 139, 204
    torture during, 142–143
    volunteering for, 135–136
    work options, 86, 129
Japanese American National Museum, 81
Japanese Americans
    arrests and interrogations, 84–85, 93, 124, 131, 149
    assembly centers, 77–81, 90, 131, 132

birth location and distinctions,
63
cultural differences between
Nisei and Issei, 81
deportment/expatriation to
Japan, 132–133, 143, 210
discrimination toward, 62–63,
67, 76, 92, 96, 104, 187–188,
196, 207–208
enemy alien classification,
65
espionage and disloyalty
allegations, 66–67
evacuation, 76, 78–79, 80–81,
87, 107, 130
evacuation opponents, 135
evacuation resistance, 223
forced evacuation in California,
70–74, 76–77, 79–80, 131
German Americans compared
to, 70, 148, 226
German prisoners of war in
Mississippi compared to, 119
government civilian policies
and directives toward, 64–65,
66, 68
Hawaiian detainees, 47–49, 59,
62
Italian Americans compared to,
70, 171, 226
lawsuits against U.S., 223–224,
226, 227–229
legal jurisdiction and military
philosophies regarding, 250
military enlistment options,
132–133
property damage or loss claims,
216–217, 225
property sales and seizures,
74–76, 131

public response to evacuation,
66, 81–83, 91, 104
redress and restitution, 226–
231, 232
release and aftermath, 204–211,
213, 215, 221–223
repatriations to Japan, 109, 133,
140
self-imposed exiles to
Colorado, 125–126
University of California
students, 70
in U.S. military (*see* Nisei
soldiers in U.S. military)
See also Japanese American
internment
Japanese Latin Americans, 229
Jefferson, Thomas, 17, 21
Jerome, Arkansas, camp, 89, 90,
103–109
Jews, 172–185, 217–219, 232
Johnson, Lyndon, 191
Jones, Evan, 31
Justice Department, U.S., 148–149,
157, 161, 204, 214, 218

Kachima, Tetsuden, 222
Kawaguchi, Tom, 196
Kellogg, Brown and Root (KBR),
255
Kennedy, Edward, 232
Kennedy-Specter Comprehensive
Immigration Bill, 232–233
Kerry, John, 261
Kibayashi, Mr., 142
Killing Time, 1–9
Kimoto, John, 75
Knox, Frank, 62, 67
Knox, Henry, 19
Korean Americans, 238

Korean War, 237
Korematsu v. United States, 223–224, 227–228
Ku Klux Klan, 104, 116, 156

La Guardia, Fiorello Henry, 162, 168
Lachlane, Margaret, 7–9
Lakota, 158
Lansky, Meyer, 164–165
Lanterns on the Levee (Percy), 116
Latin American deportations, 153–154, 229
Lavery, Hugh, 95
lawsuits, 223–224, 226, 227–229
Lazio, Rick, 231
Library Journal, 82
Lilienthal, David, 184
Lincoln, Abraham, 235
Little Turtle, Chief, 17, 18
Lone Heart Mountain (Ishigo), 128, 214
Los Angeles Times, 188
Lost Battalion, 193–194
Louisiana Purchase, 20
Lower Mississippi (Carter), 120
loyalty assessments, 109–110, 132–133, 136, 138–141, 143, 206, 208
Luciano, Charlie "Lucky," 163–165
Lungren, Dan, 227

Mafia, 163–165
Manzanar
    closure, 204
    corruption, 98
    facility descriptions, 88, 91–92, 93–94
    guards and security, 96, 97–98
    living conditions, 88–89, 92–93, 94
    newspapers, 96–97, 100
    orphanages, 94–96
    purpose and capacity statistics, 77, 89
    riots and demonstrations, 98–101
Marshall, George C., 137–138, 192
martial law, 47, 142–143, 148–149, 205
Marutani, William M., 227
Matsumoto, 95–96
Matsuo, Dorothy, 193
Mayer, Jane, 248–249
Mayer camp, 77
McCain, Henry, 116
McCain, John, 259
McCarran-Walter Act (Immigration and Nationality Act), 175, 207
McCloy, John J., 62, 90, 136–137
McKellar, Kenneth, 184
Mechecannochqua (Little Turtle), Chief, 17, 18
medical care, 79, 92–93, 156, 258–261, 260
Memoirs of His Own Life and Times (Turner), 6–7
Merritt, Ralph P., 96
Mexicans, 238, 242
Miami, 15, 17
Michener, James A., 66–67
Middle Easterners, 246–253, 256–259, 261–264
military enlistment, 150, 159, 170–171. *See also* Nisei soldiers in U.S. military
Military Intelligence Service Language School, 190
militia movements, 263
Minidoka camp, 121–122, 204

Mississippi, 115–119, 248
Mohammed, Khalid Sheikh, 249
Mohawks, 17
Mongolia (ship), 147
Morgenthau, Henry, Jr., 176
Morrissey, Thomas J., 125
Moultrie Creek, Treaty of, 27
Muslim Americans, 245–253, 256, 258–259
Mussolini, Benito, 162–163
Myer, Dillon S., 133, 135, 142, 178–179

Nagasaki bombings, 211
Nakamura, Grace, 100
National Council for Japanese American Redress (NCJAR), 226, 228
National Park Service, 232
Native Americans
    colonists' conflicts with, 16–17, 18
    German American prisoners and, 158
    interracial marriages and discrimination, 13–16
    land seizures and disputes, 18–20, 21–23
    removal and internment of, 23–25, 27–33
Nazism, 119, 146, 173
Neugin, Rebecca, 31, 33
Neupert, Emma, 151–152, 214–215
Neupert, George, 151–152, 214–215
Neupert, Rose-Marie, 151–152, 214–215
New World Order, 263
New York Times, 258, 259–260
Ng, Hiu Lui, 260–261

Niles, David, 176
9/11 attacks, 245–246
1984 (Orwell), 74
Nipponese, 76
Nisei, 63, 81, 100–101, 138–139
Nisei soldiers in U.S. military
    battalion units of, 63, 130, 191–196
    blackmail to avoid family deportation, 210
    commissioned military officer, first, 190
    editorials commemorating, 197–199
    enlistment as choice, 123–124, 132–133
    enlistment as internment release strategy, 203
    intelligence units of, 189–191
    postwar occupation of Japan, 209
    postwar treatment of, 196
    selective service policies, 136–137, 191
Nisei Writers and Artists Mobilization for Democracy, 135
Noguchi, Isamu, 135–136
Noorani, Sadru, 252–253
Northern Pacific Railroad, 158

Obama, Barack, 259, 261, 263–264
Office of Redress Administration (ORA), 228
Ogawa, Louise, 81
Old Tom, 25–26, 33–34
Olson, Culbert, 171
100th Battalion, 191–193
opera singers, 166–168
orphans and orphanages, 94–96
Orwell, George, 74

Osceola, Chief, 28, 29
Otsuk, George, 197

Pacific International Livestock
    Center, 77, 78
Palestine, 176
Palla Armata (Turner), 6, 17
Panama, 153–154
pardons, 203
paroles, 151, 168, 215
Patriot Act, 251
Pauline Frederich (freighter), 146,
    150
Payne's Landing, Treaty of, 27, 28
Pearl Harbor attack, 39–43, 61, 62,
    67, 245
Percy, William Alexander, 115–116
Perlman, Max, 180
Personal Justice Denied, 226–227
Peru, 229
petitions, and returning evacuees,
    211
Pinza, Doris, 166, 168
Pinza, Ezio, 166–168
Piscataway (Conoy) tribe, 14, 18
Polakoff, Moses, 164
Portland camp, 77, 78
postcards, 81
Poston, Charles, 129
Poston camp, 89, 129, 134–135,
    204
Prison Called Hohenasperg, The
    (Jacobs), 155
prisoner-of-war (POW) camps,
    116–119, 156
Proclamation 2525, 148
propaganda, 67, 80–81, 83, 133
property
    claims for damage or loss,
        216–217

collective loss statistics, 227
    damaged, 52
    forced sales and government
        seizures, 54–55, 74–76, 131,
        221
    Panamanian arrests and
        confiscation of, 153–154
    search and seizure of, 64–65
Pulitzer Prizes, 199
Pushmataha, Chief, 22
Puyallup camp, 77, 78, 79, 85–86

al Qaeda, 246
al-Qahtani, Mohammed, 248–249

railroad labor, 158
Rankin, Jeannette, 61–62
Rankin, John, 175
Raymondville camp, 259
Reagan, Ronald, 228, 238, 242
registration of enemy aliens, 64,
    146–147, 252
reparations and redress, 226–232
repatriations, 109, 133, 140
reservations, 20, 24–25
Reynolds, Robert, 157–158, 175
Rohwer camp, 104, 107–108, 110–
    115, 204
Roosevelt, Eleanor, 133–134
Roosevelt, Franklin
    death of, 184
    enemy alien detainment
        proclamations, 148
    German and Italian arrests and
        evacuation plans, 148–149,
        162
    Italian immigrant policies, 177
    Japanese Americans and
        military enlistment policies,
        137, 192

Japanese evacuation and
  internment orders, 61–64,
  66, 67
Jewish detainee policies, 183
Jewish immigration policies,
  175–176, 184
Jewish political appointments
  by, 176
martial law implementation on
  Hawaii, 47
Ross, John, 29, 32

Sacramento Bee, 82
Sand Island Detention Center, 48,
  49, 57–58
Santa Ana Racetrack, 77, 78, 87, 89,
  114
Sargent, Winthrop, 21
Schroder, Gertrude, 49
Scotland, 1–9
Scott, Winfield, 28–30, 32
search and seizures, 64–65, 150
Selective Service System, 136, 150,
  159, 170
Seminoles, 27–29
Senzaki, Miyo, 107–108
September 11 attacks, 245–246
Shawnees, 17, 22
Sherman, William, 34
ship seizures, 147, 148
shopping, 104–105, 126–127
Short, Walter, 47
Sichi, Marino, 168–171
Sinatra, Frank, 162
social amnesia, 222–223, 230
Social Security Act, 225
Specter, Arlen, 232
Sprague, Claire, 82–83
St. Louis (luxury liner), 173,
  174

Stimson, Henry L., 62, 64, 68, 137,
  204
suicides, 76, 175, 182

Takasugi, Leonard, 130
Takasugi, Nao, 129–130
Takei, George, 111, 112–113, 141
Takei, Henry, 110, 111
Takei, Nancy, 110, 111
Takei, Takekuma, 110–112
Tateishi, John Y., 98–99
terrorism, 242, 246, 257
Thompson, Bennie, 251, 255–256,
  257, 261, 263
Todorogi, Koji, 142
Togasaki, Yoshiye, 79, 92–93
Tolan, John H., 69–70
Topaz camp, 89, 196, 204
torture, 3, 7–9, 142–143, 247–250,
  261–262
Trail of Tears, 32–33
treaties, 19–20, 24, 27, 28
Truman, Harry S., 190, 204, 218–
  219
Tsukamoto, Marielle, 106–107
Tsukamoto, Mary, 106–107
Tsumagari, Fusa, 81
Tule Lake camp, 89, 133, 139, 140–
  143, 204
Turner, Emily (nee Bigham), 34, 35
Turner, James (son of Thomas
  Asbury Turner), 33–34
Turner, Jane, 14–16
Turner, John, 6, 9–10, 13–16, 17, 25
Turner, Joseph (son of Samuel
  Turner), 17–18
Turner, Joseph (son of Thomas
  Asbury Turner), 33–34
Turner, Richard, 15, 17
Turner, Samuel, 15, 17

Turner, Sir James, 2–6, 9–10, 17
Turner, Stephen Henry, 34–35
Turner, Thomas, 17–18
Turner, Thomas Asbury, 25, 33–34

UnCivil Liberties (Fox), 162
United States, Korematsu v., 223–224
University of California, 70
USA Patriot Act, 251

Vietnam War, 238

Wakamatsu, Shigeo, 75
Wakatsuki, Jeanne, 96
War Relocation Authority (WRA)
   camp investigations by, 108–109
   camps operated by, 157
   closure of, 204, 213
   enlistment or deportation choices of, 122–123
   inmate lists, 228
   Italian refugees, 177, 178
   Japanese American camps supervised by, 89–91
   Japanese American relocation supervised by, 69–70
   loyalty assessments by, 109–110
   opposition to concentration camps, 110

Wartime Civil Control Administration (WCCA), 71, 77
Wartime Treatment Study Act, 232
Wartime Violation of Italian Americans Civil Liberties Act, 231
Washington, George, 17, 19, 20
Washington State, 75, 77, 83–86
waterboarding, 247–248
Webb, Del, 129
Wilner, Tom, 250
Wilson, Margaret, 7–9
Work Corps, 77
work options, 86, 104, 127, 129, 157–158, 221–222
World War II camps, 173, 238, 251. *See also specific ethnic groups affected*

Yamada, Mitsuye (nee Yasutake), 37, 83–84, 121–122, 206–208, 251
Yamanaka, Al, 141
Yamanaka, Morgan, 141, 143
Yamane, Tokio, 142
Yasutake, Hide, 83–84
Yasutake, Jack, 83–84
Yasutake, Mike, 206
"yellow peril," 67, 83
Yeshii, Michael, 222
Yoshinaga-Herzig, Aiko, 87–89, 98, 103, 208–209, 225–226, 228, 230, 256